SEE YOU
ON SUNDAY

SEE YOU ON SUNDAY

A COOKBOOK FOR FAMILY AND FRIENDS

Sam Sifton

PHOTOGRAPHS BY DAVID MALOSH
FOOD STYLIST: SIMON ANDREWS

RANDOM HOUSE · NEW YORK

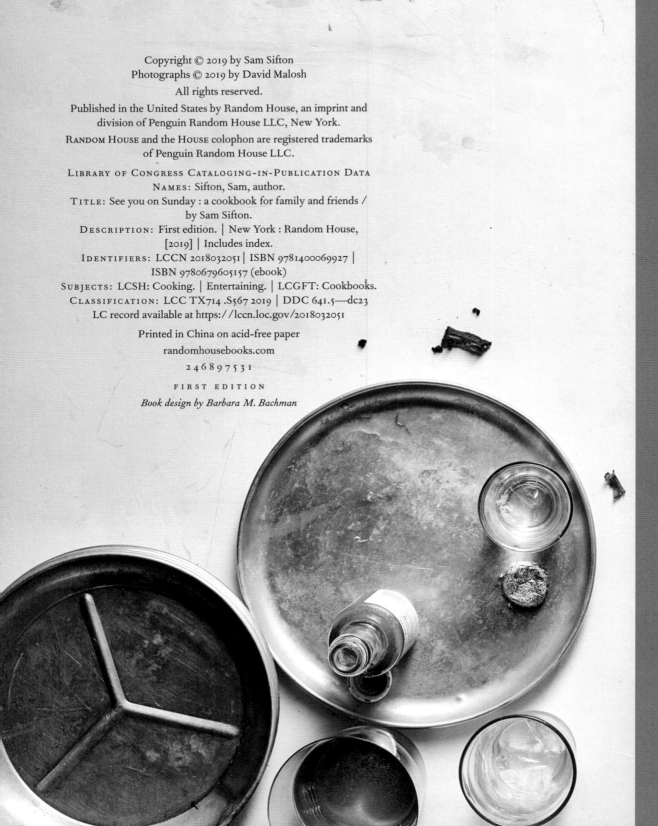

Published in the United States by Random House, an imprint and
division of Penguin Random House LLC, New York.

RANDOM HOUSE and the HOUSE colophon are registered trademarks
of Penguin Random House LLC.

LIBRARY OF CONGRESS CATALOGING-IN-PUBLICATION DATA
NAMES: Sifton, Sam, author.
TITLE: See you on Sunday : a cookbook for family and friends /
by Sam Sifton.
DESCRIPTION: First edition. | New York : Random House,
[2019] | Includes index.
IDENTIFIERS: LCCN 2018032051 | ISBN 9781400069927 |
ISBN 9780679605157 (ebook)
SUBJECTS: LCSH: Cooking. | Entertaining. | LCGFT: Cookbooks.
CLASSIFICATION: LCC TX714 .S567 2019 | DDC 641.5—dc23
LC record available at https://lccn.loc.gov/2018032051

Printed in China on acid-free paper
randomhousebooks.com

2 4 6 8 9 7 5 3 1

FIRST EDITION

Book design by Barbara M. Bachman

For
Tina Fallon,
who makes it possible,
and better

CONTENTS

———

SEE YOU
ON SUNDAY

A THEORY
OF DINNER

—

"They broke bread in their homes and ate together
with glad and sincere hearts."

—ACTS 2:46

"*See you on Sunday.*"

The dinners started years ago, in a drafty loft on an empty block in Williamsburg, Brooklyn, with a tiny gas stove and an enormous butcher-block prep table. Later they occurred in a walk-up in Greenpoint, a few miles north along the East River, with tiny babies sleeping in the hall. Big vats of pasta. Roasted chickens. Platters of ribs. Then came epic meals out on Long Island, in a little house steps off Main Street, and quieter ones on the southern coast of Connecticut, in a white kitchen out of a Cheever short story. Clams and corn, vegetables roasted on a sheet pan, ducks braised in a pot, huge briskets, many pizzas, stir-fries, ham, chili, turkey, repeat.

We gathered in Maine to eat off a wood stove, and in Florida to pick at grouper or trout as the sun fell into the Gulf. We cooked on roofs, in yards, in kitchens small and dingy, large and luxe, and beneath fluorescents in a narrow Brooklyn parish-hall galley, to feed groups of twenty, thirty, more. We cooked for family, real and imagined, informally, formally, somewhere between the two. We cooked for friends who were happy or troubled, for people in programs that had them floating a line between the two.

The point was to cook or, more accurate, the point was to gather around a table with family and eat, and to do that regularly enough that people knew it was happening, could depend on it somehow, this consistency in a world that doesn't offer a lot of that outside of work and pain. Sunday dinner. Sunday supper.

Word got around. And the calls or texts would start coming: "There dinner on Sunday?"

Yes. See you then. Bring wine or a cake, a friend, some flowers, nothing at all.

People are lonely. They want to be a part of something, even when they can't identify that longing as a need. They show up. Feed them. It isn't much more complicated than that. The point of Sunday dinner is just to have it. Even if you don't particularly like entertaining, there is great pleasure to be had in cooking for others, and great pleasure to be taken from the experience of gathering to eat with others.

Sunday dinner isn't a dinner party. It is not entertainment. It is just a fact, like a standing meeting or a regular touch football game in the park. It makes life a little better, almost every time.

There is some science to back up the assertion. We know that children who eat with their families regularly do better in school. They have better vocabularies. They are less likely to develop eating disorders, abuse drugs or alcohol, become teen parents. They have better manners. They have higher self-esteem. Have your kids eat dinner with adults—not just their parents, but friends from work, from the street, from the gas dock or library reading group—and they are likely to learn more about the human condition than children who do no such thing.

A number of years ago I cooked a dinner for a couple dozen people at a church in Brooklyn, a duty I took up a few times a season then: a Sunday dinner to follow a short, late-afternoon service. My children fumed throughout the liturgies of word and table alike, as children do. They saw the time spent in pews as silly and boring, a waste of time they might have better spent reading manga or doing homework.

Perhaps they were right. But also, as they generally did, my children shared dinner with the rest of the congregation after the service, talking with grown-ups from the neighborhood, artists and teachers, seekers and the lost. They drew crayon drawings on the paper tablecloths and played with kids they saw weekly but whose last names they did not know.

My children enjoyed these dinners, though I know they were loath to admit it. They disliked all that preceded them. "Church ought just to be dinner," one of them said that night. I smiled in response and, if I were a better parent, I might have said that this is already the case, at least in a church that sees its beating heart in the sacrament of the Eucharist: the consumption of bread and wine. But the kids were off clearing the tables by then, and asking for ice cream.

So that was a successful Sunday dinner, in my mind. They ate with others, and appreciated the experience. That's not nothing. The experiences mount.

Adults benefit from the fellowship of the table as well, as much as and probably more than children. "Life satisfaction" is a term of art used by social scientists to capture a person's overall happiness and well-being. Life satisfaction, the academics say, is strongly correlated with time spent with those who care about you and about whom you care. Dinner is a marvelous way to create that time, to mark it, to make it happen. The life satisfaction does not come from the first meal, or the fifth or the twentieth, but from the effort itself, from the accrual of experience in cooking the meal and sharing it. Regularity matters. Sunday dinners, at their best, are simply special occasions that are not at all extraordinary. They become that way over time.

See You on Sunday is a book to make those dinners possible. It is intended as a rough guide to the business of preparing meals for groups larger than the average American family, which currently hovers in the neighborhood of three. In general, then, the recipes in the book are all written for yields of around six servings (or four to eight depending on portion size), though they are all easily scaled up to feed a crowd and indeed, in some cases—gumbos, roasts, and others—they are meant expressly to feed a large group.

The recipes are mostly simple, if occasionally labor-intensive. They are largely free, I think, of fanciness. The intention is that you can make them. They derive from decades spent cooking for my family and for groups ranging from six to sixty, and from years spent talking to restaurant chefs and cookbook authors and home cooks in connection with my daily work at *The New York Times*, where I have done many things but have always written about food.

The architecture of the book is simple too, or is meant to be: chapters devoted to proteins and grains, to vegetables and dessert, as well as to the joys of exception—taco dinners and pizza parties, meals just for the family, a fine occasion for friends.

Some stipulations about what Sunday dinners mean for the home cook. First: They are not intended to be feasts in the banquet sense of the word. Food costs matter. Veal for a crowd is expensive. So is grouper, so sometimes are duck legs, and a standing rib roast of beef ought to be a rare treat. You are not a feudal landowner entertaining the serfs. You are a member of a family, real or imagined, cooking a meal. So you will see a lot of recipes within this book for cheaper cuts of meat and, along with them, exhortations that you stretch out one-pot meals with gravies and sauces. A vat of something flavorful with a pot of white rice or a tray of roasted potatoes is sometimes all you are after. Simplicity can be more than enough.

"Just throw some stuff in a pot," the Reverend John Merz said to me once. "Put that on rice. That's it." Merz runs our Episcopal parish in Greenpoint, Brooklyn. He was giving me advice before the first meal I ever cooked for his congregants and advising me to keep it simple. I've known Merz since childhood, when the last thing that could have happened was that John Merz would become a priest. Which is to say: He didn't say "stuff." I've kept the advice in mind ever since.

An equally important stipulation, from the point of view of both value and health: *See You on Sunday* offers a number of recipes for grains and vegetables that rightly ought to be seen not as side dishes to accompany a main-event protein but as equal, if not greater, players on the dining room stage. The words of Michael Pollan should ring true for Sunday dinners as in the rest of our diet: "Eat food. Not too much. Mostly plants." That may be difficult to do in the face of fried chicken or roast pork, to

be sure. (And these make terrific Sunday dinners.) But it is worth noting all the same.

I came to the belief on my own, with no intention, by accident. I was cooking a Sunday dinner out on Long Island, off the grill. It was high summer, and the farm stands nearby were thick with produce. I roasted Fairy Tale eggplants over the fire, daubed them with goat cheese, and drizzled them with olive oil. I melted onions after that, getting them soft and slightly charred. Squash got a similar treatment, and I hit them with a splash of lemon juice amid the oil. The main event was meant to be smoke-roasted chicken—I had a couple of them, beautiful local birds I'd rubbed in spice. These I put to one side of the old gas grill that had lately come into my possession, and on the other I put a pack of wood chips in a perforated envelope of aluminum foil. Fire went to that side. The chicken side I left unlighted. I put the top down and went into the house to make a pilaf and get some corn going.

But as I say, it was an old grill new to me, with balky qualities I had yet to discover. When I went out to check on the birds, they were incinerated: coal-black husks, burned beyond recognition. I quietly tipped them into the trash, returned to the kitchen, fluffed the rice, and served it with the vegetables: a vegetarian feast. A dozen people did not remark on the loss. I learned a great deal from that night, and not just about gas grills.

A third exhortation: Set the table. A degree of ceremony ought to accompany the business of a regular dinner in your home, some sense that Sunday night is unlike other nights, that there is a formality to the ritual even if the ritual isn't formal. Put out napkins, place settings, some low candles, a tablecloth. The object of a Sunday dinner is to eat, but it is not only to eat. A table set for the people who are going to share the meal has a civilizing effect.

Finally, do not take any of this too seriously. The purpose of cooking regularly for friends and family is simply to do it, and to make better the lives of all involved in the process of eating the meal. That will happen in fits and starts, not always successfully, which is just fine. A failed dinner or a not very good stew is as much part of the journey as an exceptional meal or a brilliant dish. Each takes its place in the history of your shared meals, to be remembered by all involved according to its hilarity or excellence. Each is just another stone in the foundation of a tradition. Get cooking.

HOW TO SET UP YOUR KITCHEN

YOU CAN GO YOUR WHOLE LIFE with just a few pots and pans, a cutting board, a good chef's knife, and a colander in which to drain pasta. But if you're going to cook Sunday suppers, you're going to get good at them and then people are going to start to drop by to join you in eating them, and sooner or later there are going to be quite a few people to feed. You ought to set up your kitchen accordingly. (You'll thank me come Thanksgiving.)

So to accompany that chef's knife and cutting board, that colander and your favorite pots and pans, lay in a **serrated bread knife, a paring knife,** and a good **vegetable peeler.** Keep the knives sharp with a **steel** and replace the peeler every couple of years. Get a **zester** for citrus and to turn Parmesan into snow (replace it every few years as well). You'll do well to secure a set of **mixing bowls** and an **offset fish spatula** that I guarantee you'll use for far more than fish. Heavy **kitchen tongs** will come in handy day after day, as will a couple of big **flathead wooden mixing spoons.** Do you need a **whisk?** Yes. You'd be surprised.

You've probably got a big pot you boil water in for pasta. You need a **big Dutch oven,** as well, ideally an enameled cast-iron one with a lid that fits it well. You can make stews and soups and gumbos in it, bake bread, roast chicken, mash potatoes. A **really large pan** will come in handy for frying things, in either cast iron or stainless steel. Perhaps you'll end up with one of each. I went decades without a deep cast-iron chicken fryer with a lid. Now I use it all the time.

Maybe you have a roasting pan. That'll work hard for you, but what you need on top of it is a couple of **sheet pans**, known sometimes in cookware shops as jelly-roll pans. You can roast on them, bake cookies as well, but they are not just for cooking per se. They are invaluable prep tools when cooking in bulk. Put one next to your cutting board for scraps as you peel and chop. Use another to stage the ingredients you'll need to cook on the grill, or to salt and pepper your meats in advance of cooking them. Use sheet pans below your pie plates when you're baking, so when the pies weep, they don't bubble sugar onto the oven floor. Use sheet pans once or twice for something that isn't heating through, such as frozen Tater Tots for the kids, and you'll use them for everything, again and again. Already have a sheet pan? Get another. Have two? My friend and *Times* colleague Melissa Clark was asked that once. Her answer: "Get a third."

You don't absolutely need a **bench scraper**. But it's sure nice to have one to shovel chopped onions and peppers onto a sheet pan to dump in the Dutch oven, or to sweep trimmings and waste from your cutting board onto a sheet pan while you prep. You do need a lot of **bar or dish towels,** though, so you can keep the kitchen clean as you work, and to use in addition to or in place of oven mitts when you're working with hot pots and pans.

Next, a few gadgets and machines. You should get a **pepper mill,** so you can grind black pepper and not use the batch-ground stuff that isn't as good. A **rice cooker** is a Sunday dinner standout—a set-it-and-forget-it friend. I know you can make good rice without one. I do, sometimes. But the machine always does, and holds the finished grains perfectly for hours. In the financial history of my Sunday meals, the thirty-five dollars spent on it has paid off handsomely.

A **stand mixer** is more expensive. So is a **food processor.** You can do without them, of course. But they're a joy for making doughs and blitzing up sauces and whipping things, and their cost too will amortize over time. (Or you can get yourself married. Those tools will arrive as gifts almost as surely as an awkward toast at the rehearsal dinner.)

Finally, get yourself a **digital instant-read thermometer.** There is no better tool for letting you know, quickly, what's happening inside your food. Use it to ensure perfectly cooked meats and right-temperature frying. Don't guess. Guess-work is the enemy of Sunday suppering.

If you want to understand the importance of a well-stocked pantry in this Sunday game, try cooking a meal in other people's kitchens. Their pantries come in a bunch of varieties but mostly fall between two poles: a kitchen in which the cooking is a breeze because literally everything you need is in the fridge and the cupboards, down to the tin of anchovies you decide at the last minute you'd like to use in the sauce for the cauliflower; and a kitchen in which the refrigerator is empty but for a bottle of champagne and a wilting bunch of celery, and the shelves next to the stove hold only a near-dead bottle of olive oil, fifteen boxes of herbal tea bags, and a dusty jar of Mrs. Dash.

Your own pantry may fall closer to one than the other, for reasons of circum-stance or thrift. I've worked at both ends. But if you're serious about cooking often, for yourself and your family as much as for larger groups, you would be wise to emulate the one with the healthy larder of nonperishable or semi-perishable goods. There is little more frustrating than discovering late in a recipe that you don't have any red pepper flakes, or cider vinegar, or butter, and no percentage at all in need-ing to buy olive oil each time you set out to cook. Make clam chowder someday with lobster stock fished out of the freezer and you'll experience a revelation, just as you will when you thaw out some chicken stock to use in a stew, just as you will when you drizzle hot honey over fried chicken or a savory waffle. Do you need to make your own mayonnaise? You do not. But, boy, is it good when you do.

So look down the following list and consider the recipes beyond it and, per-haps, start to chip away at the contents at the market and at the stove, so you can cook what you like, when you like, and don't find yourself cursing because you don't have any ground cumin and that damn Sifton seems to put it in every fourth recipe he writes.

PANTRY AND FRIDGE

ANCHOVIES

BAKING POWDER

BAKING SODA

BEANS, CANNED, OF MANY VARIETIES

COCONUT MILK, CANNED

CORNSTARCH

FLOUR, BOTH ALL-PURPOSE AND FINELY MILLED
    INSTANT FLOUR, LIKE WONDRA

HONEY

KETCHUP

MAPLE SYRUP

MAYONNAISE

MUSTARD, DIJON OR WHOLE-GRAIN

NUTS, A LOT OF DIFFERENT KINDS

OIL, INCLUDING EXTRA-VIRGIN OLIVE OIL;
    NEUTRAL OIL, SUCH AS CANOLA OR GRAPESEED; AND
    SESAME OIL

PASTA, DRIED

RICE OF ALL VARIETIES, WHITE AND BROWN AND WILD

SALTINES, PLAIN (UNSALTED)

SAUCES, INCLUDING CHILI-GARLIC, GOCHUJANG,
    HOT PEPPER, OYSTER, SOY, AND WORCESTERSHIRE

STOCK, IDEALLY HOMEMADE, THOUGH STORE-BOUGHT
    WORKS EVERY TIME

SUGAR, BOTH GRANULATED WHITE AND BROWN

TOMATOES, CANNED

TOMATO PASTE, TUBED OR CANNED

VINEGARS, INCLUDING BALSAMIC, CIDER, RED WINE,
    RICE WINE, AND WHITE WINE

SPICES

CHILI POWDER

CINNAMON

CORIANDER, GROUND

CUMIN, GROUND

PAPRIKA, SWEET, HOT, AND SMOKED

PEPPERCORNS, BLACK

RED PEPPER FLAKES

SALT, KOSHER

THYME, DRIED

FREEZER

CARROTS

CORN

FRUITS

PEAS

STOCKS, HOMEMADE

A NOTE ON SALT AND PEPPER

ALL THE RECIPES IN THIS BOOK were developed and tested using kosher salt and freshly ground black pepper. If you cook them with table salt and ground black pepper from a little metal can, you may well be disappointed by the results.

More specifically, all the recipes in this book were developed and tested using Diamond Crystal brand kosher salt and freshly ground black pepper. That isn't a product endorsement so much as a stipulation. Salt, after all, is salt: sodium chloride. But finely milled table salt has a significantly higher density by volume than coarse grains of kosher salt. And within the world of kosher salt, which has two main players in the United States, Diamond Crystal has an appreciably lower density by volume than its chief competitor, Morton's. Use Morton's or table salt in its place, and you will want to use less salt than I call for in the recipes. Taste as you go.

As for pepper, I'll make an aesthetic judgment. The canned stuff lacks the floral pungency of freshly ground pepper. It sits around. It gets stale. Get yourself a good pepper mill and you will use it every day.

HOW TO SET A TABLE

THERE IS A SACRAMENTAL ELEMENT TO Sunday suppers, even if you have them on Wednesday nights with just a couple of friends. You are giving a gift of yourself and receiving fellowship in kind. The table is the stage on which that transaction occurs. You should make it nice.

You can do that in a thousand ways. You could spend the afternoon ironing napkins, then set each place as if for a dinner at the finest restaurant in town, with multiple forks and knives and spoons and glasses for water, for wines. You could set out flatware and china on a sideboard for guests to assemble on their own: coffee mugs filled with utensils, piles of plates, sheaves of rumpled napkins folded as best as the children could. You might arrange candles on the table, over a damask cloth, or next to place mats, in view of flowers. Here are your grandmother's salt cellars. There is a boat for the gravy. You could make a picnic and have everyone sit on the grass and eat off milk crates or a piece of driftwood.

There are only a few rules. The most important is that you never set your table as an afterthought. Intentionality is what matters most in almost every aspect of a Sunday supper. You set the table because you care about what will happen at it, and you have thought through what that means.

So, roughly speaking, everyone needs a plate and implements to serve and eat the food. Everyone needs at least a glass for liquids, and a napkin for laps. Everyone needs elbow room. Some will need extra salt and pepper. Not everyone carries hot sauce in her bag.

If you are setting a relatively formal table, each setting should follow the same model. A napkin should be placed to the left of the plate, with a fork on top of it, tines facing up. (Two forks if you're serving an appetizer or salad before the main dish, the appetizer one smaller than the first, and set to the left of the big one.) Take

care with that napkin. It can be paper, in a pinch, but it should always be folded like a book, with the spine facing the plate. Don't fold it like a flower or put it on the plate itself. You are not a caterer. On the right side of the plate, a knife, the sharp edge facing inward toward the plate, and perhaps a spoon to its right, if you are serving soup or want to use it for dessert. Place a water glass a few inches above the knife and, if you like, a wineglass just above and to the right of the water glass.

That's it. Repeat around the table and then, if you live in a cold climate, remove the plates to the kitchen so you can heat them through and return them when you serve the food. For hot food, there is no greater indignity than a cold plate.

Now look at the table and ask yourself what's missing. Candles, maybe, but don't go crazy on their height: You want to be able to see everyone. Little votives or tea candles are the way to go here, placed down the middle of the table so you can eliminate overhead lights. (The great restaurateur Keith McNally once said that if you don't look better in his dining rooms than you do outside of them, he's failed at his job.) Maybe some low flowers. Water pitchers. Wine, opened and ready to pour. No soda bottles. Make sure there is room to place your platters of food. If there is not, make room in the kitchen or on a sideboard to do so.

And are you serving bread with your meal? There is no need for bread plates or butter knives. Just let people have at the loaf and the butter on its plate, and allow the crumbs to fall where they may. The ritual of a Sunday supper should never be solemn, and rarely formal. A little mess around the edges shows that plain. Let's eat!

HOW TO WARM PLATES

YOU DON'T HAVE TO BE A maniac about this, but it is a simple truth that putting hot food onto cold plates is not something you want to be doing. It's not being fussy to say so. You made a nice lasagna and it's piping hot, and you've let it rest a few minutes to set up, and now you're serving it to a dozen people. If everyone's waiting to eat until the last person gets her serving, and the plates are chilly, the first person served is going to be eating lasagna that's appreciably less hot than the last. Warm plates are not good etiquette, in other words. They are good sense.

Now, if you live in a warm climate, or cook in a home where someone likes the thermostat clicked up above 70°F, this advice may not apply. Your plates and platters are warm because the air in which you use them is warm. But I grew up in the Northeast, in the home of Carter Democrats who wore pilled sweaters to dinner from Thanksgiving through Easter. Before dinner, we took our plates and platters cold from the sideboard. Here are three good ways we warmed them before use.

1. Heat your oven to its lowest setting—probably 170°F or so. Then turn the oven off and put all the plates and platters you need onto the grates within it, and allow them to toast in the dying heat until you're ready to use them.

2. But you're using the oven to cook the meal! Place the plates and platters on top of the stove, in proximity to the oven vent that's probably behind the burners, and rotate the plates every ten minutes or so, until they're warm or you're ready to use them. Some stoves have shelves above them for just this purpose, and people use them instead to store spices that quickly grow stale in the heat, or to display their beautiful enameled cast-iron Dutch ovens, or stacks of stainless-steel pans. Those can be moved aside.

3. Finally, some dishwashers have a "plate warmer" function that does just exactly what you'd think it does. Just load the machine and hit the button.

ON DRINKS AND WINE

SUNDAY SUPPERS ARE NOT DINNER PARTIES. Really, they're not. They are gatherings of family and friends in the presence of food and drink, and they ought always to be festive and full of good cheer. But they are not a time to play mixologist with the tiki drinks or sommelier with a vertical tasting of Châteauneuf-du-Papes from Bonneau. That's entertaining, which is a different affair from serving a regular, if sacrosanct, meal. If you're having Sunday supper on a Sunday, probably most everyone has work or school in the morning. On a Thursday night, same. A Sunday supper is not a time to rage.

That said, there has never been a dinner not improved by some kind of aperitif, whether it be a spritz or a mug of Red Zinger tea, a gin and tonic or a tall glass

of mineral water with lime. And wine with the meal—at least if your culture allows for it or you're not working a program that keeps you alive—is not merely convivial but also an act that for some leads back down a long historical chain: to the culture of the ancient Greeks, to the blood of Christ, to the four cups of wine at the seder table, even to the mindful drinking in some Buddhist practices.

So if you can have it, have wine—have plenty—with your meal. (If you can't, go hard at iced tea, at lassis, at sugarcane juice.) Have guests bring bottles, or lay in your own. Serve plenty of still or sparkling water, as well, and perhaps iced tea or lemonade for the children. Serve beer if it matches the grub. There is no need to spend time figuring out what varietal goes best with chili (a chilled zinfandel, perhaps?) or gumbo (a Loire chenin?). Just serve cold beer, and that's the Sunday supper done. "No better form of sodality has ever been devised," Christopher Hitchens wrote in his memoirs. "The tongue must be untied."

Above all, and despite my efforts to champion moderation, try not to run out during the meal. The transubstantiation of water into wine was a miracle at Cana, one not likely to be repeated soon—and even if it is, what are the chances it happens at your Sunday supper? So do some loose math. A standard-sized bottle of wine yields around six servings, more like four in the crowds I inhabit, and you can figure dinner will run two servings per person, minimum. For beer, consider three bottles per person, even if most everyone drinks only two and a few don't drink at all. (At least there'll be some in the refrigerator tomorrow, and maybe some wine on the counter as well.) Finally, if you don't traffic in sparkling water (there, a bottle per person is good advice), make sure to have a few pitchers of still tap water on the table at the meal's start. Moderation in all things, but not water. You'll need plenty of that. Refill your pitchers as needed.

BIRDS

—

*C*hicken is where we start our journey. There is no better, more versatile, more delicious protein with which to begin an exploration of the joys of cooking for friends and family. Roast a good-sized bird in a hot oven under a shower of salt and pepper and serve the result with a salad thick with herbs, a fresh baguette, and a few pats of salted butter and you will be instantly indoctrinated into the fellowship of the Sunday supper.

Crisp skin gives way to luscious meat, and chicken juices run into the dressing on the greens, the heat melting them a little, the acidity cutting the fat ever so slightly, while the bread acts as a bridge between all three. Take a sip of wine and smile into the candlelight. A roast chicken dinner is a complete explanation of why we cook.

Fried chicken will work as well. So too will chicken baked below mustard and bread crumbs, above soft, fragrant leeks. Relatively inexpensive, relatively easy to prepare, and deeply versatile on the stove, chicken pays dividends long after the meal you've made is gone. (Save your bones: Make stock!)

And chicken is astonishingly popular. Americans love it, in all its forms. "Chicken" is generally the number-one recipe search term at the website of *The New York Times*. Strip out "pizza" and "cake" and it's the same business over at Google. When people look around for something to cook for their friends for dinner, what they're looking for more often than not is chicken.

There are other forms of poultry, and Americans love them too. This chapter includes recipes for their preparation. There are recipes here for turkey, for turkeys are delicious and feed a crowd, and ought to be cooked more often than simply on Thanksgiving. There is a recipe for goose, as well. Goose is a good thing to cook once in a while, if only to harvest the copious amount of fat that sits beneath the bird's skin and use it to roast potatoes. Duck, likewise, and more often.

But again and again, here in the United States, we return to chicken. You might as well know how to cook it well.

Start by buying a good chicken. Time was, the only chicken you could reliably find at the supermarket was the bright yellow factory model, its sad goldenrod skin slack against plastic sheathing. That chicken is still out there, but you have no need for it. Better chicken is now widely available. It ought to be the only chicken you buy.

Look at the poultry case at the best supermarket you know. There are countless options. Here's an Oberlin-educated vegan chicken with a degree in religious studies. There's an antibiotic-free all-natural chicken with an interest in Chopin who goes inside the coop only when it rains. There are hormone-free chickens. "Natural" chickens. "All natural" chickens. Kosher chickens. The terms begin to stack up, and it is difficult to know what to think.

The only label that matters, the only one that can reliably tell you anything about the chicken you are considering buying, is the one that declares the bird "USDA organic." A chicken declared to be "organic" by the United States Department of Agriculture is one that has eaten only organic feed, that has not been given antibiotics, and that has been given access to the outdoors. A chicken that is certified as USDA organic is generally speaking a good chicken. It tastes of chicken. It is better than the alternatives.

Those alternatives are crazy making in their labeling. You may see a chicken that is "vegetarian fed." Sounds good, until you consider that stale doughnuts are a vegetarian feed. So is old white bread. So are antibiotics. You might find a terrific vegetarian-fed chicken. You might not. Buyer beware. Likewise with "kosher" chicken. A kosher chicken has been slaughtered in accordance with Jewish dietary law. But it may have been raised under a different faith. Who knows?

As for a "free-range" or "free-roaming" chicken? These labels mean only that the chicken "has been allowed access to the outside," according to the USDA regulations. How much access, the government does not say.

How about a "hormone-free" chicken? The administration of hormones to chickens is illegal in the United States. You can't find a chicken that's been raised on hormones here. If a chicken is labeled "hormone-free" it is the equivalent of a sign on a banana declaring it "nut-free."

Sometimes you will run across a chicken labeled as "natural" or "all natural." Follow the regulations of the USDA closely enough and you will see that "natural" means just that no artificial ingredient or added color is in the meat. That is not much to go on.

So get the organic chicken. That is the best place to start.

Next, consider the size of the bird, and whether you should buy it whole or in parts. There are little fryer birds, sometimes called broilers. These weigh in the neighborhood of 2½ to 4½ pounds and are good for small meals; I'll sometimes roast two for six people. And there are larger roaster chickens, up in the 5- and 6-pound range, appropriate for a family or small group of friends.

For larger meals where you want chicken parts, you can buy whole chickens and butcher them—not hard. Or you can buy just the parts you need. These are sold bone-in or boneless, with skin or without. For the purposes of this book and perhaps of good cooking in general, I recommend buying whole birds when you can use them, bone-in thighs the rest of the time, and only sometimes skinless or ground chicken.

Notice I wrote "thighs." Chicken thighs appear a lot in my recipes—meat of dark complexion, dense with fat, full of flavor. You can make fantastic chicken breasts for a crowd. The ones that come off the roasted whole chickens that follow in this chapter will prove the point plain. But for a mess of chicken, for a mess of people, it is often best and almost always cheaper to cook dark meat alone. Chicken thighs are more forgiving of time spent over heat. They are generally moister, more flavorful. In the hierarchy of chicken, thighs fall right under whole birds and just above wings.

ROAST CHICKEN

THERE ARE PROBABLY AS MANY RECIPES FOR roast chicken as there are people who roast them. You can make a roast chicken pretty fancy if you like, with brines and butters, aromatics, varying oven temperatures, glazes of sweetness and fire. You can roast a chicken on top of sliced onions or potatoes or both. You could stuff quartered lemons into the bird's cavity or rub harissa beneath its skin. And someday, perhaps, you will do all of these things. But start with a simple roast chicken; serve it with a salad, some warm bread, and plenty of butter; and you'll maybe do that quite a lot: a dinner for friends, easily made. The key is a hot oven to start, a 15-minute blast of heat that helps seize tight the bird's skin, followed by a run of 45 minutes to an hour of even cooking at 350°F to arrive at a golden, burnished skin above tender, juicy meat. A single chicken serves four or five people. For a crowd, I generally double this recipe, using two cast-iron pans or a large roasting pan to hold the birds. It takes a little longer to finish, but not a great deal longer.

3 tablespoons olive oil

1 whole chicken, in the
   neighborhood of 3 1/2 to
   4 pounds, patted dry

Kosher salt and freshly ground
   black pepper

1. Put a cast-iron pan that will comfortably fit the bird into the oven and heat to 500°F. (Or two pans for two birds, or a stainless-steel roasting pan for same.) Rub the oil all over the chicken and season aggressively with salt and pepper.

2. When both the oven and the pan are hot, about 25 minutes, remove the pan from the oven, carefully put the bird on its hot surface, breast side up, and place it in the oven. Cook for about 15 minutes, until the skin has started to turn pale gold.

3. Turn down the heat to 350°F and allow the bird to cook until it is golden brown and an instant-read thermometer inserted into the meaty part of the thigh registers between 155° and 160°F. (No thermometer? Wiggle the drumstick. The chicken is done when the drumstick is loose in the socket of the thigh.)

4. Remove the chicken from the pan, tipping it to allow the juices to drain, then place it on a carving board to rest for 5 to 10 minutes. Carve and serve, drizzled with the hot juices from the pan.

PAN-ROASTED CHICKEN THIGHS

HERE IS CHICKEN AS BLANK CANVAS, a dinner you can serve with virtually any sauce, side dish, or starch that you like. All you need to do is get the skin crisp, and you've got a successful Sunday supper right there.

12 bone-in, skin-on chicken thighs
Kosher salt and freshly ground
  black pepper
¼ cup neutral oil, such as canola
  or grapeseed

1. Heat the oven to 475°F. Pat the chicken dry with paper towels and season generously with salt and pepper.

2. Place a couple large cast-iron pans or heavy-bottomed skillets over high heat, and swirl into each enough oil to coat the surface lightly. When the oil shimmers, put the chicken thighs into the pan, skin side down, and cook for 2 to 3 minutes, then reduce the heat to medium-high. Continue cooking, moving the chicken pieces around occasionally to encourage the skin to crisp and the fat to render, for a further 10 to 12 minutes, until the skin has turned a tawny brown.

3. Transfer the chicken to the oven and cook for 12 minutes or so, then return the pans to the stove top and set over a medium flame. Flip the chicken pieces and cook for 4 to 5 minutes, until the chicken is entirely cooked through. Transfer to a warmed serving plate and allow to rest a few minutes before serving.

YOU SHOULD BE MAKING CHICKEN STOCK MORE REGULARLY

YOU'VE GOT THE BONES. USE THEM. Take what you've got left over from roasting a chicken and put them in a pot with an onion and a carrot and a stalk of celery and some peppercorns and a bay leaf and, should you have them, a sprig or two of fresh parsley and thyme. Cover that with water, bring it just to a boil, then reduce to a simmer and allow it to bubble along for 6 to 8 hours, or overnight. Strain the stock through a sieve in the morning and pour it into what pint and quart containers you have lying around from take-out orders. Allow the stock to cool and then freeze it until you need it. Even if you leave out half the ingredients, or cook the stock for only a couple hours, it will still be better than any stock you buy at the market for four times the price.

ROASTED CHICKEN LEGS
with CILANTRO GREMOLATA

Sounds fancy! it isn't at all. This is a simple dinner that's easily scaled up to serve a crowd: roasted chicken legs showered in herbs and topped with what amounts to a cilantro salad, perfect with rice and beans. It is best eaten outside, with bare feet on sand, but it evokes that pleasure even in a dining room in the depths of winter.

8 chicken legs, or thighs and
    drumsticks
Kosher salt and freshly ground
    black pepper
3 tablespoons olive oil
1 tablespoon ground cumin
½ cup roughly chopped fresh
    cilantro
Juice of 2 limes
2 cloves garlic, peeled and
    minced

1. Heat the oven to 500°F. Pat the chicken dry with paper towels. Season the pieces aggressively with salt and pepper, then place them, skin side up, in a shallow baking pan and toss with a drizzle or two of the oil. Dust with the cumin and place in the oven.

2. Roast the chicken until the skin is crisp and a knife inserted and removed from the flesh of a thigh results in clear juices, 30 to 40 minutes. Remove from the oven and allow to rest for 5 minutes or so.

3. Meanwhile, as the chicken cooks, combine the cilantro, lime juice, garlic, and the remaining oil to make the gremolata. Sprinkle the gremolata over the chicken and serve, ideally with rice and beans.

CHICKEN ADOBO

YOU COULD ASK EVERY FILIPINO on the planet for a recipe for chicken adobo and receive a different answer from each, every one passionately defended as the best. It is the national dish, many Filipinos say: chicken (or pork or fish) braised in vinegar until it is pungent and rich, sweet and sour and salty at once. Sometimes the meat is crisped at the edges in high heat after braising; mostly it is served with the remaining sauce. Adobo's excellence derives from the balance of its flavors and the alchemy of the process of cooking it. The braising softens the acidity of the vinegar, which then combines with the flavor of the meat in beautiful ways. Grilling or frying intensifies the taste yet further. My recipe comes from Brooklyn, where I learned it from Romy Dorotan and Amy Besa of the restaurant Purple Yam. When I published an article about it in the *Times* in 2011, my email in-box soon flooded with emendations. You must use peppercorns! You cannot use soy sauce! Your vinegar is wrong. Fish is better. Pork is better. Chicken is just fine. Really, it is much better than that.

1 cup coconut milk

¼ cup soy sauce

1½ cups rice wine vinegar

12 cloves garlic, peeled

3 whole bird's-eye chiles or
    other fiery chile

3 bay leaves

1½ teaspoons freshly ground
    black pepper

3 to 4 pounds bone-in,
    skin-on chicken thighs

1.　Combine the coconut milk, soy sauce, rice vinegar, garlic, chiles, bay leaves, and pepper in a large nonreactive bowl or resealable plastic freezer bag. Add the chicken and turn to coat. Refrigerate overnight or for at least 2 hours.

2.　Place the chicken and marinade in a large lidded pot or Dutch oven over high heat and bring to a boil. Immediately reduce the heat to a simmer and cook, stirring occasionally, until the chicken is cooked through and tender, about 30 minutes.

3.　Heat the broiler. Transfer the chicken pieces to a large bowl, raise the heat under the pot to medium-high, and reduce the sauce until it achieves almost the consistency of cream, about 10 minutes. Remove the bay leaves and chiles.

4.　Place the chicken pieces in a roasting pan and place under the broiler for 5 to 7 minutes, until they begin to caramelize. Remove the pan, turn the chicken, baste with the sauce, and return to the broiler, 3 to 5 minutes more. Remove the chicken from the pan, return the chicken to the sauce, and cook for a few minutes more. Place on a platter and drizzle heavily with the sauce.

TRINI-CHINESE CHICKEN

Y OU CAN FIND VERSIONS OF THIS DISH all over Trinidad and Tobago, a taste of that nation's diversity of culture and commitment to the delicious. The skin is fried into a lacquered mahogany. The meat beneath it tastes of five-spice, ginger, and soy and is generally accompanied by the hum of oyster sauce mixed with the zing of the pickled Scotch bonnet pepper sauce that is seemingly omnipresent on the island's tables. Do not stint on the lime used in the marinade. It offers a tartness that helps cut the saltiness of the soy.

8 to 10 chicken thighs, legs, and
   wings (about 3 pounds total)
2 tablespoons Chinese five-spice
   powder
3 or 4 limes
3 tablespoons soy sauce
One 2-inch knob fresh ginger,
   peeled and minced
1/2 cup neutral oil, such as canola
   or grapeseed
2 tablespoons sesame oil
1/2 cup oyster sauce
1 to 3 tablespoons Scotch bonnet
   pepper sauce, such as
   Matouk's
Freshly ground black pepper
1/4 cup chopped green scallions

1. In a large nonreactive bowl, toss the chicken with the five-spice powder, then with the juice of 2 of the limes, the soy sauce, and ginger. Cover and marinate in the refrigerator for at least 30 minutes and up to a full day.

2. Combine the oils in a large skillet set over medium-high heat. There should be at least 1/4 inch of oil in the pan. When the oil is hot, remove the chicken from the marinade, allowing the excess marinade to drip back into the bowl, and fry, in batches if necessary to not crowd the pan, turning the pieces frequently, until well browned and cooked through, 15 to 20 minutes.

3. Meanwhile, make the dipping sauce. Combine the oyster sauce, 1 tablespoon of the hot pepper sauce, and the juice of the third lime and stir to combine. Adjust the seasonings with more hot sauce, lime juice, and black pepper to taste.

4. Garnish with the scallions and serve with white or fried rice, with a drizzle of the sauce over each piece of chicken and the remaining sauce on the side.

CHICKEN MILANESE

Y EARS AGO I WENT TO A COLLEAGUE'S HOUSE for a dinner party that was in its execution exactly the sort of meal that defines a Sunday supper: a collection of friends who shared superlative chicken cutlets with salad served across the top, and who then left the remnants on the table to dance the two-step in the living room. This was on a weeknight, after a busy day in the newsroom, and the meal at first seemed to be a magic trick, an exercise in defying the laws of time management. But cook this dish a few times and you'll see. Pound out the cutlets in the morning, then cook at night. The chicken cooks quickly and holds well in a warm oven, or can be served at room temperature with no diminishment of awesome. Dress some baby greens with a spray of lemon juice and olive oil and capers, then plop some on top of each cutlet served.

2 to 2½ pounds boneless,
   skinless chicken cutlets
5 large eggs
2 cups panko or other unseasoned
   bread crumbs
1½ cups all-purpose flour
Kosher salt and freshly ground
   black pepper
1½ cups extra-virgin olive oil
2 lemons, cut into wedges

1. Prepare the chicken. Place the cutlets between pieces of plastic wrap and, with the flat side of a meat pounder, pound them until they are about ¼ inch thick. If cooking right away, heat the oven to 200°F. Otherwise, wrap the chicken in plastic wrap and store in the refrigerator until ready to do so.

2. Crack the eggs into a large bowl and whisk them together. Put the bread crumbs and flour into two separate wide, shallow dishes. Season everything— eggs, flour, bread crumbs, and chicken—with salt and pepper. Working with one cutlet at a time, dip the chicken into the flour, turning to coat and shaking off the excess. Then dip into the egg, lift out, and allow the excess to drip off. Dip the cutlet into the bread crumbs, pressing firmly to help them adhere. Place the chicken on a sheet pan, separating layers with wax paper, if necessary. You can refrigerate these for a couple hours if you have time.

3. Place a large skillet over medium-high heat and swirl into it enough of the oil to coat the bottom to a depth of roughly ¼ inch. When the oil shimmers, and a bread crumb dropped into it sizzles nicely, add 2 or 3 of the cutlets to the pan, leaving plenty of space between them. Fry the cutlets until golden brown, about 2 minutes, then turn carefully and fry the other sides until also golden and cooked through, another 2½ to 3 minutes.

4. Transfer to a baking sheet covered with paper towels to drain, then to a platter. Sprinkle with some salt and place the pan in the oven to warm. Repeat with the remaining cutlets. Serve with the lemon wedges and a salad.

CHICKEN PAPRIKA

THE STANDARD RECIPES FOR THIS russet-hued stew call for the paprika common to markets in the middle of the last century, mostly sweet and never smoked. But using fiery Hungarian paprika or smoked Spanish pimentón instead gives the dish a complexity and depth of flavor that pairs beautifully with butter-slicked egg noodles. It is a meal that lends itself well to consumption on one of those cool evenings when it might be spring, summer, or fall, with rain in your recent memory.

5 to 6 pounds bone-in, skin-on
    chicken thighs and drumsticks
Kosher salt and freshly ground
    black pepper
2 tablespoons neutral oil, such as
    canola or grapeseed
1 large yellow or Spanish onion,
    peeled and diced
5 cloves garlic, peeled and minced
3 tablespoons hot Hungarian
    paprika or smoked Spanish
    pimentón
4 tablespoons all-purpose flour
2 cups chicken stock, ideally
    homemade or, if not,
    low-sodium
1 large ripe tomato, chopped,
    or 1½ cups canned tomatoes
    (or a 14-ounce can)
1 pound egg noodles
2 tablespoons unsalted butter
1 cup sour cream

1. Pat the chicken dry with paper towels. Season aggressively with salt and pepper. Heat the oil in a large Dutch oven or heavy pot set over high heat until it shimmers. Sear the chicken, skin side down, in batches in the oil, until it is golden and crisp, 5 to 7 minutes. Turn the chicken over and repeat on the other side, another 5 to 7 minutes. Remove the chicken to a plate to rest.

2. Pour off all but 3 tablespoons of the accumulated fat and oil in the pot. Return the pot to the stove, over medium heat, and add the onion. Cook, stirring frequently with a spoon to scrape off any browned bits of chicken skin, until the onion has softened and gone translucent, about 5 minutes. Add the garlic and stir again, cooking it until it has softened, 3 to 4 minutes. Add the paprika and flour and stir well to combine, then cook until the mixture is fragrant and the taste of the flour has been cooked out, 3 to 4 minutes. Add the stock and whisk until smooth. Add the tomatoes, raise the heat to high, and bring to a boil.

3. Return the chicken to the pot, skin side up, stacking it in the liquid, if necessary, and lower the heat to medium. Cover the pot loosely and cook until the chicken has cooked through and the sauce has thickened slightly, 25 to 30 minutes.

4. Meanwhile, set a large pot of heavily salted water to boil over high heat. Cook the noodles in the water until they are almost completely tender,

continued on next page

approximately 6 to 8 minutes. Drain the noodles and toss them in a bowl with the butter, then toss again to coat.

5. Serve the chicken on top of the noodles, then stir the sour cream into the remaining sauce and ladle it over the whole.

COUNTRY CAPTAIN

HERE IS A TASTE OF THE LOW COUNTRY of South Carolina and Georgia, food you'll find in restaurants and home dining rooms alike, where matrons of both Charleston and Savannah have claimed it as their city's own. It has been a staple of southeastern Junior League cookbooks since at least the 1950s and is found in various forms in older cookbooks dating as far back as the eighteenth century, a dish that can offer the sense that everything really is different in the South, that it is the one last, true regional culture in the United States. It is also a great deal of fun for a group of people to eat: Condiments galore should accompany the dish. Which ones is a decision left entirely up to the host. But definitely crumbled bacon and almonds. Diced mango or shredded coconut would not be objectionable, given the seafaring history of the residents who first cooked it, nor would a chutney or tart apple or sliced banana or yellow raisins. The resulting dish is salty and sweet, of no great spiciness, a meal that sees its roots in the exotica of curry and the beauty of one-pot cooking.

¼ cup all-purpose flour

2 teaspoons kosher salt, plus
    more to taste

1 teaspoon freshly ground black
    pepper, plus more to taste

1 teaspoon dried thyme

2 tablespoons unsalted butter

3 pounds bone-in, skin-on chicken
    thighs (about 8 pieces)

4 slices bacon

1 medium yellow onion, peeled
    and diced

1 medium green bell pepper,
    seeded and diced

2 celery stalks, trimmed and diced

1 tablespoon minced garlic

2 tablespoons best-quality curry
    powder

3 tablespoons currants

One 28-ounce can chopped
    tomatoes and their juices

3 tablespoons slivered almonds, toasted

1. Heat the oven to 325°F. Combine the flour, salt, black pepper, and the thyme in a bowl. In a large skillet, melt the butter over medium-high heat until it foams. Dredge the chicken in the flour mixture, shaking off the excess, and fry, in batches, if needed, until browned on all sides, about 8 minutes. Transfer the chicken to a plate and drain off all but 1 tablespoon of the fat in the skillet.

2. Return the skillet to medium heat, add the bacon, and fry until crispy. Transfer to a plate. Once cool, crumble and set aside.

3. Add the onion, bell pepper, celery, garlic, curry powder, and 1 tablespoon of the currants to the skillet and sauté over medium-high heat until soft and fragrant, about 7 minutes. Stir in the tomatoes and their juices, bring to a boil, and simmer over medium-low heat for 10 minutes. Season to taste with salt and pepper.

continued on next page

4. Spread 1 cup of the tomato sauce in the bottom of an oven-safe casserole large enough to hold the chicken snugly in one layer. Arrange the chicken on top. Pour the remaining sauce over and around the chicken. Cover tightly with aluminum foil and bake for 35 minutes. Remove the foil and cook for 15 minutes more.

5. Top with the crumbled bacon, the remaining 2 tablespoons currants, and the slivered almonds. Serve with rice and any other condiments you wish.

CHICKEN PROVENCAL

THIS IS A RECIPE I LEARNED FROM Steven Stolman, a genial clothing and interior designer who happens to be a top-flight home cook and whose *Confessions of a Serial Entertainer* is a useful guide to the business and culture of dinner parties and general hospitality. This recipe makes for a perfect dinner-party meal: chicken thighs or legs dusted in flour and roasted with shallots, lemons, and garlic in a bath of vermouth and under a shower of herbes de Provence—generally some mixture of rosemary, marjoram, savory, oregano, thyme, and lavender. The chicken goes crisp in the heat above the fat, while the shallots and garlic melt into sweetness below. You could serve the dish with rice, but I prefer a green salad and a lot of baguette to mop up the sauce.

4 chicken legs or 8 bone-in,
    skin-on chicken thighs
2 teaspoons kosher salt
1 teaspoon freshly ground black
    pepper
1/2 to 3/4 cup all-purpose flour
3 tablespoons olive oil
2 tablespoons herbes de Provence
1 lemon, quartered
8 to 10 cloves garlic, peeled
4 to 6 medium shallots, peeled
    and cut in half
1/3 cup dry vermouth
4 fresh thyme sprigs

1. Heat the oven to 400°F. Season the chicken with the salt and pepper. Put the flour in a shallow pan and lightly dredge the chicken in it, shaking the pieces to remove excess flour.

2. Swirl the oil in a large roasting pan and place the floured chicken in the pan. Season the chicken with the herbes de Provence. Arrange the lemon, garlic, and shallots around the chicken, then add the vermouth to the pan.

3. Put the pan in the oven and roast for 25 to 30 minutes, then baste the chicken with the pan juices. Continue roasting for another 25 to 30 minutes, until the chicken is very crisp and the meat cooked through.

4. Serve in the pan or on a warmed platter, garnished with the thyme.

CHICKEN SHAWARMA

THIS IS A HOME COOK'S VERSION of the shawarmas, doner kebabs, or gyros served out of street carts and fluorescent-lighted dives in cities across the globe, wherever Turks and Arabs and Greeks have come to live and work. All those names have similar meanings, tied to the traditional preparation of the meat on a rotisserie. "Shawarma" comes from Arabic: "turning." "Doner" is from the Turkish: "turn around." "Gyro" is Greek: "circle." Here the work of the rotisserie is done by a very hot oven, which crisps the exterior of the marinated chicken thighs while leaving the interiors moist and succulent, perfect for piling into a warm pita with a host of condiments and side dishes, from feta and olives to baba ghanoush and tahini, really whatever you like. In New York shawarma is often served with white sauce—yogurt cut through with mayonnaise and lemon juice, flecked with garlic. You can make a red sauce, as well, by simmering ketchup with red pepper flakes and a hit of red wine vinegar until it goes syrupy and thick, or just use your favorite hot sauce instead.

Juice of 2 lemons

1/2 cup plus 2 tablespoons olive oil

6 cloves garlic, peeled, smashed, and minced

1 teaspoon kosher salt

2 teaspoons freshly ground black pepper

2 teaspoons ground cumin

2 teaspoons hot paprika

1/2 teaspoon ground turmeric

Pinch of ground cinnamon

Red pepper flakes

2 pounds boneless, skinless chicken thighs

1 large red onion, peeled and quartered

2 tablespoons chopped fresh flat-leaf parsley

1. Prepare a marinade for the chicken. Combine the lemon juice, 1/2 cup of the oil, the garlic, salt, pepper, cumin, paprika, turmeric, cinnamon, and red pepper flakes in a large bowl, then whisk to combine. Add the chicken and toss well to coat. Cover and store in the refrigerator for at least 1 hour and up to 12 hours.

2. When you're ready to cook, heat the oven to 425°F. Use 1 tablespoon oil to grease a rimmed sheet pan. Add the quartered onion to the chicken and marinade and toss once to combine. Remove the chicken and onion from the marinade and place on the pan, spreading everything evenly across it.

3. Place the chicken in the oven and roast until the chicken is browned, crisp at the edges, and cooked through, 30 to 40 minutes. Remove from the oven, allow to rest for a few minutes, then slice into bits. (To make the chicken even more crisp, set a large pan over high heat, add a tablespoon of oil to the pan, then the sliced chicken, and sauté until everything curls tight in the heat.) Scatter the parsley over the top and serve with tomatoes, cucumbers, pita, white sauce, hot sauce, olives, fried eggplant, feta, rice, really anything you desire.

DEVILED CHICKEN

THE EASIEST WAY TO DEVIL CHICKEN—that is, to make it spicy—is to take a mess of thighs, shower them with salt and pepper, coat them with mustard thinned out a little bit with oil and amped up with red pepper and herbs, then roast them in a hot oven until they've gone golden in the heat and the bones pull away from the meat. The more complicated way, which Julia Child pioneered and the Los Angeles chef Suzanne Goin turned into a cultured gem of a dish, is to put the chicken, rubbed with a thyme-and-mustard-thick bread crumb topping, on a bed of sautéed leeks, then roast them until the dish becomes much, much more than the sum of its parts. It's an excellent meal to serve in celebration of a milestone, or just because you'd like to feel luxe. My recipe is an adaptation of Goin's adaptation of Child's. Life is a circle.

FOR THE CHICKEN

12 bone-in, skin-on chicken thighs

1 medium yellow onion, peeled
   and thinly sliced

4 fresh thyme sprigs, plus
   2 teaspoons thyme leaves

1 tablespoon red pepper flakes

2 bay leaves

1 cup dry white wine

4 tablespoons (1/2 stick) unsalted
   butter

2 cups fresh bread crumbs

2 tablespoons chopped fresh
   flat-leaf parsley

3 shallots, peeled and diced

1/2 cup Dijon mustard

1 large egg

2 teaspoons chopped fresh
   tarragon

Kosher salt and freshly ground
   black pepper

2 tablespoons extra-virgin
   olive oil

3/4 cup chicken stock, homemade
   or low-sodium

FOR THE LEEKS

6 large leeks, trimmed so that there is only an
   inch or two of green at the tops, cut in half
   lengthwise and well cleaned of grit

Kosher salt and freshly ground black pepper

1/4 cup extra-virgin olive oil

1/2 cup dry white wine

1 1/2 cups chicken stock, homemade or
   low-sodium

1. **Prepare the chicken:** Put the chicken in a large bowl with the onion, sprigs of thyme, red pepper flakes, bay leaves, and 1/2 cup of the wine and stir to coat. Cover and put in the refrigerator for an hour or more, up to overnight.

2. Melt 2 tablespoons of the butter in a large sauté pan and when it foams, add the bread crumbs. Toss to

combine and cook until the butter begins to go dark and smell nutty. Remove from the heat and scrape the bread crumbs into a bowl. When they have cooled slightly, toss with the parsley and 1 teaspoon of the thyme leaves. Set aside.

3. Return the sauté pan to the heat and add to it the remaining 2 tablespoons butter. When it foams, add the shallots and the remaining 1 teaspoon thyme leaves, and cook until the shallots are translucent, 3 to 5 minutes. Add the remaining 1/2 cup wine and continue to cook until the mixture has reduced nearly to a glaze. Transfer that mixture to a bowl and, when it has cooled a bit, whisk in the mustard, egg, tarragon, and a spray of black pepper.

4. Remove the chicken from the refrigerator and discard the seasonings. Pat the chicken very dry with paper towels. Season the chicken aggressively with salt and pepper, and allow to sit on the counter while you make the leeks.

5. Prepare the leeks: Heat the oven to 400°F. Turn the leeks over so that the cut sides are facing up, and season with salt and black pepper. Heat a large sauté pan over medium-high heat, then add to it the oil. When the oil begins to shimmer, add the leeks to the pan, cut side down, in batches so that they are not crowded, and cook until they are beginning to go golden in the oil. Repeat on the opposite side, then remove the leeks, cut side up, to an oven-safe casserole or roasting pan.

6. Pour the wine and the chicken stock over the leeks. It will not cover them. Put the pan in the oven and braise for 30 minutes or so, until the leeks are very tender. Set aside.

7. Now return to the chicken. Reduce the oven heat to 375°F. Heat the large sauté pan over high heat and add to it 2 tablespoons olive oil. When the oil begins to shimmer, place the chicken thighs in the pan, skin side down, and cook them, in batches, until the skin is golden brown. Turn the thighs over and cook them for an additional 2 or 3 minutes, then remove them from the pan and set them aside. When you are finished with the chicken, discard most of the fat, then add the chicken stock to the pan, scraping at the bottom to release the crispy bits. Cook for a few minutes, then pour the stock over the leeks in the casserole.

8. Toss the chicken thighs in the bowl with the mustard, then in the bread crumbs mixture, covering them completely, then arrange them on top of the braised leeks. Bake in the oven for 40 minutes, or until the chicken is done, then turn up the heat to 475°F and cook for an additional 10 minutes, until the topping is golden and crisp.

OVER-ROASTED BUFFALO CHICKEN WINGS

I FIRST COOKED CHICKEN WINGS IN bulk for a church dinner that happened to coincide with the Super Bowl. Disposable aluminum pans allowed me to get four batches into a hot oven at once, dressed with butter and Frank's RedHot hot pepper sauce. A kale salad with blue cheese dressing played the role of celery sticks and dip, and baked potatoes with a fixin's bar rounded out the roadhouse theme. I was worried at the outset that the wings wouldn't be crispy, as they are at a bar. This was a preposterous fear. Roasting at high heat tightens the skin of the wings and makes them a terrific simulacrum of the deep-fried original, particularly if you roast the chicken on top of wire racks that will allow the heated air of the oven to circulate around the wings. What follows will feed a crowd. Scale up the recipe at will.

FOR THE BUFFALO SAUCE

8 tablespoons (1 stick) unsalted
    butter
½ cup hot pepper sauce (Frank's
    is the Buffalo original, though
    others will work), or to taste
Kosher salt and freshly ground
    black pepper
Cayenne pepper

FOR THE CHICKEN

5 pounds chicken wings, tips
    removed (save for stock)
2 tablespoons neutral oil, such
    as canola or grapeseed
1 tablespoon kosher salt
Freshly ground black pepper

1. Heat the oven to 425°F. To make the Buffalo sauce, melt the butter in a small pot set over medium heat, then whisk in the hot pepper sauce and salt, black pepper, and cayenne to taste. Keep warm.

2. Put the chicken into a large bowl and add the oil, salt, and black pepper to taste. Toss well to combine. Set two wire racks on top of two large rimmed baking sheets and spread the chicken out on top of them in equal portions, in single layers. Roast the wings in the oven until they are cooked through and the skin is decidedly crispy, 45 to 50 minutes.

3. Toss the chicken with the Buffalo sauce and serve, ideally with celery sticks and some blue cheese thinned out with sour cream, though kale salad and blue cheese dressing (see page 272) is also pretty great.

DELAWARE FRIED CHICKEN

THIS IS FRIED CHICKEN CRUSTED in seasoned flour and fried in a bath of peanut oil scented with bacon. I think of it as a taste of beachside living along the Delaware shore, because that's where I learned to cook it, and it's how I cook it still. (The recipe works just as well in an apartment in the middle of the city as in a prairie farmhouse far from town. Maybe it'll be Racine Fried Chicken for you, or Chicken Coeur d'Alene.) Covering the frying pan for a time while the chicken is cooking may be controversial in your set. But I'm telling you: It concentrates the crunch of the skin and makes for a recipe to recall endless summer, wherever you eat it and when. The chicken is as good cold or at room temperature the following day, perhaps even better. Finally, please, don't worry about all the oil left when you're done. Let it cool in the pot, then drain it into an old milk container and discard.

1 whole chicken, 3 to 4 pounds,
   cut into 8 to 10 pieces
1 cup all-purpose flour
1 tablespoon kosher salt, plus
   more to taste
1 tablespoon freshly ground black
   pepper
2 tablespoons Old Bay seasoning,
   or to taste
2 to 3 cups peanut, canola, or
   grapeseed oil
¼ cup bacon drippings or
   2 slices bacon

1. Pat the chicken pieces dry with paper towels.

2. In a large sealable plastic bag or paper supermarket sack, combine the flour, salt, pepper, and Old Bay seasoning, and shake to mix. Add 2 pieces of the chicken to the bag and shake to coat. Remove them, shaking to remove excess flour, and set aside on a baking sheet or wire rack. Repeat with the remaining chicken pieces.

3. Place a large cast-iron skillet for which you have a lid on the stove and add to it the oil and bacon drippings, if you have them. Heat over medium heat for 5 minutes and, if you don't have bacon drippings, add the bacon slices. Continue to heat the pan until a candy thermometer carefully inserted into the oil reads 360° to 365°F. Remove the bacon when it's crisp and set aside.

4. Using kitchen tongs, add the chicken pieces, skin side down, to the pan. Work in batches so as not to crowd them. The temperature of the oil will dip, to between 320° and 325°F. Adjust the heat so that the oil bubbles gently around the chicken. Cover the pan and cook for about 5 minutes, then uncover the pan and cook for an additional 10 minutes. There will be some

continued on next page

spatter, but nothing you can't swipe away with a kitchen towel. Turn the chicken pieces and cover the pan again, then cook for 5 minutes. Uncover the pan and cook for an additional 5 to 6 minutes, turning occasionally, until the chicken is golden brown and cooked all the way through.

5. Drain on a wire rack, paper bags, or paper towels, sprinkle with salt, and allow to rest for at least 10 minutes. Serve with Red Pepper Honey (recipe follows).

RED PEPPER HONEY

I like a drizzle of hot honey on my fried chicken, as I do sometimes on corn bread (see page 112) as well. It's fine served at room temperature, but you can also heat it through in a small pot on the stove top to get it extra runny and to allow the fire of the red pepper flakes to bloom.

¼ cup honey
Red pepper flakes

Pour the honey into a small bowl and whisk in red pepper flakes to taste. Drizzle on fried chicken or corn bread. (Try it with cheese and crackers too.)

SLOW-FRIED TUSCAN CHICKEN

HERE IS A DEAD-SIMPLE RECIPE for a dish to serve with a generous salad, potatoes, rice, or crusty bread. Take chicken thighs, salt and pepper them generously, and rub them with freshly chopped rosemary (dried will work just fine in a pinch). Then cook them slowly in a lot of olive oil, so that they become at once crisp and dense—as much a confit as a truly fried dish. The remaining oil can be used to roast potatoes for another meal, and you can use a small bit of it in your vinaigrette for the salad.

10 to 12 bone-in, skin-on chicken
   thighs, trimmed of extra fat
Kosher salt and freshly ground
   black pepper
3 tablespoons chopped fresh
   rosemary
1/2 to 3/4 cup extra-virgin
   olive oil

1. Pat the chicken thighs dry with paper towels. Season aggressively with salt and pepper, then sprinkle the rosemary over them and press the herbs down onto the meat to get them to adhere.

2. Heat the oil over medium heat in one or two deep sauté pans that can accommodate the chicken in a single layer, then add the chicken to the pan or pans, skin side down. Allow to cook gently in the oil until they have started to brown, about 15 minutes. Turn the chicken pieces over and repeat on the opposite side, for another 15 minutes. By then the chicken should be done, but you can continue to cook the pieces for another 10 to 15 minutes to brown them further, turning them every few minutes. Serve immediately or at room temperature.

SMOKE-ROASTED CHICKEN

ROASTING A CHICKEN ON THE COOL SIDE of a covered grill with the fire set off to one side of the kettle is one of the great recipes of the pleasant-weather dinner playbook, though it'll work just as well if you're wearing a coat and standing at the fire under an umbrella. Flattening the chicken before rubbing it with spices is a technique I picked up from Chris Schlesinger and John Willoughby, two masters of outdoor cooking whose cookbooks are a priceless resource for anyone interested in the pleasures of working with live fire. The flattening leads to more even cooking of the bird—and to meat that is juicy throughout the breasts and thighs, with a definite tang of smoke, especially if you scatter wood chips over the coals before covering the grill to cook the chicken. Two birds, even three, can be made on a single large grill in this preparation. Pair the meat with corn if it is in season, corn bread if it is not, and plenty of roasted vegetables or a large green salad.

1 whole chicken, 3 to 4 pounds,
    trimmed of excess fat
2 tablespoons paprika,
    ideally smoked sweet or hot
    Spanish style
1 tablespoon ground cumin
1 tablespoon granulated sugar
1 tablespoon light brown sugar
1 tablespoon kosher salt
1 tablespoon freshly ground
    black pepper
Red pepper flakes

1.   Build a fire in your grill, leaving approximately half the grilling area free of coals. If using a gas grill, turn the burners to high and then, when you're ready to cook, turn off the burner on the side where you will place the chicken.

2.   Pat the chicken dry with paper towels, then place the bird on a cutting board, breast side up. Using both hands, one placed on top of the other, press down on the breasts as hard as you can. A cracking sound may accompany your effort, and the bird will look slightly deflated, crushed, and flatter than normal.

3.   Combine the paprika, cumin, granulated sugar, brown sugar, salt, black pepper, and red pepper flakes to taste in a large bowl, and rub the mixture all over the chicken, inside and out.

4.   When the fire in the grill has died down a little and the coals are covered with white ash, carefully transfer the bird to the cool side of your grill, breast side down, with its legs facing the fire. If you have any, scatter wood chips over the heated coals and cover the grill. Roast for 30 minutes, then carefully turn the chicken over, add a few more charcoal briquettes to the

fire, and, if using, another handful of wood chips, then cover the grill again and continue cooking until the meat is done, 30 to 45 minutes longer. (An instant-read thermometer should read 160°F at the thigh.) Allow the chicken to rest for 10 to 15 minutes before carving, and serve with Simple Barbecue Sauce (see page 78) mixed with any accumulated juices from under the bird.

BEER CAN CHICKEN

R OASTING A CHICKEN VERTICALLY, atop a half-full can of beer or other liquid, offers an exceptionally moist result, with crisp skin. A smoky-sweet dry rub adds complexity and bite. The dish can be made in an oven, in a roasting pan. (You can even buy stainless-steel vertical roasting stands if you like—I did after readers yelled at me about cooking with actual beer cans, which have an untrustworthy liner in them that, they say, is not precisely oven-safe. Whichever, I have not looked back.) What follows is a recipe for a traditional spice-rubbed version of the dish. But once you have dialed in your technique, feel free to experiment with other rubs, other liquids in place of the beer. Coating the chicken with a paste of miso, mirin, and soy, then replacing the beer in the can with sake (see page 46), is one way to start.

1 whole chicken, 3 to 4 pounds

4 tablespoons sweet paprika or
    mild smoked paprika

2 tablespoons chili powder

2 tablespoons ground cumin

1 tablespoon ground coriander

1 tablespoon light brown sugar

1 tablespoon granulated sugar

1 tablespoon freshly ground
    black pepper

1 tablespoon kosher salt

1 tablespoon chile de árbol or red
    pepper flakes, or to taste

One 12-ounce can beer, with the
    top half poured off or
    consumed

White Barbecue Sauce
    (recipe follows)

1. Build a fire in your grill, leaving approximately half the grilling area free of coals. If using a gas grill, turn the burners to high and then, when you're ready to cook, turn off the burner on the side where you will place the chicken. If using an oven, heat to 425°F.

2. Using paper towels, pat the chicken dry.

3. Combine the paprika, chili powder, cumin, coriander, brown sugar, granulated sugar, black pepper, salt, and chile flakes in a large bowl, and rub the mixture all over the chicken, inside and out.

4. Put the beer can on a solid surface. Pick up the chicken and, taking a leg in each hand, put the cavity over the can and slide the bird down onto it. When the fire in the grill has died down a little and the coals are covered with white ash, carefully transfer the bird and the can to the cool side of the grill, its back to the fire, balancing the chicken upright and using the legs to support it in this position. If using an oven, place the chicken upright in a roasting pan using the same method and place carefully in the oven.

5. Cover the grill and cook for about 1¼ hours, basting with the barbecue sauce twice during the final half hour, until the breast meat registers 165°F on an instant-read thermometer or until the legs are loose in their sockets. (If you're using an oven, you can tent the bird with aluminum foil after 45 minutes to keep the skin from getting too dark.) De-can, let rest for 10 minutes or so, and carve.

WHITE BARBECUE SAUCE

White barbecue sauce is indigenous to northern Alabama, where it adorns the chicken at Big Bob Gibson's barbecue emporiums in Decatur. It melts into a beautiful lacquer over chicken cooked on the grill or in the oven, bringing a tangy slickness to all that it touches.

1½ cups mayonnaise

⅓ cup plus 2 tablespoons cider vinegar

2 tablespoons fresh lemon juice

2 tablespoons prepared horseradish

1 teaspoon dry mustard powder

Kosher salt and freshly ground
    black pepper

Cayenne pepper

1. Combine the mayonnaise, vinegar, lemon juice, horseradish, and mustard powder in a medium nonreactive bowl, and whisk until smooth. Add salt, black pepper, and cayenne to taste.

2. Brush on grilled or roasted chicken during the end of the cooking process, and pass the remaining sauce at the table.

BEER CAN CHICKEN *with* MISO *and* MIRIN

T HIS VARIATION ON THE CLASSIC BEER CAN chicken recipe delivers a riot of umami, the mysterious fifth flavor beyond sweet and salty, bitter and spicy. The dish is excellent served with rice and grilled scallions.

1 whole chicken, 3 to 4 pounds

2 cloves garlic, peeled and minced

1 tablespoon minced fresh ginger

3 tablespoons white miso paste

2 teaspoons soy sauce

1 tablespoon neutral oil, such as canola or grapeseed

Kosher salt and freshly ground black pepper

1 empty 14½-ounce can of beans or soup from your recycling box, label removed, washed in hot water and plenty of soap, then rinsed and dried

1 cup mirin

1. Build a fire in your grill, leaving approximately half the grilling area free of coals. If using a gas grill, turn the burners to high and then, when you're ready to cook, turn off the burner on the side where you will place the chicken. If using an oven, heat to 425°F.

2. Using paper towels, pat the chicken dry.

3. Whisk the garlic, ginger, miso, soy sauce, and oil in a large bowl, and rub the mixture all over the chicken, inside and out. Salt and pepper the chicken aggressively.

4. Put the empty can on a solid surface and pour the mirin into it. Pick up the chicken and, taking a leg in each hand, put the cavity over the can and slide the bird down onto it. When the fire in the grill has died down a little and the coals are covered with white ash, carefully transfer the bird and the can to the cool side of the grill, its back to the fire, balancing the chicken upright and using the legs to support it in this position. If using an oven, place the chicken upright in a roasting pan using the same method.

5. Cover the grill or close the oven door, and cook for about 1¼ hours, until the breast meat registers 165°F on an instant-read thermometer or the legs are loose in their sockets. (If you're using an oven, you can tent the bird with aluminum foil after 45 minutes to keep the skin from getting too dark.) De-can, let rest for 10 minutes or so, and carve. Serve with grilled scallions and white rice.

DUCK *and* CARROTS

I ADAPTED THIS RECIPE FROM ONE the great British chef Fergus Henderson included in his landmark first cookbook, *Nose to Tail Eating: A Kind of British Cooking*. It does not seem particularly British, but it is excellent beyond compare. You crisp up some duck legs and nestle them in a mixture of leeks and carrots, with a chile added for heat, then pour over the whole some chicken stock and roast the stew into submission. There is a great deal of leeway afforded to the home cook by that word "chile." Henderson never specified a type. Countless runs at the recipe suggest that the best result comes from the use of a single Scotch bonnet chile pepper, uncut, placed in the very center of the pot. It imparts an enormous amount of flavor and a strong run of heat. For those made nervous by the power of a Scotch bonnet, a jalapeño can be used instead, in the same way, or a few dried chiles de árbol. Bread is the best accompaniment, and copious amounts of chilled red wine.

2 tablespoons duck fat or
    unsalted butter

6 duck legs

1 Spanish onion, peeled and diced

2 leeks, tops removed, halved,
    and cleaned, then sliced into
    half-moons

8 whole cloves garlic

12 medium carrots, peeled and
    chopped into coins

1 whole Scotch bonnet chile

1/2 bunch fresh flat-leaf parsley

3 fresh rosemary sprigs

2 bay leaves

Kosher salt and freshly ground
    black pepper

1 1/2 to 2 cups chicken stock,
    ideally homemade or
    low-sodium

1. Heat the oven to 375°F. Place a large skillet over medium-high heat and add to it the duck fat. When the fat sizzles or foams, brown the duck legs well, in batches, removing them to a platter when golden brown and crispy.

2. Add to the pan the onion, leeks, and garlic, and sauté in the rendered duck fat until soft, 5 to 7 minutes. Add the carrots and cook, stirring occasionally, for an additional 3 to 4 minutes, then pour all of the vegetables into a deep, oven-safe casserole or Dutch oven.

3. Nestle the chile into the very center of the mixture, then place the parsley, rosemary, and bay leaves on top of it. Put the duck legs, skin side up, on top of the carrots and press them down gently into the mixture. Season the top of the duck legs with salt and black pepper, then pour the chicken stock into the casserole until the liquid begins to lap at the sides of the duck legs—"like alligators in a swamp," Henderson wrote.

4. Put the casserole in the oven and cook until the drumsticks are thoroughly loose in their sockets, the skin is crisp, and the meat is easily pierced with a knife, about 1 1/2 hours. (Keep an eye on the skin for the final 30 minutes. If it threatens to get too dark, tent the dish with aluminum foil.)

EASY DUCK CONFIT

THIS IS A RECIPE TO REWARD SLOW, GENTLE COOKING: The duck cooks in its own fat. It results in crisp-skinned, luscious meat that works beautifully beside a tart salad. (You could also shred it over pasta.) Duck legs are often expensive but not always. If you see a bunch at the butcher at a reasonable rate, pounce on them. Save the rendered fat to cook potatoes or to rub on chickens you'll roast.

6 duck legs

Kosher salt

2 teaspoons neutral oil, such as
    canola or grapeseed

2 cloves garlic, unpeeled

1 bay leaf

Leaves of 2 thyme sprigs

1. Pat the duck dry with paper towels. Using a clean needle or sharply pointed knife, prick the skin of the legs all over, to allow the fat to run when the duck roasts. Stick the skin at an angle, so as to pierce just the skin and not the meat of the duck.

2. Salt the legs aggressively and allow them to sit for 20 minutes to an hour.

3. Use the oil to grease the inside bottom of an oven-safe casserole or roasting pan, and snuggle the duck legs into the pan in a single layer. It should be quite crowded in there. Add the garlic and scatter the bay leaf and thyme across the top.

4. Place the casserole in the oven and turn on the heat to 300°F. Now walk away. The idea is to cook the duck gently, until its fat has rendered and the skin is beginning to crisp, about 2 hours.

5. Now turn up the heat in the oven to 375°F and cook for another 15 to 20 minutes, until the duck's skin is a dark golden brown. Remove the pan from the oven and allow the duck to rest a further 10 to 15 minutes. Or allow to cool and then refrigerate the legs in their fat— you can pull them out later, wipe off the excess fat, and crisp them in a pan. In any event, save the leftover fat to cook potatoes or green beans, to add to vinaigrette, or to rub on chickens for roasting. Discard the garlic and bay leaf before serving.

ROAST TURKEY

IT IS MADNESS TO COOK A TURKEY ONLY once or twice a year. The whole point of Sunday suppers is to ape the fellowship and good spirits of a Thanksgiving feast. Bringing people together in the presence of a large roasted bird helps do that—and the leftovers make for days of good eating afterward. This is as basic a recipe for an herb-roasted turkey as there is, and it results in a bird of uncommon juiciness beneath its crisp, golden skin. While it rests, set the roasting pan over a low flame and whisk some instant flour into the pan drippings. Let that cook for a few minutes, stirring all the while, then add some chicken or turkey stock to make gravy. Add a splash of cream to smooth it out. With mashed potatoes and a pile of greens, you hardly need cranberry sauce, but adding some to the table would not be in error.

One 12-to-14-pound fresh turkey, giblets and neck removed

3 tablespoons kosher salt

1½ tablespoons freshly ground black pepper

6 tablespoons unsalted butter, at room temperature

1 tablespoon grated lemon zest

1 tablespoon minced fresh rosemary

1 tablespoon minced fresh sage

1 tablespoon minced fresh thyme

1 medium onion, peeled and quartered

1 lemon, quartered

1. Remove the turkey from the refrigerator an hour or two before cooking it and pat very dry with paper towels. Allow to sit on a rack in its roasting pan.

2. Heat the oven to 450°F. Rub the turkey with the salt and pepper, inside and out. Using a fork, mix the butter, lemon zest, rosemary, sage, and thyme in a small bowl. Rub this herb butter all over the turkey, inside and out.

3. Place the onion and lemon inside the turkey cavity. Tuck the tips of the wings under the bird, then truss the legs together with cotton string. Roast the turkey, uncovered, in the oven for 30 minutes.

4. Reduce the heat to 325°F. Baste the turkey with the pan juices, and add 1 cup water to the pan if it is looking dry. Continue roasting the turkey, basting every 30 minutes and tenting it with aluminum foil if the skin is turning too dark, until an instant-read thermometer inserted into the thickest part of the thigh without touching the bone registers 165°F, 2 hours and 45 minutes to 3 hours total. Transfer to a cutting board or platter and allow to rest for at least 30 minutes before carving.

TROWBRIDGE STREET ROAST TURKEY

THIS IS THE TURKEY RECIPE I've been cooking the longest, since my friend John Patrick Montaño introduced me to it in the late 1980s. It was the centerpiece of our Thanksgiving for years. It is absurdly easy to make and results in a turkey of great juiciness and amazing skin. Supermarket teriyaki sauce is an acceptable alternative to the soy and mirin and, indeed, is exactly how I made it for at least the first decade.

One 12-to-14-pound fresh turkey, giblets and neck removed
3 tablespoons kosher salt (optional)
1½ tablespoons freshly ground black pepper
1 medium onion, peeled and quartered
2 celery stalks, trimmed and coarsely chopped
6 tablespoons unsalted butter, at room temperature
3 tablespoons soy sauce, ideally light or low-sodium
1 tablespoon mirin
3 fresh rosemary sprigs

1. Remove the turkey from the refrigerator an hour or two before cooking it and pat very dry with paper towels. Allow to sit on a rack in its roasting pan.

2. Heat the oven to 450°F. Rub the bird inside and out with salt, if using. Season inside and out with the pepper. Tuck the tips of the wings under the bird. Place the onion and celery in the cavity. Rub 3 tablespoons of the butter over the turkey. Pour 4 cups water into the roasting pan and roast the turkey, uncovered, in the oven for 30 minutes.

3. Meanwhile, stir the remaining 3 tablespoons butter, the soy sauce, and the mirin (or substitute store-bought teriyaki sauce for the soy sauce and mirin) in a small saucepan over medium heat until melted and smooth. Add the rosemary. Cover and keep the glaze warm over the lowest heat.

4. Reduce the heat to 325°F. Baste the turkey with the pan juices; add more water if needed to maintain at least ¼ inch liquid in the pan. Roast for 30 minutes and baste with the pan juices. Brush lightly with the glaze.

5. Continue roasting the turkey, basting with the pan juices and brushing with the glaze every 30 minutes, tenting with aluminum foil if the skin is turning too dark, until an instant-read thermometer inserted into the thickest part of the thigh without touching the bone registers 165°F (juices should run clear when the thermometer is removed), about 2¾ hours total.

6. Transfer the turkey to a platter. Tent with foil and let rest for 1 hour before carving.

ROAST GOOSE *with* POTATOES

A ROAST GOOSE IS A NICE CHANGEUP for Sunday dinner, providing dense dark meat to all, as well as copious amounts of fat that will turn potatoes from something pedestrian into about the best potatoes you can eat on earth. Guests may raise eyebrows. Goose? Some may never have had it before. You may never have cooked it before. But roast goose is delicious and festive, an ideal holiday centerpiece, like a slender and elegant dark-meat turkey, and that fact makes it all the better for a plain-Jane Sunday supper on a weekend when it's cold out and you seek to keep dark thoughts at bay. The trick with the recipe is to prick the skin so that the fat renders while it cooks.

1 whole goose, about 12 pounds
Kosher salt and freshly ground
    black pepper
3 pounds small potatoes, ideally
    red or Yukon gold, peeled

1. Rub the goose inside and out with salt, and refrigerate on a plate, uncovered, for at least 6 hours or overnight. The next morning, pat the goose well with paper towels, then allow to sit on a rack in the kitchen for about an hour, to come to room temperature. Trim the wing tips and excess fat from the goose and reserve for another use (see page 57).

2. Heat the oven to 325°F. Using a clean needle or sharply pointed knife, prick the skin of the goose all over to allow the fat to run when the goose roasts. Stick the skin at an angle, so as to pierce just the skin and not the meat of the bird. Season the goose with salt and pepper, then place the rack in a deep roasting pan and cook for 1 hour.

3. Meanwhile, cook the potatoes in boiling salted water for 3 to 5 minutes, then drain and reserve the potatoes.

4. After an hour's roasting, remove the goose from the oven and pour off the fat from the pan, reserving it for another use. Put the goose on its rack back in the pan and add the potatoes. Roast for another hour.

5. After the goose has roasted for 2 hours total, reduce the heat to 275°F and continue roasting for 30 to 45 minutes, about 15 minutes per pound total, until an instant-read thermometer registers 165°F at the center of the breast. Remove the goose to a carving

continued on next page

board and allow to rest for 20 to 30 minutes before carving. The bird may be served at room temperature, if you like.

6. Remove the potatoes from the pan and keep them warm under aluminum foil until ready to serve. Serve with Cumberland Sauce (recipe follows).

CUMBERLAND SAUCE

An ideal accompaniment for roast goose and, indeed, perhaps the flavor that will guide newcomers into the fellowship of the goose in the first place. Cumberland sauce is also an excellent accompaniment for roast lamb and all game meats.

1 lemon

1 orange

1/2 cup port

2 tablespoons red currant jelly

2 tablespoons red wine vinegar

1/2 teaspoon Dijon mustard

Pinch of cayenne pepper

Kosher salt (optional)

1. Carefully cut off the rinds of the lemon and orange, taking care to get only the rind and not the bitter pith beneath it. Finely slice the rinds into thin ribbons and place in a small pot set over medium heat with 1/2 cup water. Simmer this mixture slowly for 5 to 7 minutes, then remove the rinds with a slotted spoon and discard. Reserve the water.

2. Squeeze the juice of the lemon and orange into the pot with the reserved water, then add the port, jelly, vinegar, mustard, and cayenne. Put the pot over medium heat and simmer for another 5 to 7 minutes. Allow to cool, adding salt, if needed.

DO YOU NEED TO WASH YOUR CHICKEN?

IN THE 1960S JULIA CHILD TOLD her viewers to rinse their chickens before roasting them, to wash off whatever bacteria were clinging to their skin. A nation abided. For decades, most recipes for chicken were preceded by language asking that the chicken be run under cool water in the sink and patted dry with paper towels. Maybe you do that yourself, out of habit and belief. I did, for years. But there is precious little science to support the claim that washing your chicken makes it any safer, and just a little more that shows it can have the opposite effect, particularly if you don't work carefully, and let the pathogen-laden water spray across your kitchen, cross-contaminating your counter, your tools, that pile of carrots sitting but three feet from the sink. Indeed, the single most important factor in cooking chicken safely has to do not with the start of the process but the end: Chicken needs to be cooked to an internal temperature of 165°F to ensure that any unwanted bacteria has been killed off by the heat. If you pull your bird from the heat at 160°F, the temperature will rise while it rests.

HOW TO CUT UP A CHICKEN

THERE IS NOTHING WRONG WITH BUYING chicken parts when you're cooking for a crowd. A family-pack tray of chicken thighs is one of the great secret weapons in a Sunday supper game plan. But there are times when it makes more sense to buy a few birds and, in the language of the professional kitchen, part them out yourself. It's cheaper, for one thing, and it yields the literal backbone of a chicken stock as well.

Here's how to do it.

1.   Put the chicken, breast side up, on a cutting board and pull one of the legs away from the body of the bird. Use a sharp knife to cut through the skin between the breast and the drumstick. Then bend the leg away from the chicken until the thighbone pops out of its socket. Use the knife to cut through the joint and skin to separate the leg entirely from the body of the chicken. Then repeat with the other leg.

2. Turn each leg, skin side down, so you can see the thin line of fat that runs between the drumstick and thigh. That's where the joint is. Cut through it to separate the two pieces of the leg.

3. To remove the wings from the chicken, turn the chicken on its side and pull a wing away from the body. Use your knife to cut through the skin and joint closest to the body. Repeat on the other side.

4. Remove the backbone. Put the chicken, neck side down, on the cutting board and cut down through the rib cage and shoulder bones to separate the breasts from the back. (Save that backbone to use in a chicken stock!)

5. To split the breasts apart, place the breasts, skin side down, on the cutting board and make a small cut into the center bone. Turn the breasts over and use your hands to press down firmly on the bone you cut into, cracking it wide. Then use your knife to cut the breasts apart, directly down the center of the cracked bone.

6. Finally, you can, if you like, turn each breast sideways and cut it into two pieces of roughly equal size. For fried chicken for a crowd, especially, this will help speed the cooking along, and it helps in matters of portioning the chicken among a large group as well.

ON MAKING STOCK

GREAT STOCKS, WE ARE OFTEN TOLD, are the product of slow and careful work, gentle heat, and a lot of skimming to remove impurities from the broth while extracting as much flavor and gelatin as possible from the ingredients used in their creation. In cookbooks written by restaurant chefs in particular, you will see pages devoted to the building of such stocks, in different concentrations, for different uses. And if you have the time and energy to devote, like, a day or two to making a robust chicken stock, a sticky veal stock, a gin-clear fish stock, a ruddy lobster stock, a bone-pure beef stock, the advice is worth following.

Most of us don't have that time, though, nor do we have the inclination. We don't make stock, because we need stock right now, not tomorrow. We need it to build a sauce, or make a braise, to flavor a pilaf or chowder, and it is far easier to pop open a store-bought container of low-sodium stock, or use a chunk of high-sodium bouillon paste, than it is to—what?—time-travel back to the day before yesterday to make the stock you didn't then know you'd need right now.

Well, yes. But here's the thing. What if you didn't make stock before dinner, but after? What if you could take all the pressure out of making it in the first place, transform it into a habit not dissimilar to doing the dishes, taking out the recycling, throwing the napkins and tablecloth into the washer before bed? What if you abandon the notion that you're making stock for French restaurants that long for starry reviews and just develop a habit of making stock out of the bones and detritus of your regular cooking, so that there's always a little of it in the freezer, in old plastic take-out containers with taped reminders on their sides: a stock of this animal or these bunches of vegetables, from a particular day and its corresponding month? That would be grand.

Some rules: Those chefs aren't wrong about gentle heat, and about gradual temperature transitions as well. Start with cold water and bring the heat up slowly. They aren't wrong about skimming, either. It's hard to do it too much. But you don't really need a recipe beyond that. Just dump the remains of your Sunday supper roast chicken into a slow cooker with a bunch of cold water, a couple carrots, and an onion, along with a bay leaf and a couple peppercorns, and set it to cook overnight. Do the same with lobster carcasses, with shrimp shells, with the wan vegetables at the bottom of the crisper at the end of the week. You'll have richly flavored water in the morning, which you can ladle through a strainer into a container set in an ice bath to cool. Cover and freeze, or put in the refrigerator to use this week.

And then do it again, after the next Sunday supper, down the months, so there is always some in the refrigerator or freezer to enhance soups and stews, to deglaze pans, and to make slightly more delicious a bowl of steamed greens or a pile of rice. Stock is a habit, same as going to the gym or smoking cigarillos on the porch after a big feed. It rewards repetition with the sense that this is how things should always be done. It becomes an old friend. Homemade stock is a Sunday supper secret weapon.

SAVE YOUR FAT

IF YOU'RE ROASTING A DUCK OR a goose, you're going to end the process with a great deal of fat. Do not discard it! There is very little to improve on potatoes roasted in the stuff, and it is a crucial ingredient in making confit as well. (When I slow-fry chicken in torrents of olive oil, I save that as well, for use the next time I make the dish or to use in vinaigrettes.) Just strain the fat into a clean jar with a tightly fitting top, and store it in the fridge. Then use it in place of oil when you're cooking a sauté, or massage some on the next roast chicken you cook, or use it in place of butter in a pan of scrambled eggs.

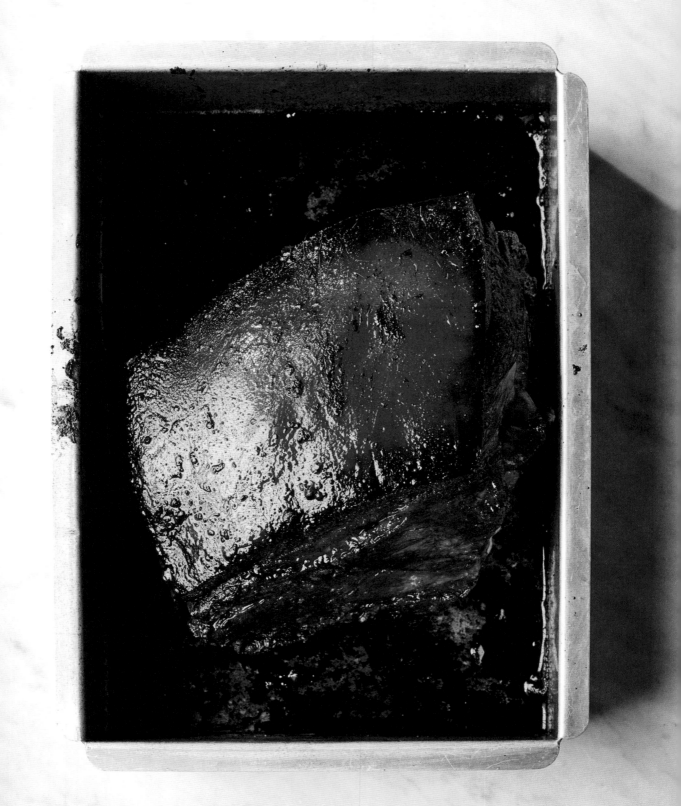

BIG MEATS

—

"The feeling of friendship is like that of being
comfortably filled with roast beef."

—SAMUEL JOHNSON

T*he British have a rich history of Sunday suppers. The meals are*
often built around a big roast—a Sunday joint, they call it—served alongside York-
shire pudding and mashed potatoes, piles of vegetables, lots of gravy.

The British have been roasting those joints for a long time. Some historians trace
the tradition back to the Middle Ages, when serfs were fed a fire-roasted ox on Sunday afternoons following church, their one day off for the week. Others cite religion
itself, and the traditional Anglican practice of fasting in advance of Sunday services.
Parishioners would return from church to an immense meal that would yield leftovers for the coming days.

Whichever or both, by the mid-eighteenth century roast beef had become a sym-
bol of British identity. Henry Fielding used it in his lyrics for *The Grub Street Opera*,
first performed in 1731: "When mighty Roast Beef was the Englishman's food, it

ennobled our brains and enriched our blood!" In 1748, William Hogarth painted a side of beef being delivered to an English tavern in the port of Calais, in front of raggedy, starving French soldiers whose only sustenance was watery soup, a raw onion, a crust of bread. The painting's title: "O, the Roast Beef of Old England."

Today, you'll find the tradition carried on in pubs and private homes alike. "There is no easier way to feed a lot of people than with a joint of meat or fowl," the jovial English cooking personality Clarissa Dickson Wright wrote at the start of the century, during the height of her *Two Fat Ladies* fame. And she was right.

Except where she wasn't.

It would be grand to serve a proper standing roast beef on Sundays, varying the menu occasionally with crown roasts of pork, platters of lamb chops, fat turkeys, and golden geese. Those would make for excellent Sunday suppers (and do). But I don't do that more than once every couple of months, and chances are you don't either. Huge portions of quality meat can wreak havoc on household budgets. The point of cooking Sunday suppers is to gather loved ones close and feed them well, to nourish them and yourself in the spirit of hospitality. It is not to go broke.

So be careful in this chapter. The secret to serving meat to a crowd is to keep the portion sizes small, and not simply for reasons of thrift. We all ought to be eating less protein and more vegetable matter—and when we do, we're happier about it both in the moment and in the hours to come.

Yes, there is a recipe that follows for a standing rib roast, rosy of hue, crackling with a salty crust. Also for buttery steaks and other cuts of meat that can take your breath away at the cash register. But you will also find many recipes that reward, again and again, those who embrace the concept of portion control.

There are a few ways to go about that in your cooking. The first is to "stretch" your meats. Make a stew where you might have made a roast (see chapter four, Big Pots), and if it's good enough (and it will be!), you'll need less meat per person than you may have originally thought. Bake a meat loaf where you might have served a steak, and you'll have money left over for an ice cream dessert. This is an excellent technique to use when you're cooking for groups of ten or more.

The second approach is to use cheaper varieties of meat. You'll see a number of recipes for pork shoulder—a hugely flavorful cut that can be the best friend of anyone who frequently cooks for a lot of people. A full pork shoulder, cooked into carnitas or shredded for sandwiches, can serve up to twenty.

The third tactic is best for groups of ten or fewer, and requires a journey deep into the paradoxical heart of modern cooking and eating. It is to spend your money on very, very good meat. Yes, that meat from the organic farm on the edge of the preserve, delivered to the market by nice young people in Carhartts and clogs, is wickedly expensive. But meat that has been raised well and dispatched humanely often tastes much better, and delivers more flavor than the feedlot protein too often sold in our supermarkets. You need less of it because its quality is high; it delivers, or I believe it does, more calories than its industrial counterpart.

Serve one expensive steak of good heritage for two people rather than two midpriced industrial ones? That's the paradox right there. It's cheaper in the long run.

Let's start with pork butts, though. The name does not imply what those sniggering tweens think it does. The butt is the upper shoulder of a pig, and there are two of them, the up-front equivalents of the hams that power the animal's rear feet. Pork butts are named for the large wooden casks, called butts, into which they were once packed in salt for storage and shipment. You see them called Boston butts sometimes. They are hefty—a full-sized pork butt runs in the neighborhood of ten or twelve pounds—but often are sold in half sizes. Deeply muscled and encased in fat, they are hugely flavorful.

Pork butts can feed a multitude. (So can so-called picnic hams, which are the lower shoulders of the pig, and which may be treated similarly.) They are inexpensive. And they are ridiculously easy to cook, requiring only time and heat to reveal their excellence. You could place one in a Dutch oven on the stove top or in a slow cooker set out on the counter, add a can of Dr Pepper to the pot, walk away for eight hours, then serve a meal that more than a few people would consider delicious. (Seriously.) Chances are you'll come back to them again and again on your journey into the delicious business of Sunday suppers.

PULLED PORK

THE SECRET INGREDIENTS IN QUALITY pulled pork are time and smoke. You'll have a good amount of the latter on the meat after a couple of hours, but it will take many more for its connective tissue to break down and for the butt to begin to collapse within its flavorful bark. I learned that at the feet of a master, the live-fire chef Chris Schlesinger, over the course of a weekend cooking with him at his home in Westport, Massachusetts, during which we only catnapped. "Barbecue Man may appear to be asleep," he roared at one point in the middle of the night, coming off the couch to stoke the grill on his deck. "But Barbecue Man is always awake and in control." The pork that followed proved the point, and subsequent adventures with barbecue men and women across the country confirm its importance. All you need is charcoal, wood chips or chunks, and plenty of time. Cook pulled pork with friends over the course of a day and the dinner that follows will see your joy multiplied for the shared experience of making it.

¼ cup Spanish paprika

¼ cup packed dark brown sugar

2 tablespoons kosher salt

2 tablespoons freshly ground
    black pepper

2 tablespoons ground cumin

2 tablespoons chili powder

2 tablespoons dry mustard
    powder

2 tablespoons ground coriander

1 tablespoon cayenne pepper

1 skin-on half pork butt,
    5 to 6 pounds

Eastern Carolina–Style Barbecue
    Sauce (recipe follows)

1. Build a small charcoal fire on one side of a grill with a cover. (You can make a barbecued pork butt on a gas grill, but it is difficult to achieve the same level of smoky excellence.)

2. Mix the paprika, brown sugar, salt, black pepper, cumin, chili powder, mustard powder, coriander, and cayenne together in a bowl. Apply the spices to the pork butt with your hands, covering the meat entirely.

3. When the flames on the fire begin to die down, leaving flickering coals, shower them with a handful of wood chips, then place the butt on the grill on the side without fire. Do not let the flames touch the meat at any time.

4. Cover the grill, vent slightly, and cook, checking the fire every 30 minutes or so and adding more fuel as necessary by bits and pieces, for 10 to 12 hours, until the meat is soft to the touch, on the verge of collapse.

5. Remove the meat from the grill, let rest for 10 minutes, then pull the meat apart with two forks. Place the pulled pork in a bowl and moisten with barbecue sauce.

EASTERN CAROLINA-STYLE BARBECUE SAUCE

In other parts of the Carolinas, barbecue sauce is made with mustard and vinegar; elsewhere with ketchup and molasses. I'm from Brooklyn, so what do I know, but this sharp and spicy vinegar sauce does much to cut the fat in a luscious pile of pulled pork, and I find that elevates its flavor all the more.

- ½ **cup distilled white vinegar**
- ½ **cup cider vinegar**
- ½ **tablespoon sugar**
- ½ **tablespoon red pepper flakes**
- ½ **tablespoon hot sauce**
- **Kosher salt and freshly ground black pepper**

Whisk the white vinegar, cider vinegar, sugar, red pepper flakes, hot sauce, and salt and black pepper to taste together in a bowl. Drizzle on barbecued meat. (Covered, the sauce will keep for about 2 months, and is excellent on simmered collard greens.)

HOW TO BUILD A FIRE

I HAVE A PROPANE GRILL AND I use it all the time. I don't make judgments about cooking over gas. It's fast and efficient. You can make delicious food on a propane grill. But if you're grilling in order to impart a good hard sear on your food, with a backing scent of smoke to it, or if you're making barbecue, which is to say if you're using wood smoke and low heat to prepare meat over a long period of time, or if you're smoke-roasting, which is a slightly speedier version of the same technique, you're going to need a fire. You should build it correctly.

Here's how. If you're using charcoal, pour it into a chimney starter, crumple two sheets of newspaper beneath it, and light. When flames lick the top of the cylinder and all the briquettes or lumps are afire, use the handle to tip the coals carefully onto one side of the grill, creating a hill of fire that runs from the grill's edge down across its bottom. This will create three zones of heat: very hot where the charcoal is mounded highest, medium in the middle of the hill, and low where it bottoms out.

The whole process takes about twenty minutes and requires roughly two minutes of active work. In contrast, if you're using lighter fluid, you'll need to spray the charcoal with it three or four times, creating huge conflagrations each time, and watch the fire carefully all the while to make sure it's catching and then rake the coals into place with a poker or tongs. That's twenty minutes of active work, where you might be happier getting your food ready to cook. Moreover, a container of lighter fluid will last three or four fires before running out. A chimney starter costs what three containers of lighter fluid do and never runs out. It simply exists, gaining rust but never losing utility. I have one that is twenty years old.

With a three-zone fire, you can sear what you're cooking on the hot side of the grill, then move it over to the cooler areas to finish cooking. You can cook what you're cooking more slowly in the area of medium heat, without scorching it, and then do the same. And you can put a whole chicken or pork butt or stack of eggplants on the side that doesn't have any flame beneath it at all, then cover the grill to allow it to roast in heat that meets it indirectly.

That last technique is barbecue, basically. You can add wood chips or chunks to the fire every half hour or so to create smoke, and a handful of charcoal every hour or so to keep the heat even and low.

Or you can use wood straight through the process: a varsity technique, not for freshmen. To build a wood fire in your grill, get some good, dry split hardwood to burn, then follow the Boy Scouts. Use some crumpled newspaper as tinder, and tepee some kindling around it, leaving plenty of space between the small pieces of wood. (For kindling, either gather dry branches from the yard or wherever you're cooking, or use a hatchet to split firewood into thin blades.) Light the newspaper and let the fire get started, then add more kindling to the tepee in stages, so the flames begin to build. You can blow on the fire if it threatens to stall. Fire loves oxygen. When the kindling is going well, crackling and well lighted, you can begin to add larger pieces. Soon enough, you'll have a good little campfire going. And as the pieces of wood turn to glowing coal, you'll be able to rake them into position for indirect heating and the sweet joy that it imparts to all that it cooks.

EASY PULLED PORK

EASY, YES, BUT ALSO AN ALL-DAY AFFAIR, requiring at least five to seven hours of roasting in a low oven so that the meat achieves a collapsing sweetness beneath a burnished crust. While the meat roasts, debate how you're going to serve it. Sandwiches are the traditional approach, with coleslaw and barbecue sauce. (I like potato buns for how they go soft but do not fall apart.) But the pork is great in tacos as well—and a taco station always makes for a great Sunday supper. Nachos? Sometimes Sunday supper is a game-day event, and the meal should be eaten recumbent on the couch or prone on the floor in front of the television. Alternatively, simply put out a huge platter of the stuff alongside some salads and bread, or rice and beans, and let people have at it. Leftovers are unlikely.

1 bone-in, skin-on pork shoulder,
    butt, or picnic ham, 7 to
    10 pounds
Juice of 1 orange
Juice of 1 lime
2 tablespoons kosher salt
2 tablespoons ground cumin
4 teaspoons ground coriander
1 tablespoon dark brown sugar
1 tablespoon freshly ground
    black pepper
4 cloves garlic, peeled and
    minced

1. Place the pork in a large, shallow bowl and pour the orange juice and lime juice over it, then turn the pork to coat. In a small bowl, mix the salt, cumin, coriander, brown sugar, pepper, and garlic. Discard the excess juice from the bowl containing the pork, then rub the pork all over with the spice mixture. Cover with plastic wrap and refrigerate until you're ready to cook or overnight.

2. Heat the oven to 300°F. Remove the pork from the refrigerator, discard any juices, and place in the bottom of a roasting pan. Cook for 5 to 7 hours, or until the pork yields easily to the tines of a fork. Allow the meat to rest for up to an hour.

3. When you're ready to serve, put the pork on a cutting board, reserving the pan juices and fat. Using two forks, shred the meat off the bone, chopping it up, if desired. Place in a large bowl and moisten with some of the reserved pan juices. Dice as much of the skin as you desire and add it to the meat, mixing to combine. You could cover that and keep it in a warm oven for an hour or so until ready to serve.

MOMOFUKU BO SSÄM

B O SSÄM IS A KOREAN DISH: a moist, fragrant collapse of roast pork beneath a tight and salty caramel crust, with juices thick beneath it, a kind of syrup that is delicious in its intensity. You tear the meat apart with forks and chopsticks, then eat the pieces wrapped in lettuce, with kimchi, rice, and condiments. The chef David Chang popularized the dish in New York at his Momofuku Ssäm Bar, then spread it across the world in a cookbook he wrote with Peter Meehan in 2009, *Momofuku*. I put a version of that recipe in the *Times* a few years later after interviewing Chang, and it soon became one of the most popular we have ever published. That position has not softened since. Here's why: It works, is insanely easy to prepare, and is hugely delicious. Pile bits of everything into the lettuce and eat.

FOR THE PORK

1 whole bone-in, skin-on pork butt
    or picnic ham, 8 to 10 pounds
1 cup granulated sugar
1 cup plus 1 tablespoon kosher salt
7 tablespoons brown sugar

FOR THE GINGER-SCALLION
SAUCE

2½ cups thinly sliced scallions,
    both green and white parts
½ cup minced fresh ginger
¼ cup neutral oil, such as canola
    or grapeseed
1½ teaspoons light soy sauce
1 scant teaspoon sherry vinegar
½ teaspoon kosher salt, or
    to taste

FOR THE SSÄM SAUCE

2 tablespoons ssamjang fermented
    bean-and-chile paste (available in
    many Asian markets and online)
1 tablespoon gochujang chile paste (available
    in many Asian markets and online)
½ cup sherry vinegar
½ cup neutral oil, such as canola or grapeseed

ACCOMPANIMENTS

2 cups plain white rice, cooked (see page 134)
3 heads Bibb lettuce, leaves separated, washed
    and dried
Kimchi, if you can find it at the market

    1. **Prepare the pork.** Place the pork in a large, shallow bowl. Mix the granulated sugar and 1 cup of the salt together in another bowl, then rub the mixture all over the meat. Cover the meat with plastic wrap and place in the refrigerator for at least 6 hours or overnight.
    2. When you're ready to cook, heat the oven to 300°F. Remove the pork from the refrigerator and

continued on next page

discard any juices. Brush off the meat to remove the bulk of the remaining sugar and salt. Place the pork in a roasting pan and cook in the oven for about 6 hours, basting hourly with the pan juices, until it collapses and yields easily to the tines of a fork. Remove the meat from the oven and allow to rest for up to an hour.

3.   Meanwhile, **make the ginger-scallion sauce.** In a large bowl, combine the scallions with the ginger, oil, soy sauce, vinegar, and salt. Mix well and taste, adding more salt if needed.

4.   **Make the ssäm sauce.** In a medium bowl, combine the chile pastes with the vinegar and oil, and mix well.

5.   Make sure the rice is cooked and the lettuce washed. Put the sauces and kimchi, if you found it, into serving bowls.

6.   When the accompaniments are prepared and you're ready to serve, turn the oven to 500°F. In a small bowl, stir together the remaining 1 tablespoon salt with the brown sugar. Rub this mixture all over the cooked pork. Place the pork in a pan in the oven for 10 to 15 minutes, until a dark caramel crust has developed on the meat. Serve hot, with the accompaniments.

PERNIL

PERNIL IS A LATIN AMERICAN TAKE on the roast pork butt, big with the taste of garlic and oregano and perfect with a plate of rice and beans. It is ridiculously simple to prepare. Hot sauce and sliced limes are the mandatory accompaniments. Bonus points for frying slices of sweet plantain to serve with it as well.

½ bone-in, skin-on pork shoulder, about 5 pounds

10 cloves garlic, peeled and minced

3 tablespoons fresh oregano leaves (or 2 tablespoons dried oregano)

1 tablespoon kosher salt

2 teaspoons freshly ground black pepper

2 to 3 tablespoons olive oil

1 tablespoon cider or red wine vinegar

1. Heat the oven to 325°F. Using a very sharp knife, score the pork diagonally left to right, then right to left, to create a diamond pattern across the meat. Mash the garlic, oregano, salt, and pepper with a mortar and pestle, or pulse briefly in a food processor. Drizzle in the oil until you have achieved a rough paste. (You may not need all the oil.) Blend in the vinegar.

2. Rub the mixture all over the pork, taking care to get it into the slits you've made in the skin. Place the pork in a roasting pan with ¼ cup water, cover tightly with aluminum foil, and place in the oven for 3 hours. Remove the foil and continue roasting, basting occasionally, until the skin is crisp and the meat is wobbly. Remove the pork from the oven and allow to rest for 10 to 15 minutes.

3. Cut the meat into rough hunks and chop the crisp skin. Serve with cut limes, hot sauce, and rice and beans.

FRESH MAPLE HAM

A SMOKED HAM IS A WONDERFUL THING to serve for a Sunday supper, an Easter in July or September, festive and pink. But I think there's something magical about a fresh ham—uncured, unsmoked, straight from the butcher—cooked slowly in the oven below a shower of salt and pepper, and glazed with maple syrup and a touch of balsamic vinegar. It's like a giant pork roast, suitable for serving a large crowd with leftovers for sandwiches in coming days. If you happen to have access to what I think of as fancy pork, heritage breeds raised on good slops from the farm and maybe some nuts from around the edges of the field, there is no need to brine the meat before cooking. Please do so, though, if you're making do with what most of us make do with most of the time: commodity pork from the supermarket, low priced and less run through with delicious fat than in times of yore. Keep the skin on the meat regardless and score it deeply with a razor or your sharpest knife. The nooks and crannies allow it to crisp all over, delightfully.

1 skin-on butt or picnic portion
    fresh ham, 10 to 12 pounds
4 teaspoons kosher salt, or more
    to taste
4 teaspoons freshly ground
    black pepper, or more to taste
1 cup maple syrup
½ cup balsamic vinegar
1 teaspoon ground cinnamon
½ cup pecans, toasted
½ cup candied ginger

1.   Heat the oven to 450°F. Using a razor blade or sharp knife, score the entire surface of the ham in a diamond pattern, cutting down just through the skin to the flesh underneath. (If you are cutting to the right depth, the skin will spread apart a bit as you cut.) Rub the outside of the ham all over with the salt and pepper, pressing into the crosshatch spaces between the skin. Put the roast on a rack in a large roasting pan and place in the oven.

2.   After 20 minutes, reduce the heat to 300°F. In a small bowl, whisk together the maple syrup, balsamic vinegar, and cinnamon. Baste the ham hourly with the mixture, as well as with fat from the bottom of the pan, roasting until the very center of the ham reaches an internal temperature of 145°F, 2½ to 3 hours total cooking time. (Begin checking at 2 hours, inserting a meat thermometer into the absolute center of the roast.)

3.   Put the toasted pecans and candied ginger into a food processor and pulse lightly until crumbled and well combined.

4. When the ham is done, remove it from the roasting pan, shower with the pecan-ginger mixture, and cover it loosely with aluminum foil. Allow the meat to rest for 20 to 30 minutes. (Its internal temperature will rise to 150°F or more as it rests.)

5. Tip the roasting pan to the side so you can spoon off all the fat from the pan juices, then place the pan on the stove top over medium-high heat. Scrape the bottom of the pan to free any browned bits, skim any film off the surface, and season the liquid as needed with salt and pepper. Pour into a gravy boat.

6. Carve the ham into thick slices, drizzle with the pan sauce, and serve, passing the remaining sauce.

CORINNE TRANG'S WOK-FRIED RIBS

RECIPES ARE SHEET MUSIC. THEY'RE INTERPRETED by the player in a thousand ways. In 1999, Corinne Trang published a version of this recipe in her essential cookbook *Authentic Vietnamese Cooking: Food from a Family Table*. It was, she said, a take on a recipe she learned from a family friend who was of Chinese and Vietnamese descent. I took it outside to a wok set over a propane burner in the yard, doubled its size, and added a pile of chopped coriander to the finished dish. Sometimes, in summer, I'll cook some clams in the wok while the pork is resting, using the same combination of hoisin and fish sauce to flavor them, and serve the two proteins alongside each other, with rice and greens and an immense bowl to receive the stripped pork bones and clamshells. Sunday suppers can get messy. This is one of the best ways to ensure that happens.

4 to 5 pounds pork ribs, cut crosswise through the bone into pieces of about 1½ inches (ask your butcher to do this with his band saw or clear some time to do it yourself with a heavy cleaver)

¼ cup neutral oil, such as canola or grapeseed

6 large cloves garlic, peeled and minced

¼ cup hoisin sauce

¼ cup fish sauce

1 bunch fresh cilantro leaves, roughly chopped

1. Bring a large pot of water to a boil over high heat. Blanch the ribs in the boiling water for 10 minutes, then drain; work in batches if necessary.

2. Heat the oil in a large wok set over the medium-high heat of a propane burner. Add the ribs and garlic and stir-fry until the ribs are beginning to get golden at the edges, about 15 minutes. Add the hoisin sauce and toss the ribs around in it so that each is well coated. Add the fish sauce and continue stir-frying until the liquid has evaporated and the hoisin sauce has started to caramelize on the ribs, an additional 20 minutes or so.

3. Remove the ribs to a large platter and garnish with the chopped cilantro.

VIETNAMESE-ISH PULLED PORK

One winter's eve, pining for the flavors of Corinne Trang's Wok-Fried Ribs (opposite), but with no desire to cook them indoors, I wondered if her combination of hoisin and fish sauces might make a good braising liquid for a pork shoulder. It was, and how. Shred the finished meat and serve on soft flour tacos with a crisp slaw, or serve on top of rice for the sort of meal that has everyone eating in happy silence, bowls in their hands, forking the food into their mouths in contentment.

1 tablespoon sesame oil

1 medium yellow onion, peeled and diced

8 cloves garlic, peeled and minced

2 tablespoons minced fresh ginger

1/2 cup hoisin sauce

1/4 cup fish sauce

1 tablespoon Sriracha sauce

1/2 bone-in pork shoulder, skin and fat removed, about 5 pounds

12 to 16 flour tortillas, warmed

1. Heat the oven to 325°F. Place a large, oven-safe Dutch oven or pot with a lid over medium-high heat. After a minute or so, swirl in the sesame oil and then the onion, stirring to combine. Sauté for about 5 minutes, then add the garlic and continue to cook until the onion is soft and becoming translucent. Turn off the heat, stir in the ginger, and set aside.

2. Add the hoisin sauce to the pot, along with the fish sauce, and stir to combine, loosening the mixture with a little less than 1/2 cup water. Add the Sriracha sauce to taste.

3. Nestle the pork on top of the liquid, then turn the meat over a few times to cover. Cover the pot and place in the oven for 4 to 6 hours, until the pork is wobbly and shreds easily with a fork. Remove the pork from the pot and allow to rest for a few minutes. Set the pot and the juices aside.

4. Shred the pork with a pair of forks. Discard the bones. Return the pulled pork to the pot and stir to combine with the juices that remain in it. Serve immediately with tortillas or cover and keep warm in a low oven for up to 3 hours.

SPEND ENOUGH TIME COOKING SUNDAY DINNERS and thinking about how you could make them better and eventually you're going to run into the acronym BTU, short for British thermal unit, the measurement of the amount of heat required to raise the temperature of one pound of water by one degree Fahrenheit. How many BTUs a stove's burner can put out has a direct effect not just on how quickly you can boil water but on how hot you can get a griddle and put a sear on a steak.

Say you're in the kitchen making a huge stir-fry for a dozen people on a summer night, working your wok as if auditioning for a job at the little spot down by the train station with the great beef and broccoli, and it's not going well. The damn wok isn't hot enough for all this pork or greens, all these clams and all this rice, though it's plenty hot enough to give the kitchen the atmosphere of a subtropical hell. And now helpful Ron, who hasn't been coming to dinner all that long because he's generally at work late making an extraordinary amount of money and who has used some of it to renovate a large home nearby, is right at your elbow, asking how many BTUs you get out of the stove. Ron's just put in a sick new Viking, he says: 18,500 BTUs on that puppy, can sear a steak hard in about 35 seconds.

Good for you, Ron. Your own stove, like most stoves, puts out only around 7,000. You stare at the wok for a while, then start to cook in batches. Dinner's delicious, if a little late. Leaving the kitchen is like departing a sauna. Ron brought good wine, though; has a few smart jokes. (He's actually a nice guy.) Sunday dinners are the best even when they're not. They're simply links in a chain. Everyone's happy.

But the whole thing may get you to thinking—it got me to thinking, anyway. I've collected a great number of cooking devices over the years and only one of them gets well and truly, brilliantly hot. It's the propane cooking hob I use to deep-fry turkeys and French fries outdoors, in a giant aluminum pot. It's just a metal frame with a burner inside it that attaches to a tank of propane gas and it ran me around fifty dollars at the start of the twenty-first century. When you fire it up, it delivers about 30,000 BTUs in a throaty roar. I was doing that but once or twice a year. But what if you could use that machine to stir-fry, or to fry fish, or to make steaks? You might cook on that thing all summer long.

You could. You should. I do. The investment in a propane hob burner and a large wok or skillet to set atop it will pay off handsomely. Using one is a dramatic and highly effective way to cook, and it has the added benefit of not smoking out your kitchen while you do. I use the hob to wok-fry ribs for a crowd, but it's excellent for making double or triple batches of fried chicken, to do the same with fried rice or deep-fried fingers of fish, to fry hot dogs, to make French fries. You cook Sunday suppers long enough, a propane hob burner is going to come in handy, and leave an impression when it does.

BARBECUED PORK RIBS

THE IDEA HERE IS NOT TO DO VERY MUCH to the meat at all, just let the smoke and heat do their work, though some people like to mist the ribs during cooking with a mixture of apple cider and bourbon. You can do that if you like. You could also cook the ribs in smoke for just an hour or two, then wrap them tightly in aluminum foil and allow an oven set to 200°F to do the rest of the work. But the best advice I can give has nothing to do with recipes and cheats and everything to do with management of space. Sunday suppers draw a crowd, so you're going to want to cook a lot of ribs. Investing in a rib rack lets you cook the ribs standing on an end, which in turn lets you fit four or six racks where you might ordinarily be able to fit only two.

2½ tablespoons kosher salt

1 tablespoon freshly ground
   black pepper

1 tablespoon hot paprika

1 tablespoon chili powder

1 tablespoon dry mustard powder

1 tablespoon light brown sugar

1 teaspoon red pepper flakes

8 racks baby back ribs, or 4 racks
   St. Louis–style spareribs
   (about 8 pounds)

1. Build a small charcoal fire, about the size of a loaf of commercial sandwich bread, on one half of a grill fitted with a cover.

2. Combine the salt, black pepper, paprika, chili powder, mustard powder, brown sugar, and red pepper flakes in a small bowl and stir to combine. Rub the spice mixture all over the racks of ribs.

3. When the flames begin to die down, leaving flickering coals, place the ribs in a rack set on the half of the grill without the burning charcoal. Do not let the flames touch the meat at any time. Add a handful of wood chips to the fire. Cover the grill, vent slightly, and cook, adding a handful of wood chips every 30 minutes or so and a bit more fuel as necessary, until the meat is crusty and pulls easily away from the bone, about 4 hours. Remove the ribs from the grill, wrap tightly in aluminum foil, and allow to rest for 10 to 15 minutes before serving, with Simple Barbecue Sauce (see page 78) on the side.

GRILLED BABY BACK RIBS

W E THINK OF RIBS AS AN ALL-DAY AFFAIR, the meat cooked in smoke and low heat until it begins to pull from the bone. But baby backs can be grilled relatively quickly, and the result is delicious. This recipe benefits from a basting technique used by the chef and barbecue madman Adam Perry Lang, who thins out his barbecue sauce with water, then paints it onto the meat he's cooking in coat after coat, allowing it to reduce and intensify rather than seize up and burn.

1 cup Simple Barbecue Sauce
    (recipe follows), or your
    favorite brand of store-bought
2 racks baby back pork ribs,
    about 2¼ pounds each
Kosher salt and freshly ground
    black pepper

1. Build a fire in your grill, leaving one side free of coals. When the coals are covered with gray ash and the temperature is medium (you can hold your hand 5 inches above the coals for 5 to 7 seconds), you are ready to cook. (For a gas grill, turn all the burners to high, lower the cover, and heat for 15 minutes, then turn the burners to medium.)

2. Meanwhile, combine the barbecue sauce with 1 cup water and stir. Set aside.

3. Slide a spoon or its handle between the membrane on the back of each rack of ribs and use the spoon to gain purchase on the meat's papery film. Pull it off the racks. Then season the ribs generously with salt and pepper and put them on the grill directly over the coals. Cook for 25 to 30 minutes, turning once every 5 minutes or so, and basting with the thinned barbecue sauce, until the ribs are cooked through, with a crust on the exterior and no pink at the center.

4. Take the racks of ribs off the grill, cut them into individual ribs, and serve.

SIMPLE BARBECUE SAUCE

I like this sauce for its smoky zing, which comes from the pimentón, or smoked Spanish paprika, used to flavor it. But you can use or doctor your favorite barbecue sauce, or make one that suits your tastes. Molasses is an appropriate substitution for the brown sugar here. (So, for that matter, is Coca-Cola.) And if you don't have smoked paprika, try red pepper flakes.

2/3 cup ketchup

1/2 cup cider vinegar

1/4 cup light brown sugar

2 teaspoons smoked Spanish paprika

1 teaspoon ground cumin

1 teaspoon kosher salt

1 teaspoon freshly ground
    black pepper

Combine the ketchup, vinegar, brown sugar, paprika, cumin, salt, and pepper in a small saucepan. Bring to a simmer over medium heat and cook for 5 to 10 minutes, until it thickens. Remove from the heat and use at will. Cooled, put in a covered jar, and left in the refrigerator, it will last a good long while.

GRILLED PORK CHOPS

A THICK, JUICY PORK CHOP IS a marvelous thing. But a thin-cut one, cooked quickly so that it becomes crisp and flavorful, can make for a terrific evening as well, and often at a much lower cost to the cook. Pick up a few family packs of thin-sliced industrial pork at the gigantimart, grill them hard and fast, then serve with a pungent salsa and a big vat of slaw. Summer suppers don't come much more enjoyable. Figure two chops per person, and eat with your hands.

FOR THE PORK

12 thin pork chops, 1/2 inch thick or less

Kosher salt and freshly ground black pepper

2 tablespoons chopped fresh mint

2 tablespoons chopped fresh cilantro

FOR THE SALSA

1 1/2 cups fresh pineapple, peeled and diced

1 jalapeño pepper, stemmed, seeded, and diced, or to taste

2 tablespoons minced fresh ginger

2 tablespoons roasted sesame oil

1 tablespoon Asian fish sauce, or to taste

Juice of 1 large lime

1. **Prepare the pork.** Prepare a charcoal grill or set a gas grill to high. Season the pork chops aggressively with salt and pepper.

2. **Make the salsa.** Combine the pineapple, jalapeño, ginger, sesame oil, fish sauce, and lime juice in a large nonreactive bowl and stir to mix. Taste and add more fish sauce, if desired.

3. When the charcoal is gray and the flames have just started to die, or when the grill is very hot, put the pork chops on the grill. Cook for roughly 3 minutes a side until well seared on the outside and done on the inside.

4. Arrange the pork chops on a warmed platter, spoon the salsa into the center of the platter, sprinkle with the mint and cilantro, and serve.

CROWN ROAST *of* PORK

NOT ALL OF THE DINNERS AT WHICH YOU play host should be casual. Sometimes you want to encourage a certain formality, to salute either a person or a holiday, or just to play dress up. That could just be me, but a crown roast of pork makes a stunning centerpiece for such a meal. (The knife work behind building one is a little complicated, so get your butcher to do it for you.) Cooking the roast is not difficult if you use little foil caps on the Frenched ends of the ribs to keep them from burning, and an oven-safe thermometer to keep an eye on the internal temperature of the meat. You'll want to pull the roast when the temperature hits 145°F.

Do you want a dressing to serve in the center? (You do. A recipe follows on the opposite page.) Cook it separately and then spoon it into the open cavity just before you serve the meal. Cooking a dressing within the walls of the meat slows down the cooking and, I think, diminishes the flavor. The result is the rare roast you will want to carve at the table and not in the kitchen.

2 tablespoons fresh thyme leaves

2 tablespoons fresh sage leaves

3 cloves garlic, peeled

1 tablespoon kosher salt

2 teaspoons freshly ground black pepper

¼ cup extra-virgin olive oil

1 crown rib roast of pork, 8 to 10 pounds

Crown Roast Dressing (recipe follows)

1. Combine the thyme, sage, garlic, salt, and pepper with a mortar and pestle or in a food processor, and pound or pulse to combine. Stream in the oil and pound or pulse to make a paste.

2. Massage the herb paste all over the meat, making sure to coat both the middle and the crevices between the ribs. Place the roast in a large roasting pan and allow to sit at room temperature for an hour or so.

3. Heat the oven to 450°F. Roast the pork for 20 minutes, then turn down the heat to 350°F and roast for 1½ to 2 hours longer, until the internal temperature of the meat, measured between the bones, registers 145°F. Let rest for 10 to 15 minutes before placing the meat on a warmed platter, adding dressing to the center of the roast, and taking it to the table.

CROWN ROAST DRESSING

This is a fairly rustic dressing for such an upscale cut of meat, but I like the way the apples and prunes (call them dried plums if you like!) highlight the sweetness of the pork.

10 slices good bread

6 tablespoons unsalted butter

Kosher salt and freshly ground black pepper

1 medium yellow onion, peeled and diced

4 tart, sweet apples, such as Granny Smith, peeled, cored, and diced

1 cup pitted dried plums, chopped

3 tablespoons sage leaves, roughly chopped

4 cloves garlic, peeled and minced

3 tablespoons light brown sugar

1. Heat the oven to 325°F. Put half the bread into a food processor with 1 tablespoon of the butter, a good pinch of salt, and a grinding of pepper, and pulse until finely ground. Transfer to a rimmed baking sheet, then repeat the process with the remaining bread, 1 tablespoon butter, and some more salt and pepper. Transfer to the same baking sheet and spread the crumbs out evenly.

2. Place the baking sheet in the oven and cook until the crumbs are golden brown, about 15 minutes, stirring once or twice along the way. Remove the baking sheet from the oven and set aside.

3. Meanwhile, melt 2 tablespoons of the remaining butter in a large sauté pan set over medium-high heat. When the butter melts and foams, add the onion and apples to the pan along with a little salt and pepper and stir to combine. Cook until the onion has started to turn clear and the apples have softened, about 10 minutes. Add the dried plums, sage, garlic, and brown sugar, and stir to combine. Cook until fragrant, another couple of minutes. Stir the bread crumbs into the apples and onion and remove the pan from the heat.

4. Pour the dressing into a baking dish greased with 1 tablespoon butter. Cut the remaining tablespoon butter into small pieces and scatter over the top of the dressing. Bake until the top and sides are browned, 40 to 45 minutes.

THE BEST GLAZED HAM

YOU CAN SERVE THIS HAM AS A HOLIDAY showstopper with scalloped potatoes and greens, or as a sideboard sandwich station (just add mustard and potato rolls) for any event from a wedding to a funeral, with the definite exception of a bar or bat mitzvah. It looks festive, tastes great with its sweet and fiery crust above the salty meat, and is near impossible to screw up.

1 bone-in ham, 7 to 8 pounds
Whole cloves
1½ teaspoons dry mustard
   powder
1 cup packed light brown sugar
¼ cup dry sherry

1. Heat the oven to 325°F. Place the ham on a rack in a large roasting pan. Score the ham diagonally left to right, then right to left, to create a diamond pattern across the meat. Stud each diamond with a whole clove.

2. Add a cup or two of water to the bottom of the pan, then bake the ham, uncovered, 25 minutes to the pound if it is ready to cook, about half that if it is ready to eat.

3. Combine the mustard powder and brown sugar in a bowl, then add the sherry to make a thick paste. Spread the mixture over the ham about 20 minutes before it is ready to be removed from the oven, then bake until a crust has formed. Serve hot or at room temperature.

HOW TO CARVE A HAM

LOOKS TRICKY. IT ISN'T, REALLY. JUST cut a couple slices from the bottom of the thinner side of the ham, parallel to the long shank bone that sticks out of the meat like a cartoon handle, to create a flat base for carving. Place the ham on that base and use a sharp fork to hold it there. Make vertical slices into the meat, perpendicular to the bone, starting from the narrow shank end. Now cut along the bone to release the slices and serve. Cut only what you need, as the leftovers will stay moister on the bone than off.

SPLIT PEA SOUP

THEY SAY A DEFINITION OF ETERNITY is two people and a ham. Eventually, though, you're going to be down to nothing, and that's when it's time to make split pea soup. Recipes for the dish abound, but I like this pressure-cooker version: Clean and trim and chop the white parts of 3 big leeks. Sauté these in butter until they are soft, then season them with salt, black pepper, a little cumin, and some red pepper flakes. Tip that into the pot of the pressure cooker with a pound of split peas, the ham bone, and about 6 cups stock or water. Cook that on high pressure for 20 minutes, then release the steam manually. Pull the ham bone out and strip what meat you can from it, chop the meat, and return it to the pot. Check the seasonings and serve.

SUNDAY ROAST BEEF

ROAST BEEF IS AMONG THE SIMPLEST of all main dishes to prepare well, especially if you invest in a good thermometer to make sure you don't overcook the meat. Pulling a roast when its interior temperature approaches 125°F, then allowing it to rest, will yield perfectly rare slices of beef (for medium-rare, remove the roast from the oven when its interior temperature rises toward 130°F). Making a roast beef even if the crowd for dinner is going to be small is no error: The leftovers make for excellent sandwiches and breakfast hash. This recipe calls for a relatively inexpensive sirloin tip or chuck roast, and covers it with a simple dry rub that contains a whisper of garlic. The result pairs nicely with roasted root vegetables or mashed potatoes, and always with grated horseradish.

**1 sirloin tip or chuck roast, 3 to
    5 pounds**
**2 cloves garlic, peeled and
    smashed**
2 teaspoons kosher salt
**1 tablespoon freshly ground
    black pepper**
2 teaspoons dark brown sugar
Red pepper flakes (optional)

1. Heat the oven to 350°F. Line a rimmed baking sheet with aluminum foil.

2. Place the roast on the baking sheet and rub all over with the garlic cloves, then season with the salt, black pepper, brown sugar, and, if using, the red pepper flakes.

3. Place the beef in the oven and roast for 50 minutes to an hour before checking its internal temperature with a thermometer. Depending on the size of the roast, you may need to continue cooking for another 15 to 30 minutes. Remove the roast from the oven at 125°F for rare, closer to 130°F for medium-rare, and allow to rest, loosely tented under aluminum foil, for at least 20 minutes before slicing.

FANCY ROAST BEEF

HERE IS THE GOLD-STANDARD RECIPE for a fancy dinner for up to a dozen people: a standing rib roast of beef, simply dressed in salt and pepper, with a cloaking of butter and flour that helps it develop a crust. The process is simple, but the stakes are high; it's an expensive cut of meat. Lessen the anxiety by making sure to have a good thermometer at hand, so that you can pull the meat at your desired level of doneness. The clear fat that runs into the pan below the meat is a perfect vehicle for cooking potatoes.

**One 3-to-4-rib roast of beef,
    8 to 10 pounds**
2 tablespoons unsalted butter
¼ cup all-purpose flour
2 tablespoons kosher salt
**2 tablespoons freshly ground
    black pepper**

1. Remove the roast from the refrigerator 2 or 3 hours before cooking.

2. Heat the oven to 450°F. Rub the butter on the cut ends of the roast.

3. Combine the flour, salt, and pepper in a small bowl, then massage the mixture all over the meat.

4. Set the roast, rib side down, in a shallow roasting pan (the ribs act as a natural rack), and place in the oven. Roast for 20 to 30 minutes, until the roast is nicely darkened. Reduce the heat to 350°F and continue to roast, basting every 15 to 20 minutes, until the roast reaches an internal temperature of 125°F for rare, closer to 130°F for medium-rare.

5. Remove the roast to a cutting board and let rest for 20 minutes before carving into either huge slabs or thin slices, depending on your tastes.

OFF-OVEN ROAST BEEF

A S MUCH A LEAP OF FAITH AS AN EXERCISE in actual cooking, this roasting method calls for placing a beef roast into a wickedly hot oven for 5 minutes per pound, then turning the oven off entirely and allowing it to rest, undisturbed, until it is done. Snaking the wire of an oven-safe meat thermometer out of the oven and onto the countertop will offer a fail-safe guarantee against overcooking. Remove the beef when its temperature reaches in the neighborhood of 125°F. Magic!

1 beef roast, such as top, eye, or
    bottom round, about 3 pounds
1 tablespoon kosher salt
1 tablespoon freshly ground
    black pepper
3 cloves garlic, peeled and minced
1 tablespoon olive oil
Red pepper flakes

1. Remove the roast from the refrigerator an hour or so before you intend to cook it. Heat the oven to 500°F.

2. In a small bowl, mix together the salt, black pepper, garlic, oil, and red pepper flakes to taste to create a kind of paste. Rub this all over the roast. Place the beef in a roasting pan or cast-iron skillet, fat side up, and put it in the oven. Cook, undisturbed, for 5 minutes per pound, about 15 minutes.

3. Turn off the oven. Do not open the oven door. Leave the roast to continue cooking, undisturbed, for approximately 2 hours, or until its internal temperature rises to around 120°F. Remove the roast from the oven. Oh, it's rested. Slice and serve.

BARBECUED BEEF RIBS

Y OU DON'T NEED MUCH TO BARBECUE BEEF RIBS but fire, smoke, and time, which in the right weather makes the dish an excellent weekend meal. For a rehearsal dinner before a friend's wedding once, I showered about twenty pounds of beef ribs with salt and pepper, then tipped them onto a big Weber grill with a tiny fire below it, and fed it a single small chunk of oak each hour for the better part of a day. The result was spectacular. Here I get a lot of smoke on the ribs early, then finish them in the even heat of a low oven. My spice rub adds a little bit of brown sugar to the equation, and some fiery smoked Spanish paprika. These are not strictly necessary, but they add a nice dimension to the crust of the meat. About which, one note: Order the ribs from a butcher instead of searching for them in a market. Except for at Christmas and New Year's, when there's a rush on roasts, you don't see them that often in the wild. Ask for "back" ribs—the bones behind the rib roast or rib-eye steaks. Each rack will be approximately six ribs wide.

2 racks beef ribs, 5 to 7 pounds
    total
3 tablespoons kosher salt
2 tablespoons freshly ground
    black pepper
2 tablespoons dark brown sugar
1 tablespoon smoked Spanish
    paprika

1. Build a small charcoal fire, about the size of a loaf of commercial sandwich bread, on one half of a grill fitted with a cover.

2. Place the ribs, meat side down, on a baking sheet or cutting board and remove the papery membrane from the back of the rack by inserting a small knife beneath it and levering it up to give you enough to gain purchase with a dish towel. Peel off the membrane and discard.

3. Combine the salt, pepper, brown sugar, and paprika in a bowl, breaking up the brown sugar with a fork. Using your hands, cover the meat entirely in this rub.

4. When the flames begin to die down, leaving flickering coals, place the rib racks, meat side up, on the half of the grill without the burning charcoal. Do not let the flames touch the meat at any time. Add a handful of wood chips to the fire. Cover the grill, vent slightly, and cook, adding another handful of wood chips every 30 minutes or so and a bit more fuel as necessary, until the meat is crusty, soft to the touch, and well browned, about 2½ hours.

continued on next page

5. Put two large sheets of heavy-duty aluminum foil onto a rimmed baking sheet and place one set of the ribs on it, meat side up, then wrap the ribs, sealing the package tightly. Repeat with the second set of ribs, then return the meat to the grill to cook for another hour or so, until the meat has completely collapsed beneath its barky exterior. (Alternatively, you can heat your oven inside to 200°F and "hold" the ribs there for a couple of hours.)

6. Cut the racks into individual portions and serve, or return to the grill and cook for 15 minutes or so per side, mopping the racks with barbecue sauce, if you like. Serve with a lot of napkins.

BARBECUED BRISKET

MAKE MY BRISKET IN THE TEXAS TRADITION and, truth be told, I probably cook it a little faster than most. You can bring the heat down in your smoker or grill to around 250°F or so and let it go for close to ten hours if you like. Either way, you need to cook with confidence. Time and smoke are going to do their work, melting the meat and giving it a nice crusty bark as well. So don't just spend the better part of the day's cooking standing around feeding fuel to the fire and worrying. Instead, make side dishes of beans and coleslaw, heading out between tasks to check on the temperature and get the smoke up on the grill. It all adds up to a really pleasant day into a delicious evening. I love serving the finished meat with Simple Barbecue Sauce (see page 78), pickles, and slices of cheap white sandwich bread, as they do at actual barbecue joints. The bread is like a napkin and mop, all at once.

2 tablespoons kosher salt

2 tablespoons freshly ground
    black pepper

2 tablespoons dark brown sugar

2 tablespoons paprika

1 piece beef brisket, with a thick
    layer of fat, 5 to 6 pounds

1. Build a small charcoal fire, about the size of a box of cereal, on one half of a grill fitted with a cover. If you're using a gas grill, light only one of the two burners, or two of the three, and get the temperature to around 325°F.

2. Combine the salt, pepper, brown sugar, and paprika in a bowl, breaking up the brown sugar with a fork. Place the brisket in a foil roasting pan just large enough to hold it and, using your hands, cover the meat entirely in the rub.

3. When the flames in the charcoal grill begin to die down, leaving flickering coals, place the pan and brisket on the half of the grill without the burning charcoal. (If you're using a gas grill, place the pan over the part of the grill that doesn't have heat beneath it.) Add a handful of wood chips to the fire. (For a gas grill, you can put chips into an envelope of aluminum foil. Pierce it with a fork and place it over the live burner.) Cover the grill, vent slightly, and cook, adding a handful of wood chips every 30 minutes or so and a bit more fuel as necessary, until the meat is crusty, soft to the touch, and well browned, 5 to 7 hours. If the brisket begins to brown too much, tent it with a sheet of foil.

continued on next page

4. Transfer the cooked brisket to a cutting board, cover with foil, and allow to rest for 15 minutes or so, reserving the pan juices. Use a sharp knife to slice the brisket across the grain. Serve with white bread, pan juices, crisp pickles, and your favorite barbecue sauce.

CHEATER'S BRISKET

AN HOUR OR SO AT THE GRILL, then ten hours of unattended cooking in the oven—there are times when this is the best option for delivering an immense amount of smoky brisket to the table at the end of the day while still attending to the business of weekend living. This recipe is a cheat on the whole culture of Texas barbecue, yes. But it's delicious all the same. Serve with barbecue sauce, baked beans, white sandwich bread, pickles, coleslaw, whatever you like.

1/3 cup packed dark brown sugar

3 tablespoons smoked paprika

3 tablespoons kosher salt

3 tablespoons freshly ground
   black pepper

2 tablespoons ground cumin

1 beef brisket, ideally untrimmed,
   about 10 pounds

1. Combine the brown sugar, paprika, salt, pepper, and cumin in a small bowl, then rub it all over the brisket, coating it entirely. (You can apply the rub the night before cooking and allow it to season, wrapped, in the refrigerator.)

2. Build a fire on one side of a charcoal grill, or set one of the burners on a gas grill to high. When all the coals are covered with gray ash or the gas grill is hot, place the brisket, fat side up, on the cooler side of the grill, add a handful of wood chips to the hot side, if you have any, and put the cover down. Cook for 30 minutes. Flip the brisket over, add a second handful of wood chips to the hot side, and cook for an additional 30 minutes. Remove the brisket and wrap tightly in two sheets of heavy-duty aluminum foil, fat side up.

3. Heat the oven to 225°F. Put the foil-wrapped brisket in a large roasting pan and place in the oven to cook, unattended, for the next 9 to 10 hours, until extremely tender. (The internal temperature of the meat will be around 165°F.) Unwrap the meat carefully, still in the roasting pan, and save the accumulated juices. Slice against the grain and pour the juices on top of the result.

SWEET *and* SOUR BRISKET

Y OU CAN BE A CHRISTIAN HOLY ROLLER, an Easter Catholic, a Dharma brat, or a devout Muslim—someday, somehow, you're going to need a Passover recipe, for yourself or someone else. Mine, a regular of our Sunday supper rotation, derives from a recipe that Joan Nathan, the cookbook writer and historian of Jewish cooking, gave me for brisket—oven-braised in a tart, tangy medium of onion, ginger, garlic, mustard, and wine, as well as two secret ingredients. These are soy sauce and a can of Coke. Passover celebrants have rejoiced at the results of the alchemy achieved, but not only they. I've served this dish in an Episcopal church for Epiphany meals as well, to great effect.

1 medium onion, peeled and
    quartered

One 3-inch knob fresh ginger,
    peeled

8 large cloves garlic, peeled

¼ cup Dijon mustard

½ cup dry red wine

One 12-ounce can Coca-Cola

1 cup ketchup

¼ cup honey

¼ cup cider vinegar

¼ cup soy sauce

½ cup olive oil

Large pinch of ground cloves

1 tablespoon coarsely ground
    black pepper, or to taste

1 first-cut brisket, 6 to 7 pounds,
    rinsed and patted dry

1.   Heat the oven to 350°F. Place everything but the brisket into a food processor or blender, and process until smooth.

2.   Place the brisket, fat side up, into a heavy roasting pan just large enough to hold it, and pour the sauce over it. Cover tightly with aluminum foil and roast for 2 hours. Turn the brisket over and roast, uncovered, for 1 to 2 more hours, until the meat is fork-tender and collapsing. Remove the brisket from the oven and, ideally, allow to cool, then cover and refrigerate overnight.

3.   The next day, heat the oven to 350°F. Transfer the brisket to a cutting board, lift out the congealed fat on the braising liquid, and cut the meat, against the grain, into thick slices.

4.   Set the pan over two burners on the stove top. Turn the heat to high and allow the sauce to heat through. It may need some reducing. If so, boil it down. Return the meat to the sauce and place the pan in the oven for 15 to 20 minutes, until it is heated through.

GRILLED RIB-EYE STEAKS

I LEARNED TO COOK THESE DRY-RUBBED STEAKS from Alan Ashkinaze, the executive chef of Gallagher's Steakhouse in Manhattan. The rub on it delivers an impressive crust that is forgiving of the sorts of not-quite-prime steaks that we often run into at the supermarket, and makes for an excellent grilling-weather meal. The recipe calls for four big steaks. Sliced before serving, which is how you ought to deliver the meat to the table, these will serve eight to ten people. Put the bones out as well, for those who like to gnaw. I enjoy grilled salad to go with it, and potatoes.

2 tablespoons kosher salt

2 tablespoons freshly ground
   black pepper

2 tablespoons light brown sugar

1 tablespoon sweet paprika

2 teaspoons garlic powder

2 teaspoons onion powder

1 tablespoon chili powder, ancho
   if you can find it

1 teaspoon celery seeds

1 teaspoon ground cumin

1/2 teaspoon cayenne pepper, or
   to taste

4 rib-eye steaks, 1 1/2 inches thick,
   12 to 14 ounces each

1. Build a fire in your grill. If using a gas grill, turn all the burners to high.

2. Combine the salt, black pepper, brown sugar, paprika, garlic powder, onion powder, chili powder, celery seeds, cumin, and cayenne in a medium bowl. Rub the steaks all over with the mixture and set aside.

3. When the coals are covered with gray ash and the fire is hot (you can hold your hand 6 inches over the grill for only a few seconds), put the steaks on the grill directly over the coals and cook until deeply seared, 5 to 6 minutes. Turn the steaks over and cook for 6 to 8 minutes more for medium-rare.

4. Remove the steaks from the grill and allow to rest for 5 to 7 minutes before slicing the meat off the bone and against the grain into thick slices. Place on a warmed serving platter and dress with the accumulated juices on the carving board.

PAN-ROASTED STEAKS
with GARLIC *and* THYME BUTTER

A CLASSIC RESTAURANT PREPARATION ADAPTED TO the home—bistro cooking for a gathering of friends after work or play. Serve with smashed potatoes or roasted root vegetables, with a salad. The better the steak, the more expensive your meal will be, so go heavy on the side dishes and reduce the portion size of the meat accordingly. A sixteen-ounce steak, pan-roasted in butter, will easily serve four if the vegetables are delicious, and doubly so if you offer loads of bread, butter, and cheese to finish the meal.

1 to 4 beef steaks, such as strip, rib-eye, flat-iron, chuck-eye, hanger, or skirt, roughly 1 pound each
Kosher salt and freshly ground black pepper
2 tablespoons unsalted butter per steak, cubed
1 clove garlic per steak, peeled
1 thyme sprig per steak

1. Remove the steaks from the refrigerator and pat dry with paper towels. If you have the time, allow them to sit at room temperature for 30 minutes or so. Pat dry once more.

2. Heat the oven to 375°F. Place a large, oven-safe skillet on the stove top over medium-high heat. Two steaks should fit comfortably in it; if you're cooking more than two steaks, use two pans. Scatter a teaspoon or so of salt into the skillet and allow to heat for 2 to 3 minutes more. Place the steaks in the pan and cook for 1 minute, then turn them over and do the same on the other side, moving them around a little so that they become well salted. Grind pepper over the steaks and sprinkle a little more salt on them, if necessary.

3. Turn the steaks over again and place the skillet in the oven to roast for 3 to 4 minutes, then remove the pan and place on the stove top over low heat. Check for doneness, either with an instant-read thermometer, which should read around 120°F at this point, or by touch: The meat should be softly firm but not slack. Turn off the heat under the pan. Add to the pan 2 tablespoons butter for each steak you are cooking, along with the garlic and thyme sprig per steak. When the butter has melted and started to foam, tip the pan away from you so that the liquid pools at that side of the pan and, using a long-handled spoon, quickly and repeatedly baste the meat with the melted butter until

the butter turns nutty and brown. Remove the skillet from the heat and the steaks from the skillet. Allow the steaks to rest on a cutting board for 5 minutes before slicing. Place the meat on a warmed platter and drizzle with the butter left in the pan.

PAN-ROASTED STEAKS
with HOT-SAUCE BUTTER

Y OU COULD MAKE THIS RECIPE with one of the classic American hot sauces—your Frank's or Texas Pete, your Tabasco or Crystal. But I prefer the fruitier and more fiery condiments of the Caribbean basin, like Matouk's and Baron, where the floral taste of Scotch bonnet chile peppers dominates and the sauces are often thickened with the squash known on some islands as pumpkin and others as calabaza. Married to butter, that can become a steak sauce of uncommon excellence.

1 to 4 beef steaks, roughly 1 pound
    each, such as strip, rib-eye,
    flat-iron, chuck-eye, hanger,
    or skirt

Kosher salt and freshly ground
    black pepper

2 tablespoons unsalted butter per
    steak, cubed

1 clove garlic per steak, peeled

1 to 2 tablespoons of your favorite
    hot sauce, or to taste

1.   Remove the steaks from the refrigerator and pat dry with paper towels. If you have the time, allow them to sit at room temperature for 30 minutes or so. Pat dry once more.

2.   Heat the oven to 375°F. Place a large, oven-safe skillet on the stove top over medium-high heat. Two steaks should fit comfortably in it; if cooking more than two steaks, use two pans. Scatter a teaspoon or so of salt into the skillet and allow to heat for 2 to 3 minutes more. Place the steaks in the pan and cook for 1 minute, then turn them over and do the same on the other side, moving them around a little so that they become well salted. Grind black pepper over the steaks and sprinkle a little more salt on them, if necessary.

3.   Turn the steaks over again and place the skillet in the oven to roast for 3 to 4 minutes, then remove the pan and place on the stove top over low heat. Check for doneness, either with an instant-read thermometer, which should read around 120°F at this point, or by touch: The meat should be softly firm but not slack. Turn off the heat under the pan. Add to the pan 2 tablespoons butter for each steak you are cooking, along with the garlic per steak and the hot sauce. When the butter has melted and started to foam, tip the pan away from you so that the liquid pools at that side of the pan and, using a long-handled spoon, quickly and

repeatedly baste the meat with the melted butter until the butter turns nutty and brown.

4. Remove the steaks from the skillet. Allow them to rest on a cutting board for 5 minutes before slicing. Place the meat on a warmed platter and drizzle with the hot-sauce butter left in the pan.

PAN-ROASTED STEAKS *with* GINGER *and* SOY

MY FRIEND MARK BITTMAN HAS BEEN cooking steaks with ginger and soy ever since he picked up the technique from the chef Jean-Georges Vongerichten at the dawn of this century. Mark's method is even simpler than mine. He doesn't roast the steaks at all, but cooks them in the pan at a lower temperature, flipping them repeatedly in the butter, soy, and ginger until they're done. I like my technique, but try Mark's sometime and measure the result against the one you get here. Plain white rice goes very well alongside, with sautéed greens.

1 to 4 beef steaks, roughly 1 pound each, such as strip, rib-eye, flat-iron, chuck-eye, hanger, or skirt

Kosher salt and freshly ground black pepper

2 tablespoons unsalted butter per steak, cubed

1 tablespoon minced fresh ginger per steak

1 tablespoon soy sauce per steak

1.   Remove the steaks from the refrigerator and pat dry with paper towels. If you have the time, allow them to sit at room temperature for 30 minutes or so. Pat dry once more.

2.   Heat the oven to 375°F. Place a large, oven-safe skillet on the stove top over medium-high heat. Two steaks should fit comfortably in it; if cooking more than two steaks, use two pans. Scatter a teaspoon or so of salt into the skillet and allow to heat for 2 to 3 minutes more. Place the steaks in the pan and cook for 1 minute, then turn them over and do the same on the other side, moving them around a little so that they become well salted. Grind pepper over the steaks and sprinkle a little more salt on them, if necessary.

3.   Turn the steaks over again and place the skillet in the oven to roast for 3 to 4 minutes, then remove the pan and place on the stove top over low heat. Check for doneness, either with an instant-read thermometer, which should read around 120°F at this point, or by touch: The meat should be softly firm but not slack. Turn off the heat under the pan. Add to the pan 2 tablespoons butter for each steak you are cooking, along with the ginger. When the butter has melted and started to foam, tip the pan away from you so that the liquid pools at that side of the pan and, using a long-handled spoon, quickly and repeatedly baste the meat

with the melted butter and ginger. Add the soy sauce and continue basting another five or six times.

4. Remove the steaks from the skillet. Allow them to rest on a cutting board for 5 minutes before slicing. Place the meat on a warmed platter and drizzle with the ginger and soy butter left in the pan.

OVEN-ROASTED LAMB

L AMB LOVES SMOKE, BUT IF YOU DON'T, or you don't have access to a grill, a buttery glaze scented with fennel and coriander, along with some honey, vinegar, and chile, is a worthy substitute. It's a trick I picked up eating at the late restaurant DBGB in New York, where the chef Jim Leiken applied just such a sauce to lamb ribs, before sprinkling them with lemon zest and chiles. On a rolled and tied boneless leg of lamb, this makes for an astonishing dinner.

FOR THE LAMB

1 boneless leg of lamb, rolled
    and tied, 3 to 4 pounds
4 teaspoons kosher salt
2 teaspoons freshly ground
    black pepper
6 cloves garlic, peeled and finely
    diced
Leaves of 6 thyme sprigs
Leaves of 3 rosemary sprigs
1 tablespoon unsalted butter
1 lemon
1 cup dry white wine
2 bay leaves

FOR THE GLAZE

½ cup sherry vinegar
½ cup honey
2 teaspoons fennel seeds, cracked
2 teaspoons coriander seeds,
    cracked
2 teaspoons freshly ground
    black pepper
2 teaspoons red pepper flakes
2 tablespoons unsalted butter,
    cold

FOR THE SPRINKLE

2 tablespoons coriander seeds, toasted
    and cracked, or 1 tablespoon
    ground coriander
2 teaspoons red pepper flakes
2 teaspoons kosher salt, or to taste
Zest of 1 lemon
1 tablespoon fresh flat-leaf parsley,
    finely chopped

1.   **Prepare the lamb.** Heat the oven to 425°F. Place the lamb in a large roasting pan. Use a small sharp knife to make 8 to 10 incisions, each about 1 inch deep, through the top of the meat. Mash together the salt, black pepper, garlic, thyme, and rosemary until it is a kind of paste and rub it into the incisions. Rub the butter over the top of the meat. Squeeze the lemon over the top of the meat and pour the wine into the pan. Add the bay leaves.

2.   Place the pan in the oven and roast for 15 minutes, then reduce the heat to 350°F. Continue roasting until the meat is tender and cooked through to an internal temperature of 135°F for medium-rare, about 1 hour. Remove the pan from the oven and set aside.

3.   Meanwhile, **make the glaze.** Combine the vinegar and honey in a small saucepan over medium heat. Add the fennel seeds, coriander seeds, black pepper, and red pepper flakes and bring to a slight simmer. Lower

continued on next page

the heat and allow the mixture to reduce by half. Remove from the heat and whisk in the cold butter.

4. Heat the broiler. **Make the sprinkle.** Combine the coriander, red pepper flakes, salt, lemon zest, and parsley in a small bowl and set aside. Using a pastry brush, coat the lamb lightly with the glaze and place it in the oven, turning occasionally, until the meat begins to turn golden and crisp, 5 to 7 minutes. Remove the meat to a platter and top with the reserved sprinkle. Let rest for 10 minutes or so before slicing.

BARBECUED LEG *of* LAMB

HERE IS A DELICIOUS WAY TO FEED A CROWD: a large butterflied leg of lamb smoke-roasted over charcoal and wood chips or pecan shells, if you can find them. The meat takes beautifully to the fire, and the fat that caps it helps keep it moist while adding crispness along the edges. You can carve the meat into bits for the makings of a pita sandwich or serve it alongside rice or rice pilaf for a more elegant meal, with lots of sliced tomatoes and cucumbers, and perhaps some yogurt cut through with lemon juice. Either way, it's a forgiving recipe, with parts of the lamb cooked to well-done and others to rare. Something for everyone is a hallmark of a successful Sunday supper, on whatever evening you happen to serve it.

4 cloves garlic, peeled and finely
    chopped
2 tablespoons fresh rosemary,
    finely chopped
2 tablespoons olive oil
1 boneless leg of lamb, 5 to
    6 pounds, butterflied
Kosher salt and freshly ground
    black pepper

1.   Combine the garlic, rosemary, and oil in a bowl. Season the lamb with salt and pepper, then massage with the garlic and rosemary mixture and put the meat in the bowl. Cover and allow to marinate for 30 minutes or so.

2.   Meanwhile, build a fire in your grill, leaving half of the cooking area free of coals.

3.   When the coals are covered with gray ash and the fire is hot (you can hold your hand 6 inches over the grill for only a few seconds), sprinkle wood chips over the fire and place the lamb, fat side down, on top of the fire. Sear each side of the lamb for about 4 minutes each, then move the lamb to the side of the grill without coals and roast, covered, for 30 to 40 minutes.

4.   Tent in aluminum foil for 10 to 15 minutes to rest, then serve as you like.

A GOOD MEAT LOAF

Y OU CANNOT BEAT MEAT LOAF for a family meal, so long as you don't overcook it. Watch that internal temperature closely! If you're nervous going into the process, add fat and flavor: some strips of bacon across the top of the loaf, say, or a glaze of maple and mustard. I've cooked this recipe with Italian sausage cut into the mix; with a small dice of ham; with shredded prosciutto or diced mortadella; even with soft-boiled eggs baked into the center of the meat. Meat loaf is by its nature a meal you can stretch. Try this basic recipe, easily doubled into two loaves if you've got more than ten people coming, then make it your own.

1/2 cup bread crumbs

1/2 cup whole milk

2 pounds ground beef or a
    mixture of beef, veal, lamb, or
    pork (if you're using chicken
    or turkey, you might want to
    add a few slices of chopped
    bacon or pancetta for fat)

1 large egg, lightly beaten

1 teaspoon soy sauce or
    Worcestershire sauce

1/2 cup grated Parmesan cheese

1 small bunch fresh flat-leaf
    parsley, leaves only, roughly
    chopped (about 1/4 cup)

2 cloves garlic, peeled and minced

1 medium yellow onion, peeled
    and cut into small dice

1 medium carrot, peeled and cut
    into small dice

2 tablespoons unsalted butter,
    cut into cubes

Kosher salt and freshly ground
    black pepper

1. Heat the oven to 350°F. Put the bread crumbs in a large bowl and pour the milk over them, then mix to combine.

2. When the milk has absorbed into the bread crumbs, which takes about 5 minutes, add the meat to the bowl, along with the egg, soy sauce, Parmesan, parsley, garlic, onion, and carrot, and mix carefully to combine. Shape the mixed meat into a loaf and place on a greased baking pan. Dot with the butter and season the top with salt and pepper.

3. Bake for 45 minutes to 1 hour, basting a few times with the rendered pan juices, until the meat loaf is well browned and an instant-read thermometer inserted into its center reads 155°F. Allow the loaf to rest, loosely tented with aluminum foil, for 10 minutes or so before slicing.

MEAT LOAF *for* NORA

A FEW YEARS BEFORE SHE DIED IN 2012, I was invited to a dinner to celebrate the journalist, filmmaker, and cooking icon Nora Ephron. Not the idea of her. The actual woman, for whom each guest was to make a dish inspired by her work. I drew meat loaf. I made a very fancy one, run through with whispers of pancetta, the Italian cured bacon. The guy at the deli sliced it for me, but left the plastic sleeve on the outside of the meat, something I did not notice until I pulled the meat loaf from the oven in advance of heading up to the Upper West Side, which is of course where a dinner celebrating Nora Ephron would be held. There were little plastic hairs all over the thing. It looked like a dandelion loaf. I had two hours to improvise a replacement. This is the recipe I came up with, adapted on the fly from a meatball recipe the chef Mark Ladner used to cook at Lupa restaurant in Manhattan. Ephron was given to party games and competition, so of course there was a vote at the end of the dinner to determine the winning dish. Here is your champion.

8 cloves garlic, peeled and minced

1 tablespoon finely chopped fresh
    rosemary

Red pepper flakes

1 cup fresh bread crumbs

Kosher salt and freshly ground
    black pepper

¼ cup whole milk

1 pound ground turkey

1 pound sweet Italian pork
    sausage, crumbled

¼ cup extra-virgin olive oil

4 ounces bacon, chopped

1 medium red onion, finely chopped

One 28-ounce can whole
    tomatoes, preferably
    San Marzano, seeds removed

1 cup dry red wine

¼ bunch fresh mint, roughly
    chopped

1. Heat the oven to 450°F. Combine two-thirds of the garlic, the rosemary, red pepper flakes to taste, the bread crumbs, and liberal amounts of salt and black pepper. Add the milk and mix. Add the turkey and sausage and mix once more to combine; don't overmix. Transfer onto a board and shape into a fine meat loaf, about 9 inches long and 4 inches wide.

2. Place on a greased baking pan with high sides, drizzle with about 2 tablespoons of the oil, and bake for 25 minutes, turning the loaf halfway through to brown evenly. Remove the pan from the oven and reduce the heat to 325°F.

3. Meanwhile, fry the bacon in the remaining 2 tablespoons oil until it starts to curl and its fat is rendered. Add the onion and the remaining garlic, cooking until the onion is translucent, about 4 minutes. Add the tomatoes and wine and bring to a boil.

4. Pour the sauce over the meat loaf, cover tightly with aluminum foil, and bake until a meat thermometer inserted at the center reads 150°F, 20 to 30 minutes. Remove the foil and allow the loaf to rest for 10 to 15 minutes before slicing. Spoon sauce over the slices and scatter with the mint.

BIG POTS

—

For a number of years I cooked Sunday suppers on actual Sundays, to serve a small church congregation after a short service of evening prayers. This was in Greenpoint, in Brooklyn, on a grand street that runs wide under towering plane trees, with a view of the East River to the west. We ate in the moldering parish hall behind the church, off long folding tables we set with plates and cutlery, napkins, candles, sometimes flowers, always bottles of water filled from the sink in the kitchen.

The crowd varied in size. There could be a dozen people present, or three times that: strangers, neighbors, people who sat quietly on the fence between the two. Families arrived and departed on tides pulled by their children's activities, homework, interest. (When they were there, the kids wanted bread, butter, crayons.) The homeless came on currents of need. Here suddenly would be someone new to the city, there a woman who'd lived on the block her whole life. You might see a person you hadn't seen in six months, serve an old friend, or sit next to a couple eating silently, impervious to smiles and offers of seconds. There was no religious component to the meal, no spiritualism beyond the fellowship of it. (Or there was. You brought to it what you wanted.) The parish hall on Sunday nights was most like a bar, an actual public house: a gathering place, a place to go, to be. The people who came were hungry. We fed them.

We fed them big pots. There is no easier way to feed a crowd, particularly one that could be bigger than you think, than to build a big, steaming pot of stew or chowder, something rich and slightly mysterious, and serve it alongside rice or potatoes, vegetables, bread and butter to stretch each plate. A secular miracle happens every time, a lay translation of the parable of loaves and fishes: There is always enough. (Verily, this is so!)

More than this: Big pots are easy. You can cook them well in advance, working serially over the course of an afternoon or evening, then leaving them to cure in your refrigerator, allowing their flavors to meld and deepen, before reheating them on a subsequent day. Your work is spread out, but so are the pleasures of your intentions, and the joy of the work itself.

The recipes that follow speak to the traditions of New England swamp Yankees and the cooks of the Acadian diaspora, to the larders of the Caribbean basin and the ones of Europe, to flavors celebrating the wide diversity of American culinary tastes. They do not make for mild eating, in the main. They are rib-stickers. They are rich. But they have been tested on the plates of strangers, offered in peace to people who did not ask what they were eating and who asked for more when they were done. That's not nothing.

CHICKEN BOG

This rich and peppery stew hails from the coastal plains of the Carolinas, and takes its name from the way in which the pieces of chicken sit in the pot, like hummocks in a bog. It is a favored big-table meal in my house, and among my children's all-time family favorites. Recipes for bog are as various as Carolinians themselves. Mine derives from a version I picked up years ago from the chef Robert Stehling of the Hominy Grill in Charleston, South Carolina, and has evolved slowly over the years to include a wide variety of meats, from Polish kielbasa to smoked beef, ham to breakfast sausage, occasionally all four. In contrast to recipes in which you want to prepare all your ingredients before you start cooking, this is one that can be made serially, adding each new ingredient to the pot as it is ready, in the order specified below. The fried chicken livers floated into the pot at the end, crisp at their edges, are optional. The cider vinegar and mustard are not. Nor, to end at the beginning, are the minced chicken gizzards with which you start the recipe. You need not mention these to anyone until well after you have been complimented on the meal. But they impart a fantastic texture and deep flavor to the dish. Serve over rice.

3 tablespoons bacon fat or neutral
    oil, such as corn or canola
3/4 pound chicken gizzards and
    hearts, pulsed in a food
    processor until minced
Kosher salt and freshly ground
    black pepper
2 medium green bell peppers,
    seeded and diced
2 medium red bell peppers,
    seeded and diced
4 medium to large white onions,
    peeled and diced
4 celery stalks, trimmed and diced
2 tablespoons minced garlic
1 cup dry red wine
One 28- or 35-ounce can
    tomatoes, with liquid, chopped

6 tablespoons unsalted butter
1/4 cup all-purpose flour
1 pound mixed sausages and cured meat,
    such as kielbasa, Italian sausage,
    chorizo, diced ham, or bacon
2 cups chicken stock, ideally homemade,
    or low-sodium if store-bought
1 fresh thyme sprig
1/4 teaspoon red pepper flakes,
    or to taste
2 bay leaves
1 pound chopped chicken meat,
    preferably from the thigh
8 chicken livers, trimmed and cut in
    half (optional)
1 tablespoon cider vinegar
1/2 cup Dijon mustard

continued on next page

1.   Put the fat in a large, heavy-bottomed pot over medium-high heat. When the fat shimmers, add the gizzards and hearts and cook until quite brown and sticking to the pan, 3 to 5 minutes. Stir once, sprinkle with salt and black pepper, then continue cooking until the gizzards are very brown. Add the bell peppers, onions, celery, and garlic and cook, stirring occasionally, until the vegetables are soft, about 10 minutes. Add the wine and tomatoes, bring to a boil, and adjust the heat so the mixture simmers, for another 10 minutes or so.

2.   Meanwhile, melt 4 tablespoons of the butter in a small skillet or saucepan over medium heat. Add the flour and stir until smooth. Cook, stirring often, until the mixture turns quite brown, about 10 minutes. Add this roux to the simmering stew, stir, and cook for a few minutes.

3.   Add the sausages and cured meats, stock, thyme, red pepper flakes, and bay leaves to the pot and cook at a lively simmer, stirring occasionally, for about 40 minutes. Add the chicken meat and cook for another 15 minutes or more (at this point the stew can sit on the stove, simmering, for hours; add a little water or stock if it threatens to dry out).

4.   If you're using the chicken livers, heat the remaining 2 tablespoons butter in an 8- or 10-inch nonstick skillet over medium-high heat. When the butter foam subsides, add the livers and cook until quite brown on one side, sprinkling with salt and black pepper. Turn and brown on the other side.

5.   Stir the vinegar and mustard into the stew. Add the livers, if using, and stir.

TEXAS CHILI

CHILI IS A MAKE-AHEAD DISH that improves in taste and character as it cures for a day or two in the refrigerator. Reheat the pot gently at suppertime and serve with corn chips and chopped raw onion, with sour cream, if you like, and a sprinkle of grated cheddar. (If more people show up than you'd planned to feed, you can fold a few cans of pinto beans into the mix to add a few servings, at least if there aren't any Texans present to ridicule you for doing so.)

You can make this particular recipe with the chili powder that's in your spice rack and it'll be terrific. You can make it with the chili powder they sell at the bodega or suburban supermarket and it'll be terrific. But it won't be your own chili recipe until you make it with a chili powder you've selected because you like that chili powder particularly, and you won't know which one that is until you've tasted a lot of them and made a lot of chili. That's excellent, I think. You're not running a restaurant. You don't need to be consistent. Me, I like an ancho chili powder, mild and full-bodied. There's also a generic one sold by my local supermarket that I'm partial to, dark and rich, that I think employs pasilla peppers. Sometimes I use a chili powder mix a friend came up with—ancho and habanero, along with some monosodium glutamate—and this is powerfully good as well. Try the chili powder that you have, then try another. Play the field as long as you like. The result will be good chili, every time, until it becomes the best chili, which is your own.

4 pounds beef chuck roast or
    steak

1 teaspoon kosher salt, or more to
    taste

3 tablespoons neutral oil, such as
    canola or grapeseed, plus
    extra as needed

1 large yellow or white onion,
    peeled and diced

4 large cloves garlic, peeled and
    minced

4 large green jalapeño peppers,
    or to taste, seeded and diced

1 corn tortilla, torn into pieces

3 tablespoons ground chili powder

1½ tablespoons ground cumin

1 tablespoon ground coriander

1 tablespoon dried oregano

One 12-ounce bottle beer, ideally dark

One 28-ounce can diced tomatoes

1 tablespoon dark brown sugar

1. Cut the beef into 2-inch cubes and sprinkle with the salt.

2. Swirl the oil into a large, heavy-bottomed pot set over high heat. When the oil starts to shimmer, add the meat in batches, browning it on all sides. Remove the browned meat to a sheet pan.

continued on next page

3. Lower the heat in the pot to medium and add to the remaining fat the onion, garlic, jalapeños, and torn-up tortilla, along with the chili powder, cumin, coriander, and oregano. Cook, stirring occasionally, until the onion has started to soften and turn translucent, 7 to 10 minutes.

4. Add the browned meat to the pot along with the beer, tomatoes, brown sugar, and 1 quart water, then bring the mixture to a gentle simmer and allow to cook until the meat is tender, about 90 minutes. Taste and add salt, if needed. Serve with chopped onions, chopped jalapeños, sour cream, cilantro, corn chips, or warm tortillas.

CORN BREAD

I started eating this corn bread in college, at the East Coast Grill in Cambridge, Massachusetts, and learned to make it years later at the elbow of the restaurant's then chef and owner, Chris Schlesinger, in the small kitchen of his house just up the road from Buzzards Bay. It is a little more cakelike and sweet than a traditional southern corn bread, and I asked him where the recipe had come from, how he'd developed it, how it had come to be. "The restaurant was opening, and I realized we needed a corn bread recipe," he told me. "I think it came off the back of the cornmeal box." He shrugged. "People loved it. We could never change it." But I do. I always add corn kernels to the batter for texture, and sometimes some diced jalapeño, as well. You could stir in a cup of shredded cheddar, if you like. You're not running a restaurant where if you change something about a recipe, people get mad. You can make this corn bread however you like. Serve with chilis and gumbos and bogs, or for breakfast, drizzled with hot honey (see page 40).

2 cups all-purpose flour

1 cup yellow cornmeal

3/4 cup sugar

1/2 teaspoon salt

1 tablespoon baking powder

2 large eggs

1 1/2 cups whole milk

1 1/2 tablespoons vegetable oil

4 tablespoons (1/2 stick) unsalted butter, melted

2 cups fresh or frozen corn kernels

1. Heat the oven to 350°F. Lightly oil a 9-inch cast-iron skillet and put it in the oven to get hot.

2. In a large bowl, sift together the flour, cornmeal, sugar, salt, and baking powder. In another bowl, whisk together the eggs, milk, and oil. Pour the wet ingredients over the dry ingredients, add the melted butter and corn, and stir together until just mixed.

3. Remove the hot cast-iron pan from the oven and pour into it the batter, then give the pan a smack on the countertop to even it out. Return the pan to the oven and bake for about 1 hour, until the corn bread is browned on top and a toothpick or a thin knife inserted into the top comes out clean.

GUMBO

THE BASIS OF ALL GREAT GUMBOS IS ROUX, a thickening agent created by heating equal parts flour and oil until—for gumbo, anyway—it is nutty and brown. You can make a delicious roux with butter or bacon fat, but for this dish I use a straight neutral oil such as canola or peanut, and quite a lot of it, for the big pot. Get the flour into the hot oil and stir until it reaches the hue you desire, which in my case is somewhat darker than café au lait. (The darker the roux, the more deeply flavored your gumbo, but the less thickening power it has. Seek moderation in all things.) You can make gumbos with chicken or duck, crabs, sausage, or shrimp. I've done well with doves and pheasant. What follows, though, is a family favorite, and one of my favorite things to spend the bulk of a weekend afternoon cooking: chicken and smoked sausage. Serve with rice, of course. The gumbo cures beautifully overnight and is easily reheated.

1 cup neutral oil, such as canola or peanut

1 cup all-purpose flour

2 large Spanish onions, peeled and diced

1 large chicken, cut into a dozen pieces, or 12 bone-in, skin-on chicken thighs

2 teaspoons celery salt

1 teaspoon kosher salt

1 teaspoon freshly ground black pepper

1 teaspoon sweet paprika

1 teaspoon garlic powder

1 teaspoon onion powder

1/2 teaspoon cayenne pepper

Pinch of ground allspice

2 pounds smoked beef or pork sausage, sliced into thick coins

2 celery stalks, trimmed and diced

2 green bell peppers, seeded and diced

1 red bell pepper, seeded and diced

1 medium tomato, seeded and chopped

2 cloves garlic, peeled and minced

2 to 3 quarts chicken stock, homemade or low-sodium

3 fresh thyme sprigs

2 bay leaves

1 tablespoon Worcestershire sauce

Hot pepper sauce

1. Make the roux. Heat the oil in a large Dutch oven set over high heat until it is shimmering. Whisk the flour into the hot oil, where it will immediately begin to sizzle. Reduce the heat to medium and continue to whisk until the roux has darkened to the color you like, 10 to 15 minutes. Add the onions and stir to combine. Reduce the heat and continue to cook until the onions and roux have gone a shade darker again, 10 to 15 minutes.

continued on page 116

2. Season the chicken with the celery salt, kosher salt, black pepper, paprika, garlic powder, onion powder, cayenne, and allspice, and add the pieces to the pot. Raise the heat and cook, turning the chicken frequently, until it has browned, about 15 minutes.

3. Add half of the sausage to the pot and stir, then add the celery, bell peppers, tomato, and garlic, and stir again. After a minute or two, add the stock, along with the thyme and bay leaves. Bring the mixture to a boil, then reduce the heat to a bare simmer and cook for 45 minutes or so, stirring occasionally. If fat rises to the surface, skim it off.

4. Add the rest of the smoked sausage and the Worcestershire sauce to the gumbo, along with hot pepper sauce to taste, and continue to cook for a further 45 minutes. Remove the bay leaves and thyme. Serve immediately or, to greater effect, the next day, over white rice.

BEEF STEW

HERE IS A BEEF STEW AS STANDARD and delicious as they come, a recipe I rejigger constantly to match what's available in the market or refrigerator. The only constants are the beef and the use of flour as a thickening agent. You don't need to use the flour. Some people don't like what it does to the gravy. But you must use the chuck. Taken from the cow's shoulder, it melts beautifully in the wine and stock. Those who like the qualities brought to the stew by red wine should reserve a half glass to stir into it at the end of the cooking process, which adds a bright, acidic note to the meal. As for those who like peas in their stew? Add a cup or two along with the Worcestershire sauce, and let them heat in the gravy. Make this stew your own.

4 pounds boneless beef chuck

Kosher salt and freshly ground
    black pepper

¼ cup olive oil

2 cloves garlic, peeled and finely
    chopped

2 medium yellow onions, peeled
    and diced

2 celery stalks, trimmed and
    chopped

6 tablespoons all-purpose flour

4 cups dry red wine

2 cups chicken stock, ideally
    homemade, or low-sodium
    if store-bought

3 whole cloves

1 bay leaf

1 fresh thyme sprig (or
    ½ teaspoon dried)

6 fresh flat-leaf parsley sprigs, plus
    chopped parsley for serving

6 large carrots, about 1½ pounds,
    trimmed and cut into 1-inch
    lengths

6 new potatoes, cut into quarters

1 tablespoon Worcestershire sauce

1. Cut the meat into 2-inch cubes. Season to taste with salt and pepper.

2. Heat the oil in a large, deep skillet or Dutch oven set over medium-high heat. When the oil shimmers, add the beef cubes in batches, and cook, turning often, until they are well browned all over, about 10 minutes. Set the browned pieces aside in a medium bowl.

3. Lower the heat to medium. Add the garlic, onions, and celery and cook, stirring occasionally, for another 10 minutes, until the onions have started to turn translucent. Return the meat to the pan, sprinkle with the flour, and stir to coat the meat evenly. Cook for an additional 5 minutes.

4. Add the wine and stir until the mixture boils and thickens. Stir in the stock (or water, if you don't have any stock). Add the cloves, bay leaf, thyme, and parsley. Cover the pot and simmer for 1 hour.

5. Add the carrots and potatoes to the beef. Cover and continue cooking for 30 minutes, or until the vegetables are tender. Add the Worcestershire, stir, and taste, adjusting the seasonings as needed. Fish out the bay leaf and thyme and parsley sprigs. Serve, sprinkled with chopped parsley.

STEAK *and* GUINNESS STEW

H ERE IS A HEARTY, STOUT-INFUSED, and cheese-thickened stew that is excellent for serving to large crowds, essentially a British steak and kidney pie without the kidneys and piecrust. The gravy stretches nicely over buttered noodles, so three pounds of meat goes a long way. You could tip it into a baking dish and top with puff pastry or mashed potatoes if you're bound for a potluck; you could definitely make a batch and put it in the freezer against the knowledge that some day soon you're going to need it to feed a crowd on the quick. It delivers big, big flavor whenever it's served. Serve with buttered noodles or mashed potatoes—something starchy and rich.

4 tablespoons (½ stick) unsalted butter

2 large red onions, peeled and diced

4 cloves garlic, peeled and minced

2 carrots, peeled and chopped

2 celery stalks, trimmed and chopped

10 button mushrooms, trimmed and sliced

3 pounds brisket (preferably second cut) or stew meat, chopped into bite-size pieces

Kosher salt and freshly ground black pepper

1 fresh rosemary sprig

2 tablespoons all-purpose flour

Two 12-ounce cans stout

8 ounces grated cheddar cheese

1. Heat the oven to 375°F. In a large, oven-safe pan fitted with a lid, heat 2 tablespoons of the butter over medium-low heat. When the butter melts and begins to foam, add the onions and garlic and cook, stirring frequently, until soft, about 10 minutes.

2. Add the carrots, celery, mushrooms, and the remaining 2 tablespoons butter and cook over medium heat, stirring frequently, until the mushrooms are dark in color and the moisture released by them has evaporated, about 15 minutes.

3. Season the beef pieces all over with salt and pepper. Add the beef and rosemary to the pan, then sprinkle the flour over them and cook over high heat, stirring often, for about 5 minutes.

4. Add enough Guinness just to cover the beef. Cover the pan and put it in the oven for 1½ hours. Remove from the oven and stir. Return to the oven and cook for 1 hour more. If the sauce remains thin, set the pot over medium-low heat, remove the lid, and reduce the liquid. Season to taste with salt and pepper. Fold in the cheese and stir to combine.

JAMAICAN OXTAIL STEW

YOU'LL FIND OXTAIL STEW ALL OVER the Caribbean basin and wherever its residents have moved. My recipe comes from one I learned from the family who built the Golden Krust bakery and restaurant chain in New York, which I adapted into something more easily made in the home. The gravy it creates, slopped over rice and peas, is a sustaining taste of island life in a big, messy city or wherever you reside. It makes for a fantastic, savory meal for a large group of friends and family. Watch that sugar blackening at the bottom of the pot at the beginning. It creates exquisite flavor, but can wreak havoc on the pot.

3 pounds oxtails, cut into
    segments by a butcher
Kosher salt and freshly ground
    black pepper
3 tablespoons light brown sugar
2 Spanish onions, peeled and
    diced
4 cloves garlic, peeled and
    minced
3 tablespoons minced fresh
    ginger
1 whole Scotch bonnet chile
3 fresh thyme sprigs
12 allspice berries
1 bunch scallions, green and white
    parts, trimmed and chopped
2 tablespoons granulated sugar
3 tablespoons soy sauce
1 tablespoon Worcestershire sauce
3 tablespoons all-purpose flour
3 tablespoons ketchup
1 cup butter beans, or one
    10½-ounce can, rinsed and
    drained

1. Season the oxtails aggressively with salt and pepper. Heat a large Dutch oven or a heavy-bottomed pot over medium heat. Add the brown sugar to the pot and melt, stirring with a wooden spoon, until it darkens and starts to smoke—about 5 minutes. Then add 2 tablespoons boiling water. (Careful! It will splatter.) Stir to mix.

2. Add the oxtails to the pot, working in batches, stirring to cover them with blackened sugar, then allowing them to cook, turning occasionally, until they are well browned. Remove the oxtails to a bowl and keep warm.

3. Add half of the onions, half of the garlic, and half of the ginger to the pot, along with the chile, thyme, allspice, and one-third of the scallions, and stir to combine. Allow to cook until softened, about 5 minutes.

4. Return the oxtails to the pot along with any accumulated juices and put water into the pot so that the oxtails are almost submerged. Bring to a simmer and then cook, covered, for about 1 hour, stirring occasionally.

5. Add the remaining onions, garlic, and ginger to the pot, along with another third of the scallions. Add the granulated sugar, soy sauce, and Worcestershire. Stir to combine and continue to cook until the meat is yielding and loose on the bone, about 1 hour longer.

6. Remove about 1 cup of liquid from the pot and place in a small bowl. Add the flour to this liquid and stir to combine, working out any lumps with the back of a spoon. Add this slurry to the pot, along with the ketchup, then stir to combine and allow to cook another 15 minutes or so. Remove the Scotch bonnet and thyme sprigs. Fold the butter beans into the stew and allow these to heat through. Scatter the remaining scallions over the top. Serve with rice or rice and peas.

MISSISSIPPI ROAST

I T WAS ONE OF MY COLLEAGUES at the *Times,* Margaux Laskey, who first told me about this amazing slow-cooker beef dish. She'd seen it on Pinterest, read about it on mom blogs, made it herself, and fallen in love: a tangle of slow-cooked beef in a sauce made with packages of dry ranch mix and "au jus" gravy, a stick of butter, and a couple peperoncini. I fell for it too, and eventually tracked down its creator in the small town of Ripley, Mississippi.

She is a home cook named Robin Chapman, who started making the dish as a variation on one her aunt made with packaged Italian dressing. "Roast," she told me she called the dish. The story spooled out from there. A friend of Robin's, Karen Farese, started making the recipe soon after, and eventually contributed it to her church's cookbook, calling it "roast beef." Another congregant made the dish for family, and a cousin who was visiting took a shine to it. That woman, Laurie Ormon, of Bentonville, Arkansas, took the recipe and wrote about it on her blog, where she called it "Mississippi Roast." Her post got picked up by another blog and another blog and another blog, and by the time I started to dig into its history and track down its origin for an article in the newspaper, the recipe had been "pinned" on Pinterest more than a million times.

You can make Mississippi Roast as Robin did and does, and it's fantastic and about as simple to prepare as a cup of tea. Or you can follow my lead and flour and brown the meat instead of using the packaged gravy, and make your own ranch. I also cut back the butter by half and increased the number of peperoncini. That makes me a city slicker, I guess, but the recipe delivers an amazing dinner of sandwiches on potato buns or a topping for slick egg noodles. It is still dead simple to prepare: the easiest recipe for Sunday supper in this book, maybe anywhere. And if you don't have a slow cooker, you can make it in a pot on the stove, set over very low heat.

1 boneless chuck roast or top or
   bottom round roast, 3 to
   4 pounds
2 teaspoons kosher salt, plus
   more to taste
1½ teaspoons freshly ground
   black pepper, plus more to
   taste
¼ cup all-purpose flour
3 tablespoons neutral oil, such as
   canola or grapeseed
4 tablespoons (½ stick) unsalted
   butter
8 to 12 peperoncini
2 tablespoons mayonnaise
2 teaspoons cider vinegar
½ teaspoon dried dill
¼ teaspoon sweet paprika
1 teaspoon buttermilk
Chopped fresh flat-leaf parsley

1.   Place the roast on a cutting board and rub the salt and pepper all over it. Sprinkle the flour all over the seasoned meat and massage it into the flesh.

2.   Heat the oil in a large sauté pan set over high heat until it is shimmering and about to smoke. Place the roast in the pan and brown on all sides, 4 to 5 minutes a side, to create a crust. Remove the roast from the pan and place it in the bowl of a slow cooker. Add the butter and peperoncini to the pot. Put the lid on the slow cooker and set the machine to low.

3.   As the roast heats, make a ranch dressing. Combine the mayonnaise, vinegar, dill, and paprika in a small bowl and whisk to emulsify. Add the buttermilk, or a splash of milk and a splash of lemon juice if you don't have any buttermilk, then whisk again. Remove the lid from the slow cooker and add the dressing. Replace the lid and allow to continue cooking, undisturbed, for 6 to 8 hours, until you can shred the meat easily using two forks. Mix the meat with the gravy surrounding it. Adjust seasoning to taste. Garnish with parsley and serve with egg noodles or roast potatoes, or pile on sandwich rolls, however you like.

BEEF STROGANOFF

ORGET WHAT YOU THINK YOU remember about this putatively Russian dish, which saw its heyday in American kitchens during the 1950s and its nadir in school cafeterias two decades later. Beef Stroganoff makes for an outstanding Sunday supper: a vat of tender sautéed meat in a silken gravy studded with caramelized mushrooms, alongside a huge tangle of buttered noodles. Be careful when adding the cream at the end—especially if you use sour cream, since it so easily curdles in the heat. Crème fraîche or heavy cream will offer smoother results. This recipe is easily halved or doubled, depending on the size of your dinner. As written, it serves around eight.

3 pounds sirloin roast or beef tenderloin, if you're feeling fancy, well trimmed

1/4 cup all-purpose flour

1 tablespoon kosher salt, plus more to taste

1 tablespoon freshly ground black pepper, plus more to taste

1 tablespoon hot paprika

2 tablespoons neutral oil, such as canola or grapeseed

6 tablespoons unsalted butter

1 pound button mushrooms, cleaned and cut into quarters

3 medium shallots, peeled and thinly sliced

1/2 cup dry white wine

2 cups heavy cream or crème fraîche

1 tablespoon Worcestershire sauce

1 tablespoon Dijon mustard

24 ounces wide egg noodles (2 large bags)

1. Cut the tenderloin into 1/2-inch slices against the grain, pound lightly, then cut those slices into 1-inch-wide strips.

2. Combine the flour, salt, pepper, and paprika in a large bowl and toss to combine. Dredge the slices of meat in the flour mixture, shaking them to remove excess flour, and set the pieces on a rimmed baking sheet.

3. Place a large skillet over high heat and swirl into it the oil. When the oil begins to shimmer, sauté the beef slices, in batches if necessary, until they are well browned all over but rare inside. Remove the meat to the baking sheet. Turn the heat down under the pan slightly.

4. Add 2 tablespoons of the butter to the pan and, when it has melted and started to foam, add the mushrooms and toss to coat them with the fat. Cook, stirring frequently, until they have released their moisture and are a deep, dark brown, 12 to 15 minutes. About halfway into the process, add the sliced shallots and stir to combine.

5. When the mushrooms and shallots are soft and caramelized, deglaze the pan with the wine, scraping at all the stuck-on bits on the pan's surface. When the wine has reduced by about half, slowly stir in the cream, followed by the Worcestershire and mustard.

Add the meat, along with any accumulated juices under it, and stir to combine. Taste and adjust the seasonings. Cook for an additional 2 to 3 minutes, until the dish is hot and the beef is cooked through and medium-rare.

6. Meanwhile, cook the noodles in a large pot of boiling water until they are just done, about 10 minutes. Drain and toss with the remaining 4 tablespoons butter. Serve under or alongside the Stroganoff.

MAPO RAGÙ

THIS IS MY TAKE ON A DISH THAT WAS developed at the Momofuku Ssäm Bar in Manhattan a long time ago by the chefs David Chang and Tien Ho, and which is almost literally a mashup of Korean, Chinese, and Italian flavors and techniques. After cooking it approximately a bajillion times, I wrote about it for my day job at the *Times*, and have cooked it as many times since. It is endlessly adaptable, depending on your larder or access to ingredients. The original recipe calls for the use of cylindrical Korean rice cakes and the red pepper paste known as gochujang, also for Sichuan peppercorns and silken tofu. Those may not be a part of your family-cooking routine. They may be hard to find where you live. So you can omit the rice cakes and serve the meat sauce over rice or noodles instead. You can bail on the gochujang and replace it with miso paste. Likewise the Sichuan peppercorns. Swap their numbing qualities for some chiles or red pepper flakes. And you don't need the silken tofu at all, though boy, howdy, does it add a luxurious dimension to the meal. It's a dinner to open eyes and genuinely surprise people. When you cook it, raise a glass to Chang and Ho every time. It's the right thing to do.

1/3 cup neutral oil, such as canola or grapeseed

3 large yellow onions, peeled and sliced

1 teaspoon kosher salt, or to taste

2 pounds ground pork

8 cloves garlic, peeled and minced

2-inch piece fresh ginger, peeled and chopped

1/4 cup gochujang, or to taste

2 tablespoons low-sodium soy sauce

4 teaspoons light brown sugar

1 tablespoon Sichuan peppercorns (optional)

2 bunches kale or any hearty cooking green, roughly chopped

One 12-ounce box silken tofu, drained and whisked

15 to 20 frozen cylindrical rice cakes (optional)

1 bunch scallions, green and white parts, thinly sliced

1. Heat around half of the oil in a wok set over medium-high heat. When the oil shimmers, add the onions and a pinch of salt. Cook, stirring occasionally, until the onions have released their moisture and are starting to brown, about 10 minutes. Then turn the heat down to low and continue to cook, stirring every few minutes, until the onions have turned golden brown and sweet, an additional 20 to 30 minutes.

2. Tip the onions into a bowl, and return the wok to high heat on the stove. Add the remaining oil, then the pork, and cook, breaking the meat up with a spoon, until it is just cooked but not yet browning, about 15 minutes. Add the cooked meat to the reserved onions.

continued on page 128

3. Meanwhile, put a large pot of salted water over high heat and bring to a boil.

4. Return the wok to the stove over medium heat and cook the garlic and ginger in the fat remaining from the pork (add an extra splash of neutral oil, if necessary). When the garlic and ginger soften, add the gochujang, soy sauce, brown sugar, and Sichuan peppercorns, if using. Add around 1 cup water, enough to loosen the gochujang and make a sauce, then return the pork and onions to the wok and stir to combine. Adjust the seasonings.

5. Bring the sauce to a simmer and add the chopped greens, then stir to combine and cook until they have started to soften, about 5 minutes. Tip the whisked silken tofu into the sauce and stir to combine.

6. Meanwhile, put the rice cakes, if using, into the boiling water for 3 to 5 minutes to soften, then drain them and add to the wok. Or just serve the ragù with steamed rice, rice noodles, or pasta. Garnish with the sliced scallions and serve.

CORNED BEEF

MAYBE YOU'VE MADE THE CORNED BEEF they sell in the supermarket—a white plastic bag of industrial-brined point-cut brisket and a bag of spices with which to simmer it into pink submission, alongside wedges of cabbage, peeled potatoes, and carrots. It's not terrible. But it's not fantastic. Home-cured corned beef, on the other hand, *is* fantastic, and more easily made than you might imagine. I learned how to do so from the food writer and raconteur Michael Ruhlman, and have not turned back to the package since. Yes, corned beef requires some planning. But not a terrible amount of work—only time. You can slide wedges of cabbage and lengths of carrot into the burbling liquid as the beef cooks, about thirty minutes before serving.

2 cups kosher salt

½ cup sugar

5 cloves garlic, peeled and smashed

5 tablespoons pickling spices

4 teaspoons pink curing salt (sodium nitrite)

1 beef brisket, 4 to 5 pounds

Two 12-ounce bottles good beer

Two 12-ounce bottles good ginger beer

1. Brine the brisket: In a medium pot set over high heat, combine about 1 gallon water, the salt, sugar, garlic, 3 tablespoons of the pickling spices, and the pink curing salt. Stir the mixture as it heats until the sugar and salt are dissolved, about 1 minute. Transfer the liquid to a container large enough for the brine and the brisket, then refrigerate until the liquid is cool.

2. Place the brisket in the cooled liquid and weigh the meat down with a plate so it is submerged. Cover the container and place it in the refrigerator for 5 days, or up to 7 days, turning every day or so.

3. To cook the brisket, remove it from the brine and rinse under cool water. Place in a pot just large enough to hold it and cover it with one of the beers and one of the ginger beers. If you need more liquid to cover the meat, add enough of the other beer and other ginger beer to do so. Add the remaining 2 tablespoons pickling spices. Bring to a boil over high heat, then turn the heat to low so the liquid is barely simmering. Cover and let cook until you can easily insert a fork into the meat, about 3 hours, adding water along the way if needed to cover the brisket.

4. Keep warm until serving, or let cool in the liquid and reheat when you're ready to eat, up to 3 or 4 days. (It's good for sandwiches, obviously, and tacos too: Combine with a hearty slaw.)

CHAPTER

FIVE

RICE AND
BEANS

—

This is by far the most economical of Sunday suppers, and among the most flavorful: a vat of simmered beans, baked beans, beans studded with sausage or run through with turkey fat, built above mixtures of onions and garlic and peppers and herbs, with tomato paste or orange juice, molasses or lime, alongside a pile of rice. You can make the beans quickly, out of cans, or you can make them slowly, with soaked dried legumes and a day spent tending to them as they soften and yield. The beans can be served without rice, as in a cassoulet or a traditional New England baked bean supper. Likewise, you can build a Sunday supper out of rice and leave the beans aside, as in paella, or with a soubise that outshines the meat you place beside it. Make rice and beans together, though, and you'll discover what the nutritionists call a "complete protein," containing all that a body needs to survive.

I like to cook in all three lanes, according to my mood, to the time of year, to the ingredients I have on hand, to the time I have to cook, to the relative health of my bank balance. You should do the same. Cook a few Sunday suppers of roast beef or fried fish or duck, and you may find yourself heading into the next one with a sense of exhaustion or worry that the project is getting out of hand. I know: That fish turned out to be expensive, but not so expensive as the beef. And, man, those ducks give off a lot of fat! Am I really expecting you to do this *regularly*? A dinner of rice and beans, or a dinner built around beans or rice, can be a fine antidote. With the exception of paella and cassoulet, perhaps, such a meal is simple and inexpensive to prepare. Much of the world exists on rice and beans. It is no shame to join them.

A few stipulations. First, there is nothing wrong with canned beans. If you have the time to get the dry ones and soak them, you'll perhaps get even better results than you do from the canned varieties. Dried beans are cheaper than canned ones. They often taste better. And if you are interested in cooking with heirloom beans, which is a fine way to blow minds in matters of flavor and texture, not to mention to support the farmers who have staked their businesses on reviving them, you are not going to find them in cans. The heirloom Marfax beans I like to bake with maple syrup and salt pork certainly don't come in cans. But I can buy two pounds of them for twelve dollars over the Internet from a small family farm in Maine and turn them into at least a few meals. I can't do that *tonight*, though. I can't do that on the night that I realize I need to cook Sunday supper despite having forgotten all about it because of meetings at work, and there are seven people coming to dinner and I've got only a couple hours to jam.

What I can do is crank open a few cans of black beans instead, pour them on top of a sofrito made from the heel of bacon that's in the back of the fridge, a couple onions, all the garlic left in the house, some tomato paste and cumin, hot pepper sauce, and a big glug of orange juice. That and some rice, some buttered toast, hot sauce on the side? There is nothing wrong with canned beans.

Second, a case for rice cookers. For a long time I made rice on the stove top. It isn't hard to do. Bring 2 cups of salted water to a boil and add 1 cup of rice. Lower the heat so the water is just simmering, cover the pot, and cook for around 16 minutes, until the rice is tender and all the liquid has been absorbed. Turn off the heat and let the rice continue to steam, covered, for another 10 minutes or so, then fluff with a fork and serve. The recipe scales easily. Two cups of rice, 4 cups of water. Three cups of rice, 6 cups of water. Easy.

But it isn't always awesome. What you want from a bowl of rice is perfection: earthy, nutty, aromatic grains, each separate from the other but part of a whole. The truth is, even for terrific home cooks, it doesn't always come out that way on the stove top. Use the wrong pot, or the wrong burner, and you'll end up with scorched rice, gloopy rice, toothy rice.

That doesn't happen with a rice cooker. The whole point of the machine is to make perfect rice, every time, and I've found that even with the dodgiest dollar-store rice cooker, perfect rice is what you get, many more times than not. And it stays that way for a long, long time, thanks to the "warm" function even the dodgiest dollar-store rice cooker offers as part of its design. So get a rice cooker and watch yourself cooking a lot more rice, a lot more often. Add a protein, some vegetables, and you've got a fine Sunday supper, right there.

Of course, there are many more meals than rice and beans to make out of rice and beans. Recipes for some of those follow, and don't lend themselves well to canned goods, nor to labor-saving machines. So make paella sometimes, fried rice often, cassoulet at least once a year. The point ought to hold regardless. It is okay to cut corners, sometimes, in order to put food on the table for your family and friends. Project cooking is a big part of Sunday suppering. But not all Sunday suppers are or should be projects. Sometimes what you want is just comfort and sustenance. That's rice and beans.

WHITE RICE

BOWL OF PLAIN WHITE RICE IS—or can be—an astonishing thing: fluffy, soft, with a slight nuttiness. Served plain, or with a pat of butter (or with a pat of butter and a splash of soy sauce; or with a pat of butter, a splash of soy sauce, and a fried egg), it is a nourishing comfort. It is a friend to sautéed vegetables, a lover of gravy, a great base into which to stir onions, nuts, and dried fruit. And it is, in our house, one of the staple starches of our supper repertoire. Cooking rice is daunting to some. It needn't be. My *Times* colleague Kim Severson worked out that 17 minutes in a 350°F oven, followed by 10 minutes of rest on the stove top, is the ideal timing for can't-miss rice. And it is. You'll maybe never go back to stove-top rice again. (Kim adds a couple teaspoons of salt, if you want to go that way.) Still, a small investment in a rice cooker will pay huge dividends if you cook a lot of rice; the machines, even the cheap ones, deliver perfect rice every time off a ratio of one part rice to two parts water. Save whatever's left over for frying later. It freezes nicely in a freezer-safe plastic bag. You'll get about six cups of rice out of this recipe. Scale up as needed.

2 cups long-grained white rice

2 tablespoons unsalted butter

1. Heat the oven to 350°F. Rinse the rice well in a sieve and shake to remove excess water.

2. Heat the butter over medium-high heat in a medium oven-safe pot with a tight-fitting lid, until it is foaming. Add the rice to the pot and stir until the grains are glossy and covered with fat.

3. Add 4 cups water to the pot and bring the mixture to a boil. Put the lid on the pot and place the pot in the oven for 17 minutes. Then remove the pot and allow to stand a further 10 minutes without removing the lid. Fluff the rice with a fork and serve.

BROWN RICE

O KAY, HIPPIES, HERE IT IS: a fail-safe recipe for brown rice that yields firm-tender grains of nutty goodness and will leave you wondering why you avoided cooking the stuff ever since eating it in that lame Chinese vegetarian place near campus, way back when. The key is in the ratio of water to rice. Many packages of brown rice call for the same one you'd use for white: 2 cups water to each cup of rice. This leads to mushy rice. Instead, try 1¼ cups water to each cup of rice. Then cook slowly over medium-low heat, and leave lots of time for the rice to rest after it has simmered through. Then make sure to fluff it well at the end. Brown rice enjoys salt. I add some to the cooking liquid.

2 cups brown rice

1 teaspoon kosher salt

1. Rinse the rice well in a sieve and shake to remove excess water. Bring 2½ cups water and the salt to a boil in a wide pot with a tight-fitting lid. Lower the heat to a bare simmer, cover the pot, and allow to cook slowly until all the water is absorbed, 30 to 40 minutes.

2. Remove the pot from the heat and allow to stand for a further 10 minutes without removing the lid. Fluff the rice with a fork and serve.

SHORT-GRAINED RICE

SHORT-GRAINED WHITE RICE IS OFTEN labeled "sushi rice" in stores, and it is in fact just the thing for making sushi. It yields perfect little pearls, especially if you attend well to the rinsing of it at the start of the process. But it is equally if not more fantastic as a luxuriously plain accompaniment to many other dishes, and popping some into a rice cooker after breakfast yields a terrific easy meal at the end of the day. Caramelize some onions and then hit them with a little teriyaki or soy sauce, then put that on the rice with a fried egg. Or just add butter and a splash of soy sauce. I like it, as well, as an accompaniment to Mapo Ragù (see page 126).

2 cups short-grained white rice

1. Pour the rice into a bowl and cover it with an inch or so of water. Using a spoon or your fingers, swirl the rice around in the water to help it release any dust or starch, then carefully pour off the clouded water through a sieve. Repeat until the rinsing water runs clear.

2. Place the rice in a medium pot with a tight-fitting lid. Add 2 cups water to the rice, put the lid on the pot, then bring the water to a boil over medium-high heat. Reduce the heat under the pot to low and cook, covered, until the rice has absorbed all the water, 18 to 20 minutes.

3. Remove the lid from the pot or rice cooker and, using a wooden spoon or rice paddle, fluff the rice around a little, then loosely replace the lid and allow the rice to sit for an additional 10 to 15 minutes before serving.

WILD RICE

WILD RICE, LIKE RISOTTO, CAN ABSORB a lot of liquid. Unlike risotto, wild rice does not throw off a lot of starch—once popped open by the heat, the grains take on a chewy consistency that is of a piece with its intensely nutty flavor. What follows is a recipe for plain wild rice, which goes beautifully with turkey, duck, or goose (or venison, if you have it). Once the rice is made, you can fold sautéed mushrooms into it or dried cranberries, or make like a Minnesotan and use it as the base for a casserole by tearing some cooked poultry into it, adding a splash of stock and a handful of grated cheddar across the top, then putting it in a hot oven for 20 minutes or so. Wild rice can have vastly different cooking times depending on the source of the grains. So start checking on it after 20 minutes or so of simmering.

2 cups wild rice

1 tablespoon kosher salt

1. Rinse the rice well in a sieve and shake to remove excess water. Put 8 cups water into a large pot with the salt and bring to a boil.

2. Add the rinsed rice to the pot and cover the pot, then lower the heat to a simmer and cook until the rice is tender but not mushy, 20 to 40 minutes.

3. Uncover the rice, fluff with a fork, and continue to cook at a simmer for an additional 5 minutes. If there is any excess liquid in the pot, drain it off and allow the rice to rest for 5 minutes before fluffing again and serving.

SOME NOTES ON WILD RICE

WILD RICE IS TERRIFIC PLAIN. BUT it can be astonishing if you treat it like a pilaf or a casserole. To make **wild rice with mushrooms**, sauté a pound or so of sliced mushrooms of the best available variety or interesting taste in a lot of unsalted butter with a healthy pinch of salt and a few grinds of pepper, until they have given off all their liquid and started just to caramelize. Then deglaze the pan with wine or sherry, allow the wine to evaporate, and stir the mushrooms into the finished wild rice, on page 137. I like sometimes to make **wild rice with apples**, using the same methodology as with the mushrooms. Or, for a more substantial vegetarian main course meal, you can make **wild rice with peppers and cream.** Just sauté some diced red bell peppers with carrots and onions, then add these to the finished wild rice along with a cup of heavy cream and—this is cool—a few tablespoons of strong mustard. Pile that into a casserole and let the top get slightly crisp in a hot oven.

RICE PILAF

"PILAF" IS A PERSIAN WORD, and there are versions of the dish served all over the Middle East, indeed all over the world: rice cooked in seasoned stock, with vegetables, herbs, sometimes with meats. The recipe here is for a basic version, European in aspect, with onions, garlic, and parsley, a little thyme, some bay leaves, and chicken stock. Having mastered its preparation, you can begin to experiment with adding dried fruits and nuts, with adding diced chicken thighs, with deploying saffron, cumin, mint, or whatever flavors you wish to marry to the rice. As written here, the pilaf is an excellent accompaniment to a simple roast chicken or some fillets of fish. Your larder and imagination can take it in other directions. And of course you can make pilaf in a rice cooker. Simply sauté the aromatics in a pan in advance of adding the rice and putting the whole thing into the machine with the stock.

4 tablespoons (½ stick) unsalted butter

1 small onion, peeled and cut into small dice

1 clove garlic, peeled and minced

2 cups white rice

3 cups chicken stock, ideally homemade or low-sodium, or water

6 fresh flat-leaf parsley sprigs, plus 2 tablespoons chopped leaves

2 fresh thyme sprigs (or ½ teaspoon dried)

2 bay leaves

Kosher salt and freshly ground black pepper

1. Set a deep saucepan with a tight-fitting lid over medium heat and add to it 2 tablespoons of the butter. When the butter foams, add the onion and garlic. Cook, stirring, until the onion begins to turn translucent, 5 to 7 minutes.

2. Add the rice to the pan and stir to coat the grains with butter.

3. Add the stock, stirring to combine. Add the parsley sprigs, thyme, and bay leaves. Bring to a boil, then cover with the lid and simmer for 17 minutes, or until all the liquid has been absorbed into the rice.

4. Remove the lid and discard the parsley and thyme sprigs and the bay leaves. Add the remaining 2 tablespoons butter and use a fork to stir it in and fluff the grains. Add the chopped parsley and stir to combine. Season to taste with salt and pepper and serve right away, or cover and keep warm for 30 minutes or so.

FRIED RICE

FRIED RICE CAN BE WHATEVER it is you want it to be. What follows is a canvas to which you could add a smear of sauce at the end—soy sauce and gochujang, the Korean red pepper paste, is one option—and into which you could stir leftover chopped brisket, bâtons of bacon, shredded chicken, cubes of tofu, ground pork or lamb dusted with cumin. The idea is simply to cook each ingredient quickly and well, then fold them all together with rice that has been cooked and, ideally, well chilled, so that the grains do not clump in the wok.

3 tablespoons neutral oil, such
    as canola or grapeseed
1 medium onion, peeled and
    roughly chopped
1 red bell pepper, stemmed,
    seeded, and roughly chopped
2 carrots, peeled and cut into
    small dice
1 cup fresh or frozen peas
1 tablespoon minced garlic,
    or to taste
1 tablespoon minced fresh ginger,
    or to taste
3 to 4 cups cooked white rice
    (see page 134), cold
2 large eggs, lightly beaten
¼ cup Shaoxing wine (a Chinese
    rice wine), or Japanese rice
    wine, or water
2 tablespoons low-sodium
    soy sauce
1 tablespoon sesame oil
Kosher salt and freshly ground
    black pepper
¼ cup fresh cilantro leaves
¼ cup chopped scallions, both
    green and white parts

1. Put 1 tablespoon of the oil in a wok or large skillet, and turn the heat to high. When the oil begins to shimmer, add the onion, bell pepper, and carrots and cook, stirring occasionally, until softened and beginning to brown, 5 to 10 minutes. With a slotted spoon, remove the vegetables to a bowl.

2. Add the peas to the wok and cook, stir-frying with a large spoon, for about 1 minute if the peas are fresh, 2 or 3 if frozen, until hot. Remove them to the bowl.

3. Put the remaining 2 tablespoons oil in the wok, followed by the garlic and ginger. When the mixture is fragrant, about 15 seconds later, add the rice, breaking up clumps with a spoon as you go along and tossing it with the oil. When the rice is well coated, make a well in the center and add the eggs. Scramble these, then stir them into the rice.

4. Return the vegetables to the wok and stir to integrate. Add the rice wine and cook, stirring, for about 1 minute. Add the soy sauce and sesame oil, then taste and add salt and black pepper, if necessary. Turn off the heat, spoon the rice onto a warm platter, and scatter the cilantro and scallions across the top.

RISOTTO

ISOTTO IS MOST COMMONLY MADE from round-grained Italian rice, such as arborio or carnaroli: high in starch, with the ability to absorb a great deal of stock. Seemingly endless stirring over a low flame results in a creamy, rich mélange of rice and liquid, almost a velvet porridge. (We call that the risotto dance.) When you've gotten to that state, just add a little more butter and some freshly grated Parmesan cheese and serve. In Italy risotto is often served as a first course. For a Sunday dinner, though, it can be a main dish, accessorized with any number of vegetables, herbs, and spices, from mushrooms, corn, lettuce, and carrots, all the way to lobster and saffron. Make it as follows in this plain recipe, then do as the self-help books say and follow your bliss, adding aromatics at the start with the onions to flavor the base.

6 cups vegetable or chicken stock (or lobster or shrimp stock, or a mixture of 4 cups stock and 2 cups dry white wine), ideally homemade, or low-sodium if store-bought

6 tablespoons unsalted butter

1 medium yellow onion, peeled and diced

2 cups arborio rice or other round-grained Italian-style rice

½ cup grated Parmesan cheese

Kosher salt and freshly ground black pepper

1. Heat the stock in a large pot set over medium heat until it is barely simmering. Turn off the heat.

2. In another large pot set over medium heat, melt 3 tablespoons of the butter until it foams. Add the onion and stir to coat with the butter, then cook, stirring occasionally, until soft and translucent. You do not want any color on it. Add the rice and stir to coat it evenly with the butter.

3. Turn the heat to medium-low. Add the stock to the rice, 1 cup at a time, stirring slowly to combine and to allow the liquid to be absorbed into the grains, and to allow the starch to come off the grains, creating a creamy consistency. This takes a while, 20 to 30 minutes, so exercise patience.

4. When the dish has come together into a tender, creamy whole, remove it from the heat and stir in the remaining 3 tablespoons butter and the Parmesan, continuing until all has been incorporated. Season to taste with salt and pepper and serve as soon as you can.

NOTES ON RISOTTO

THE RECIPE ON PAGE 142 IS for a plain if luxurious version of the dish. To make a **saffron risotto**, add a few strands of the spice to the first cup of stock you add. To make a **lobster risotto** (or a shrimp or crab one, for that matter), steam a lobster, then crack it open and harvest its meat. Then replace the vegetable or chicken stock with the one created by cooking the lobster, and stir the reserved meat in at the end, with the cheese. You can make a **red pepper risotto** by cutting a couple of red bell peppers into very thin strips and sautéing these with the onion at the start of the process; by the end, the strips will have basically disappeared, leaving only a beautiful red hue on the rice, and a bright sweetness against the cheese and the richness of the grains. You could stir in some chopped sautéed mushrooms for a **mushroom risotto**, or some sweet peas for a **pea risotto** (or both, which is a delightful combination). I like a **sausage risotto**, with sautéed crumbled Italian sausage mixed in at the end, along with some chopped parsley. In the summer, add some peeled, seeded, and chopped tomatoes at the end, with torn basil, for a **tomato risotto**. You see how it goes.

GRILLED PAELLA

M Y FRIEND MANNY HOWARD GOT me started with paella and specifically with the notion of cooking the dish over an open fire: a peasant's feast in the Spanish style, tended by men outside in a field, in the dying light of a late afternoon. He jumped into the project with abandon. He bought two carbon-steel paella pans, wide and shallow with dimpled bottoms, each one slightly smaller than the diameter of a large Weber kettle grill. He bought short-grain rice, for great paellas demand it, rounded and small but capable of absorbing large quantities of the stocks in his freezer. He found fine saffron, sweet onions, and good olive oil. He acquired chorizo and chicken thighs and went to the fish market for clams and shrimp. He bought much more. The grill was hardly large enough for his ambitions.

His paella took a little while to put together, in the end and particularly in the beginning. He had no recipe. He was just flying blind as the best artists do, scaring people. But dozens ate the resulting meal, men and women and children crowded smiling around the pans, loading paper bowls with a kind of smoky perfection that covered the seafood as fog does a tidal pond.

I was one of those people. And I've been cooking the dish ever since, both outside and inside, on the stove, which works just as well, if less smokily: more a Brooklyn paella than a Valencian one. Wherever you cook the dish, the whole game is in the preparation, what the professionals call *mise en place*. It is a project to make paella, but it is not an insurmountable one. Just read the recipe two or three times before you get started, and make sure you have everything ready before you even light the fire. Your overall time will improve with practice. But the flavors will be sublime from the very first attempt.

Large pinch of saffron

2¼ quarts chicken stock, ideally homemade, or low-sodium if store-bought

¼ cup extra-virgin olive oil

2 pounds bone-in, skin-on chicken thighs

Kosher salt and freshly ground black pepper

1 pound dried Spanish chorizo, sliced in half and cut into half-moons

1 medium yellow onion, finely chopped

1 tablespoon minced garlic

4 cups short-grain rice, such as arborio

1½ pounds jumbo shrimp, peeled, deveined, and roughly chopped

1 cup fresh or frozen peas

24 littleneck clams, cleaned

2 tablespoons finely chopped fresh flat-leaf parsley

continued on page 147

1.   Stir the saffron into the chicken stock in a large pot set over medium heat on the stove. Once the stock is hot, lower the heat and keep warm.

2.   In an 18-inch paella pan, heat the oil over medium-high heat, also on the stove. (A large, wide, shallow, flameproof saucepan may be substituted—or, in a pinch, an enameled Dutch oven.) Season the chicken thighs all over with salt and pepper and brown on all sides in the hot oil. Transfer to a plate. Cook the chorizo in the same pan until it starts to brown. Transfer to a second, paper towel–lined plate. Remove the pan from the stove.

3.   Light a charcoal grill with about a large cereal box's worth of charcoal. Return the paella pan to the stove and set over medium-high heat. When the pan is hot, add the onion and cook until translucent, about 4 minutes. Add the garlic and stir until fragrant, then add the rice and stir to coat. Season with salt and pepper.

4.   Bring the stock, paella pan, chicken, chorizo, and other ingredients to a table near the grill. When the fire is at its peak heat (all of the coals are lit and you can hold your hand over the hottest part of the fire for only 3 or 4 seconds), quickly stir the shrimp, chorizo, and peas into the rice, then add 2 quarts of the stock. Add the clams, hinge side up, so that when they open in the heat, their juices are released into the rice. Nestle the chicken on top.

5.   Scatter wood chips over the fire. Quickly set the paella pan on the grate. Cover the grill and cook the paella until all the liquid has been absorbed, 25 to 30 minutes. If the rice is underdone, add the remaining cup of stock and return the pan to the fire for 5 to 7 more minutes. Season to taste with salt and pepper and top with the chopped parsley.

ONION SOUBISE

SOUBISE IS TRADITIONALLY A THICK WHITE SAUCE of pureed onions, traditionally used in France to anoint fish or eggs. This version, which gets its thickness from long-cooked short-grained rice, is another gem I first cooked out of Suzanne Goin's invaluable restaurant cookbook, *Sunday Suppers at Lucques.* I've made it with any number of types of onion and sorts of rice. But the combination of sweet Spanish onions with a short-grained risotto rice is best to me. It is, yes, absurdly rich. I like it with roast chicken.

4 tablespoons (½ stick) unsalted butter

3 pounds Spanish onions, peeled, 2 cups diced and 12 cups thinly sliced

2 tablespoons fresh thyme leaves

Kosher salt and freshly ground black pepper

½ cup short-grained rice, such as arborio

½ cup grated Gruyère cheese

⅔ cup heavy cream

3 tablespoons fresh flat-leaf parsley, roughly chopped

1. Heat the oven to 300°F. Melt the butter in a large Dutch oven set over medium heat and, when it foams, add the onions, thyme, and salt and pepper to taste. Cook slowly for 15 to 20 minutes, stirring often and turning the heat down if it threatens to scorch the butter, until the onions are soft and translucent.

2. As the onions cook, bring a small pot of water to a boil and add the rice to the pot. Cook the rice for 5 to 6 minutes, then drain it. Add the rice to the onions and stir to combine.

3. Cover the Dutch oven tightly and place it in the oven. Allow the soubise to cook, undisturbed, for 30 to 35 minutes. Remove from the oven and allow to sit for 30 minutes more.

4. Before serving, remove the top of the Dutch oven, stir the rice, and place over a medium-low flame to reheat. Stir in the cheese and cream and cook, stirring occasionally, until the dish is hot. Sprinkle with the parsley and serve on a warmed platter.

RICE *and* PEAS

A CLASSIC WEST INDIAN SIDE DISH that pairs well with grilled meat and fish, rice and peas can also be a fine partner for stews with a little spice on them and, indeed, can be great on its own, with sautéed greens and hot sauce.

4 tablespoons (½ stick) unsalted butter

2 small yellow onions, peeled and cut into small dice

4 cloves garlic, peeled and minced

4 cups white rice

2 tablespoons fresh thyme leaves

Two 13-ounce cans coconut milk

1 whole Scotch bonnet chile (optional)

Two 15½-ounce cans pigeon peas, or 2 cups cooked pigeon peas

¼ cup chopped scallions, green parts only

Kosher salt and freshly ground black pepper

1. Melt the butter in a medium saucepan set over low heat. When the butter begins to foam, add the onions and garlic, stir, and allow to soften in the heat, 3 to 5 minutes.

2. Add the rice and thyme, and stir to combine. Add the coconut milk and 5 cups water, and turn the heat to high. Bring the liquid to a simmer, then lower the heat. If using the Scotch bonnet, place it in the center of the pot. Cover and cook until the liquid is absorbed and the rice is soft, 25 to 30 minutes.

3. Remove the pan from the heat and fluff the rice with a fork. If using the Scotch bonnet, remove it. Add the pigeon peas and scallions, then stir to combine. Season to taste with salt and black pepper, then cover the pot again, heat through, and keep warm until you're ready to serve.

RED BEANS *and* RICE

IN AND AROUND NEW ORLEANS, where this dish is most popular, red beans and rice is traditionally meant for eating on Monday nights, seasoned with the ham bone left over from the previous night's meal. But, man alive, it is good eating on a Sunday night as well, or on any evening when you can gather a mess of family or friends around the table to feed. My recipe is derived from one I learned from the great Louisiana storyteller Pableaux Johnson, whose Monday suppers are legendary and whose hand at the stove is nonpareil.

1 pound dried red kidney beans, rinsed and picked over to remove any stones

2 tablespoons extra-virgin olive oil or neutral oil, such as canola or grapeseed oil

1 pound smoked sausage or andouille sausage, cut into rounds if it's smoked, or diced if it's andouille

2 medium yellow onions, peeled and diced

6 cloves garlic, peeled and minced

1 medium green or red bell pepper, seeded and diced

3 celery stalks, trimmed and diced

3 bay leaves

2 teaspoons kosher salt, or to taste

1½ teaspoons freshly ground black pepper, or to taste

1 tablespoon dried basil

1 tablespoon Creole seasoning (Johnson uses Tony Chachere's) or a healthy

pinch each of paprika, cayenne pepper, dried oregano, kosher salt, black pepper, granulated garlic, granulated onion, and dried thyme

½ tablespoon distilled white vinegar

Hot sauce

½ cup fresh flat-leaf parsley, chopped

1 bunch scallions, both green and white parts, trimmed and chopped

Cooked white rice (see page 134)

1. Place the beans in a large bowl and cover with cold water, then allow to sit out on the countertop overnight; or if pressed for time, simmer over medium-low heat, covered, until the beans are tender, about an hour. (Or, if really pressed for time, substitute three 15½-ounce cans red kidney beans, drained.)

2. Heat a large, heavy-bottomed pot over medium-high heat. Add the oil and, a few moments later, the sausage. Cook, stirring occasionally, until the meat has started to crisp, 5 to 7 minutes.

3. Lower the heat to medium and add the onions and garlic. Cook, stirring occasionally, until the vegetables have softened and begun to go translucent, 5 to 7 minutes. Add the bell pepper and celery and stir to combine, cooking until they begin to soften, a further 5 to 7 minutes.

4. Add the bay leaves, salt, black pepper, basil, and Creole seasoning to the mixture in the pot and stir to combine, then add the beans, along with a splash or two of water, the vinegar, and hot sauce to taste. Lower the heat and allow to simmer softly for an hour or so, until the beans are soft. For an enhanced creaminess, remove 1 cup of the beans before serving, mash them in a bowl with a fork, and return them to the bean pot. Scatter the parsley and scallions over the top, stir, simmer for a final 10 minutes or so, remove the bay leaves, and serve over white rice, with more hot sauce on the side.

CUBAN-STYLE BLACK BEANS

A VAT OF THESE BEANS ADDS an enormous amount of protein to the dinner table on whatever night you serve it, along with a profusion of rich, garlicky flavor. Those who eschew pork can replace the ham hock and bacon with a smoked turkey wing. Those who avoid meat altogether can add a little salt at the end. The beans are superlative with white rice, which can make for a meal in itself, especially if paired with a crisp green salad and, crucially in my view, buttered toast. Hot sauce is mandatory.

1 pound dried black beans, rinsed and picked over to remove any stones

¼ cup extra-virgin olive oil

4 slices slab bacon, diced

1 medium Spanish onion, peeled and diced

1 head of garlic, cloves peeled and diced

2 small green bell peppers, seeded and diced

1 jalapeño pepper, seeded and diced

1 tablespoon kosher salt, or to taste

½ teaspoon freshly ground black pepper

1 teaspoon dried oregano

½ teaspoon ground cumin

3 tablespoons distilled white vinegar

1 smoked ham hock

2 bay leaves

1 tablespoon dark brown sugar

1. Place the beans in a large bowl and cover with cold water, then allow to sit out on the countertop overnight; or if pressed for time, simmer over medium-low heat, covered, until the beans are tender, about an hour. (Or if really pressed for time, substitute three 15½-ounce cans black beans, drained.)

2. When you're ready to cook the beans, put the oil in a large, heavy-bottomed pot set over medium-high heat and allow to come to a shimmer. Add the bacon and cook, stirring occasionally, until the fat has begun to render out of the bacon and the meat is beginning to crisp, about 5 minutes. Add the onion, garlic, bell peppers, and jalapeño, and stir to combine. Continue cooking until the vegetables have begun to soften, 5 to 7 minutes. Add the salt, black pepper, oregano, and cumin, and stir to combine. They will absorb the heated oil in the pan and grow fragrant, 3 to 5 minutes.

3. Add the vinegar to the pot and stir to combine, then allow to cook off until it is mostly gone. Add the ham hock, bay leaves, brown sugar, the beans, and a splash or two of water, and stir again.

4. Lower the heat and allow the beans to cook, stirring occasionally, for an hour or so, until the beans are very soft and the meat on the ham hock is pulling away from the bone. (Add a little water to the pot if it seems to be getting dry.)

5. When the beans are done, remove the ham hock and the bay leaves; discard the bay leaves and tear the

continued on page 154

meat from the hock. Chop this meat and return it to the bean pot. Stir, taste, and adjust the seasonings. (The mixture can keep, softly bubbling on the stove, for hours. Add a little water, if necessary. Stir occasionally.) Serve with rice and hot sauce.

ISLAND BEANS

THESE BEANS HINT AT SOME of the flavors of the West Indian larder without being doctrinaire about it. The recipe's parentage lies in the steam-table restaurants of the Caribbean diaspora in New York, and pairs exceptionally well with grilled and roasted meats, and rice piled high. (And it is pretty good without the meat!) Add hot sauce to taste.

1 pound dried red kidney beans, rinsed and picked over to remove any stones

2 tablespoons extra-virgin olive oil

4 slices slab bacon, diced

1 medium yellow onion, peeled and diced

3 cloves garlic, peeled and minced

1 medium red bell pepper, seeded and diced

2 tablespoons ground cumin

1 tablespoon ground coriander

1 cup fresh orange juice

1/2 cup pineapple juice

Kosher salt and freshly ground black pepper

1. Place the beans in a large bowl and cover with cold water, then allow to sit out on the countertop overnight; or if pressed for time, simmer over medium-low heat, covered, until the beans are tender, about an hour. (Or if really pressed for time, substitute three 15½-ounce cans red kidney beans, drained.)

2. Heat a large, heavy-bottomed pot over medium-high heat. Add the oil and, a few moments later, the bacon. Cook, stirring occasionally, until the fat has begun to render out of the bacon and the meat is beginning to crisp, about 5 minutes.

3. Lower the heat to medium and add the onion, garlic, and bell pepper. Cook, stirring occasionally, until the vegetables have softened, 5 to 7 minutes.

4. Add the cumin and coriander. They will absorb the heated oil in the pan and grow fragrant. Stir for 1 to 2 minutes and then add the orange juice and pineapple juice. Raise the heat to high until the mixture begins to simmer, then lower the heat and reduce by about a third. Add salt and black pepper to taste.

5. Stir in the beans, along with a splash or two of water. After 5 minutes, stir again, then taste and adjust the seasonings. (The mixture can keep, softly bubbling on the stove, for hours. Add a little juice or water, if necessary. Stir occasionally.)

BOSTON BAKED BEANS

RECIPES FOR BOSTON BAKED BEANS are as varied as those who make the dish and call it their own. James Beard cooked his version with ribs. Some old sharpies prefer salt pork. Mine was, for years: Crank open a can of B&M baked beans and cook it, in the can, over an open fire, for a taste of Maine that goes back more than a hundred years, a comfort food that binds generations. All those make for excellent dinners. But for years now I've been returning to a recipe I learned from the Rhode Island chef Steve Johnson, who goes whole hog with his beans, using pork butt to run the dish through with fat and flavor. You could easily cut back on the amount of meat or, as Beard did, use four or five pork ribs instead, nestling them into the bottom of the pot, below the beans. (I use navy beans here because they're widely available, but if you can get your hands on some heritage pebblers from New England, some Yellow Eyes or Jacob's Cattle, go to!) Traditionally the accompaniment for the dish is steamed Boston brown bread. I prefer crackers and cheddar. As with any bean preparation, you can pull a cup of the mixture from the pot just before serving, mash it with a fork in a bowl, and return it to the pot to increase the overall creaminess of the dish.

1 pound dried navy beans, rinsed and picked over to remove any stones

2 tablespoons neutral oil, such as canola or grapeseed

1/2 pound slab bacon, cut into 1/2-inch cubes

3 pounds boneless pork butt or shoulder, trimmed of excess fat and cut into 2-inch cubes

Kosher salt

2 teaspoons freshly ground black pepper, plus more to taste

2 large yellow onions, peeled and diced

4 cloves garlic, peeled and diced

1 tablespoon tomato paste

2 teaspoons dry mustard powder

2 tablespoons maple syrup

2 tablespoons molasses

2 bay leaves

1 1/2 cups chicken stock, ideally homemade, or low-sodium if store-bought

1. Place the beans in a large bowl and cover with cold water, then allow to sit out on the countertop overnight; or if pressed for time, simmer over medium-low heat, covered, until the beans are tender, about an hour. (Or if really pressed for time, substitute three 15 1/2-ounce cans navy beans, drained.)

2. Heat the oven to 350°F. On the stovetop, put the oil in a large casserole or Dutch oven, and turn the heat to medium-high. When the oil begins to shimmer, add the bacon and cook, stirring occasionally. When the

bacon is nicely browned, add the pork, a bit at a time, and cook until nicely browned, sprinkling with salt and pepper as it cooks.

3. Add the onions and garlic and cook until they soften and begin to turn translucent, then add the tomato paste, mustard powder, maple syrup, molasses, bay leaves, and the 2 teaspoons pepper. Stir to combine, then add the drained beans and the stock. Stir and add water barely to cover the beans, then bring to a bare simmer on the stove.

4. Cover the pot and place in the oven. Cook for 2 hours, the first hour with the lid on, the second with the lid off. Check occasionally, adding a splash of water, if necessary. When the beans are creamy and cooked through, check for seasoning, adding salt, if necessary. Remove and discard the bay leaves. Serve immediately, or keep warm in a low oven or over a low flame, or refrigerate and reheat when you're ready to serve.

PASTA

—

"Keep an eye on the sauce."

—HENRY HILL, *Goodfellas*

First-night pasta is a tradition in my house as inviolate as that of Sunday supper itself. It refers to the dinner we make on the first night we arrive somewhere in a whirl of gear and exhaustion, in pursuit of adventure: fish, forest, sea, mountain, beach, snow. The ingredients are simple: pasta, red sauce studded with sausage or ground beef, a shower of cheese, plenty of bread to mop everything up. A first-night pasta dinner is simply a marker: We made it and we are together.

That is a fine description of any good Sunday supper, as it happens. And so that is where we will start. But pasta for Sunday supper can be so much more than simple red sauce and spaghetti. You might, for instance, make your own pasta (see page 169). This is a project to fill a day with joy and activity, ideal for keeping a family occupied when rain is falling and mud is everywhere, in advance of company. There is the Italian American tradition of Sunday gravy to explore as well—a meal cooked in pieces over the course of a day and served with ziti sometime after church, maybe during the ball game, to siblings and cousins and grandparents and those two kids from down the block who come because they always come, automatic. You can make that meal beautiful even if you're as Italian as a bag of nickels. The process is what matters, the time spent and the attention paid. In a steamy kitchen perfumed with tomatoes and simmering pork, we are all Italian. That dish belongs to America.

There are lasagnas to make a day or so before you serve them, because you won't have the time on the day itself and because the flavors set up so nicely when you let them rest overnight. There are ragùs that burble along on the stove, sauces scented by crabs, or by ducks shot by friends, or purchased at the store. If that's too complicated for the supper you're planning, try a simple tangle of pasta with butter and Swiss cheese, or peas and mint. The next week you can roll meatballs for spaghetti and understand bliss.

Finally, it is worth pointing out that pasta for a Sunday supper is one category in which we can end up relying more heavily than we might ordinarily on ingredients that were created or packaged by others: on dried pasta, for instance, if you're not making your own; on canned tomatoes, if you don't put up your own in mason jars each summer because who has the time; on canned tomato paste; on tinned anchovies; on big hunks of Parmesan or globes of mozzarella.

Save for using Parmigiano-Reggiano cheese, an appellation for the region in north-central Italy in which it is made, I won't be bossy about brands or provenance. (I do call it Parmesan here, though.) The palate wants what it wants. So try different dried pastas until you find a manufacturer you like, then see if you can't stick with it. Same deal with canned tomatoes, if you're not using fresh; with tomato paste; with anchovies and mozzarella. Good cooking is about consistency. As you'll see if or when you make a first-night pasta with what you found at the Winn-Dixie twenty minutes before closing, consistency is not always easy to achieve, even if the eating ends up being great. Cooking Sunday supper with a degree of nervousness about how it's all going to turn out is part of the adventure of travel.

At home, though, you might as well try to stack the odds in your favor.

FIRST-NIGHT PASTA

THIS IS THE MEAL MY CROWD EATS on our first night of arrival in a new place with old friends, extended family, anywhere a lot of people have gathered to be together for holidays, graduations, weddings, adventure trips, weekend getaways, and funerals alike. As you'll see from the instruction below, it's not so much a recipe as an idea: browned Italian sausage and beef in a deep-red tomato sauce that you can make fiery with red pepper flakes or scent with cinnamon or both. Sometimes I make it with sausage alone. Sometimes I add wine, if there's wine around. You can really do to it whatever you like. It's a welcoming dish. Serve mixed into pasta in a big, warm bowl, with garlic bread.

2 tablespoons extra-virgin
    olive oil
1 medium yellow onion, peeled
    and diced
4 cloves garlic, peeled and minced
1 pound Italian sausage, hot or
    mild or a mixture, cut into
    coins or crumbled
1 pound ground beef
One 6-ounce can tomato paste
1 stick cinnamon, if you have one
2 teaspoons red pepper flakes
    (optional)
1 teaspoon fennel seeds, if you
    have them
2 teaspoons dried basil, if you
    have them
One 28-ounce can peeled whole
    or crushed tomatoes
A big glug of red wine, if there is
    some to hand
Kosher salt and freshly ground
    black pepper

1 pound dried pasta of your choice
1 handful of fresh basil leaves,
    roughly torn, if you have them
1 cup grated Parmesan cheese

1. Set a large saucepan or Dutch oven over medium heat and swirl into it the oil. When the oil shimmers, add the onion and cook, stirring occasionally, until softened and beginning to turn translucent, 3 to 5 minutes. Add the garlic and cook until it becomes fragrant, 30 seconds or so, then add the sausage and beef. Cook, stirring occasionally, until the meat has browned, 5 to 7 minutes. Drain off excess fat if you like, but I really never do.

2. Use a spoon to clear a space in the center of the pan and add the tomato paste, stirring to break it up. Then add the cinnamon, red pepper flakes, fennel seeds, and dried basil, if you're using any of those. Stir to combine, then add the tomatoes, along with the wine. Add a spray of salt and a few grinds of black pepper.

3. Lower the heat under the pan and allow the mixture to simmer quietly for 30 minutes or more, then cook the pasta and toss it with the sauce. Garnish with the fresh basil and serve alongside the Parmesan. We made it.

ON THE IMPORTANCE OF GARLIC BREAD

THERE IS NO BETTER ACCOMPANIMENT TO a dinner of pasta with red sauce than a large lacquered loaf of hot bread sliced almost but not entirely through, redolent of bruised garlic and sweet butter. Save, perhaps, two or more loaves. Children thrill to garlic bread in particular, and few adults can avoid its charms. You'll need only Italian bread or a country loaf, butter, garlic, and, if you like, a lot of mixed herbs.

For a traditional loaf, simply take a stick of unsalted butter and place it on your cutting board to soften. Then peel and mince garlic, as many cloves as you deem necessary, up to a full head. When the butter has softened, use a fork to mash the garlic into it, creating a paste that may appear to be equal parts garlic and butter. Add a little coarse kosher salt and mix again. Then use a bread knife to score the bread deeply, thick slices that end right before the bottom crust of the loaf. Spread the garlic butter on each side of each slice, making sure to get it down deep toward the bottom crust. Use the remaining garlic butter to anoint the exterior of the loaf, then wrap the whole thing in aluminum foil. Bake it in a 350°F oven for around 20 minutes, a little more if your oven temperature is lower, then serve.

Or if you'd like a more luxe and fragrant version? Follow the teachings of my colleague Samin Nosrat, who cuts a wide variety of herbs—parsley, thyme, and chives, say—into the butter she uses on the bread, then stuffs yet more fresh herbs of the same variety into the finished bread before she serves it. It's like a salad, then. And ridiculously delicious.

SUNDAY GRAVY

"EVEN IF YOU'RE CATHOLIC," LENNY BRUCE ONCE RIFFED, "if you live in New York, you're Jewish." His distinction was cultural, not religious. To be from New York is to live amid and within the cultures of the city's inhabitants. It doesn't matter where your parents were born, or theirs. As a result, all New Yorkers are, at some point, Dominican. They're Irish, African American, French, German, Chinese. On Sundays, a lot of them are Italian, and make a big pot of red sauce, then stir it carefully, often, to make sure it doesn't stick. I'm as Italian as your uncle Sven, but I'd put this recipe up against a nonna's. It will serve six for sure, more if you stretch it, and it's easily doubled to serve twelve to fifteen. Cook whatever odd cuts of pork or beef you see at the butcher or market to accompany the sausages—I often use marrow bones on top of what I call for below, and they nicely velvet the sauce. Serve with garlic bread because it's Sunday gravy and that's how it's done.

¼ cup olive oil

1 tablespoon unsalted butter

6 Italian sausages, sweet or hot

3 pounds pork spareribs or beef ribs or marrow bones or a combination

2 medium onions, peeled and diced

2 carrots, peeled and diced

5 cloves garlic, peeled and minced

Kosher salt and freshly ground black pepper

1 teaspoon red pepper flakes, or to taste

3 tablespoons tomato paste

1 cup dry red wine

Two 28-ounce cans peeled whole tomatoes, ideally San Marzano

2 cups fresh basil leaves

1 pound dried ziti, shells, spaghetti, or the pasta of your choice

1 cup grated Parmesan cheese

1. Put a large Dutch oven or heavy-bottomed pot over medium-high heat and add the oil and butter. When the mixture begins to shimmer and foam, add the sausages, in batches if necessary, and brown them, turning occasionally, until they are a deep golden brown on all sides, 8 to 10 minutes. Transfer the sausages to a platter or sheet pan and repeat the browning process with the spareribs, or whatever meats you've assembled, removing them to the platter or sheet pan when they are done.

2. Turn the heat to medium and add the onions and carrots to the pot, stirring occasionally until they begin to soften, but do not allow them to brown, 6 to 8 minutes. Add the garlic, salt, black pepper, and red pepper flakes to taste and cook for an additional 5 minutes or so, then add the tomato paste and stir to combine.

3. Add the wine to deglaze the pot and, using a wooden spoon, scrape at the bottom to dislodge all the browned bits. Then add the tomatoes, using the wooden spoon to crush them roughly, and allow the mixture to come to a fierce simmer. Return the browned meats to the pot, reduce the heat so that the mixture is at a low simmer, cover, and allow to cook until the meat is fork-tender and coming off the bone, 1½ to 2 hours. Stir in the basil and keep warm until you're ready to use.

4. When you're ready to eat, bring a large pot of heavily salted water to a boil. Remove the sausages and other meats to a warmed platter and drizzle a little sauce over them. Add the pasta to the pot of water and cook until just al dente, 8 to 12 minutes. Drain in a colander and serve, dressed with the remaining sauce and the grated Parmesan, alongside the platter of meats.

SPAGHETTI BOLOGNESE

SPAGHETTI BOLOGNESE ISN'T FOUND IN ITALY, really. Meaty Bolognese sauce there is most often combined with wider, flatter pasta, such as tagliatelle, or as the base of a lasagna. The dish is nonetheless popular all over the world and perhaps especially in Britain and Australia, where "spag bol" is a kids' menu standby. (Trivia tip: Harry Potter and Hermione Granger shared a dinner of spaghetti Bolognese in *Harry Potter and the Deathly Hallows*.) I like it for chilly days when I can have the pot of sauce burbling on the stove for hours, in front of evenings when the crowd runs to young and old, and I want to serve a pasta sauce that is hearty and rich, with a soft undertone from the milk and cheese. (If you want to double down on that experience, do as Craig Claiborne did and add a few chopped chicken livers to the pot when you sauté the beef. This adds a velvety thrum to the sauce that there is no reason to explain to the children.) Make sure to shower the finished sauce and pasta with grated Parmesan, and do not forget to accompany the meal with garlic bread. Encourage messiness! This is kids' food for grown-ups.

2 tablespoons neutral oil, such as
    canola or grapeseed
6 tablespoons unsalted butter,
    plus 2 tablespoons for serving
3 medium red onions, peeled and
    diced
3 celery stalks, trimmed and diced
3 carrots, peeled and diced
1½ pounds ground beef, or
    1 pound ground beef and
    ½ pound ground pork
Kosher salt and freshly ground
    black pepper
1 tablespoon tomato paste
2 cups whole milk
1 nutmeg for grating
2 cups dry red wine

One 28-ounce can peeled whole
    tomatoes, with their juices
½ to ¾ cup chicken or beef stock,
    ideally homemade or low-sodium,
    or water
1 tablespoon red wine vinegar, or to taste
2 pounds dried spaghetti
Grated Parmesan cheese

1. Place a large, heavy-bottomed, high-sided pot or Dutch oven over medium heat and swirl into it the oil and then the butter. When the butter is foaming, add the onions and cook, stirring often with a wooden spoon, until they begin to turn translucent, 5 to 7 minutes. Add the celery and carrots and cook for another 5 minutes or so, stirring often to coat them with the fat.

2. Add the meat, along with a healthy spray of salt and pepper, and cook, stirring to break up the meat,

until it releases its liquid and is about to brown, 5 to 7 minutes. Use your spoon to create an opening on the bottom of the pot and add to it the tomato paste. Stir this around in small circles until it begins to melt and caramelize, about 2 minutes, then stir the pot to incorporate it into the whole.

3. Add the milk and stir to combine, then cook at a low simmer, stirring occasionally, until it has reduced almost entirely, about 20 minutes. Then grate some nutmeg over the top—six or so strokes on a Microplane, or about ¼ teaspoon—and stir to combine.

4. Add the wine to the pot and stir to combine, then repeat the process of reducing it until it is mostly gone, another 15 minutes or so. Stir in the tomatoes, breaking them up with the spoon, and reduce the heat to the barest of simmers. Add the stock and cook, uncovered, stirring occasionally, for as long as you can stand it: 2 or 3 hours is good. If the sauce threatens to dry out, you can add a few splashes of water or, better yet, more stock. Add some more salt, if needed, and stir in the vinegar just before serving.

5. Meanwhile, set a large pot of salted water to boil over high heat. Cook the pasta until it is just al dente, approximately 8 to 12 minutes, then drain, reserving 1 cup of the water on the side. Toss the sauce with the pasta and the remaining 2 tablespoons butter in a large, warmed bowl, loosening it if necessary with a little of the reserved pasta water. Serve with lots and lots of grated Parmesan on the side.

SPAGHETTI *and* TOMATO SAUCE

Y OU CAN'T MAKE A PASTA DINNER MUCH SIMPLER unless you dress the pasta in butter and dust it with Parmesan. But it can thrill all the same, either as a side dish or simply as a foil for garlic bread on a night when you're running late and just want to feed a bunch of people on the fly. The key is the sauce, which is a version of the one the great Italian cook Marcella Hazan made famous: good canned tomatoes, butter, and onion. Some will prefer to dice the onion and keep it in the sauce, but Hazan's original recipe calls for it to be discarded at the end and that's pretty neat: The onion leaves a sweet whisper, no more.

4 cups peeled whole tomatoes,
    essentially two 28-ounce cans,
    with their juices
8 tablespoons (1 stick) unsalted
    butter
1 onion, peeled and halved
Kosher salt
2 pounds dried spaghetti

1. Set a large saucepan over medium heat and add to it the tomatoes, butter, and onion, then add a pinch of salt.

2. Bring the tomatoes to a bare simmer and cook, stirring occasionally with a wooden spoon and pressing down on the tomatoes to crush them, for about 45 minutes, or until the sauce is velvety and rich. Season to taste with salt.

3. Set a large pot of heavily salted water over high heat. When it comes to a boil, add the pasta and cook until it is just al dente, approximately 8 to 12 minutes. Use a mug to reserve a cup or so of the pasta water and then drain the pasta in a colander.

4. Return the cooked pasta to the pot and dress it with the tomato sauce, using a splash of the cooking water if necessary to loosen it, then serve.

HOW TO COOK PASTA

PEOPLE TELL YOU TO SALT YOUR pasta water. They are right. The salt helps enhance the flavor of the pasta you are cooking. It gives it a little lift.

But how much salt, and in how much water? There is no precise ratio. What you are looking for is water that is salty, but not so salty as the sea. Figure out what that means for you and your tastes once, and you'll never really have to measure again. It'll take but a few minutes. You can do it before bed. Just take the large pot in which you cook pasta and fill it with hot water from the tap, to the level you generally use when you're cooking pasta. Add a big pinch of salt to it, and stir to dissolve. Taste. It may barely be salty. Add another big pinch and taste again. There should be some tang. Add a little more, but not so much more that you're being reckless, and taste a third time. You are probably pretty close. That's how much salt you should use, going forward.

Next time, add that amount of salt and bring the water to a boil to cook your pasta. There may be cooking times listed on the box or bag, if it's dried pasta, but they're not precise. So cook until the pasta is just al dente—meaning, it's still got a little bite to it. (If you're cooking fresh pasta, you need to cook it all the way through, but just barely, and that state is going to arrive in just three or four minutes. So look lively.) And when the pasta is done, drain it in a colander, using a coffee cup to reserve a little of the pasta water in case you need it to loosen your sauce. Give that colander a good shake to relieve it of steam, and get to the sauce.

As for that sauce: It is best to think of the process of finishing a pasta dish as one similar to the act of dressing a salad. You want to do it so that the pasta is enrobed by the sauce but not drowning in it, so that it is, above all else, in balance, a homogeneous whole. (That pasta water you saved can come in handy here.) Then add fresh herbs and cheese, off the heat, and serve. Nothing to it.

HOW TO MAKE YOUR OWN PASTA

Making your own pasta for company is an advanced-level activity, not something you want to do for the first time a few hours before your friends arrive. That is not because it is particularly difficult work, but because doing it well takes practice, and rewards experience. So start with a half batch on an afternoon when you don't have a large crowd due for dinner. Cook the result and dress it in butter and Parmesan and marvel at your success. But don't stop there. Do it again in a couple weeks, a few times over the course of a few months, and you'll begin to understand what the pasta should feel like when you roll it out, and how thin you can take it when you do. It's something to do with children or friends, working side by side in a cloud of flour, in advance of a meal, a recipe that yields a dough that you can use for fettuccine or ravioli, for sheets of lasagna, for whatever shape of pasta you like.

4 cups all-purpose flour, or more as needed

1 teaspoon kosher salt

6 large eggs

4 large egg yolks

Semolina or all-purpose flour, for dusting

1. Put the flour and salt in a mixing bowl or the bowl of a stand mixer. Beat the eggs and yolks together in a separate bowl, add them to the flour, and mix with a wooden spoon or the paddle attachment of the mixer until the dough comes together, about 1 minute. If the dough seems dry or crumbly, add 2 or 3 tablespoons cold water, just enough to keep the dough together.

2. Turn the dough out onto a cutting board and knead to form a ball. Flatten that ball to a 1-inch-thick disk, then wrap in plastic wrap and allow to rest at room temperature for at least 1 hour and up to 3 or 4.

3. Divide the dough into 8 pieces. Knead each piece until smooth. Then roll with a rolling pin or pasta machine until each piece is a smooth, thin sheet that is not quite paper-thin. Cut each sheet in half, and you'll have 16 sheets. Dust them with semolina flour or, if you don't have any, all-purpose flour, to keep them from sticking, and cut to shape, either with the pasta machine, by stacking a few pieces together, rolling them loosely, and cutting them into noodles, or just trimming for use in lasagna.

4. Place the finished pasta on a flour-dusted sheet pan and refrigerate, uncovered, until you're ready to cook.

DUCK RAGÙ

THIS IS MY TAKE ON A RAGÙ I once ate at the restaurant Esca in Manhattan, an off-the-menu staff-meal experiment that the chef Dave Pasternack ginned up out of wild-shot brant off the Great South Bay on Long Island: a wine-dark jam of tomatoes and heavy shreds of meat—poultry that looked like pork and tasted of fish, a combination to reel the mind. If you can lay your hands on geese or ducks of maritime provenance, you can omit the anchovies and the juniper berries from the sauce, but most cannot, so don't. The result is amazingly complex, a little feral, absolutely delicious. It benefits from an overnight rest in the refrigerator both to allow the flavors to marry and for the excess fat to rise to the top of the dish and congeal. Peel it off the next day and then reheat the sauce over a medium flame, or in a 250°F oven. Pasternack served his version with polenta. I serve mine more often with ziti or shells.

8 duck legs, trimmed

2 tablespoons extra-virgin olive oil

6 celery stalks, trimmed and cut into small dice

4 medium carrots, peeled and cut into small dice

2 medium red onions, peeled and cut into small dice

8 cloves garlic, peeled and minced

16 salted anchovy fillets, rinsed, dried, and minced

12 juniper berries

3 cups dry red wine

1 cup red wine vinegar

¼ cup tomato paste

4 cups chicken stock, homemade or low-sodium

Kosher salt and freshly ground black pepper

2 tablespoons minced fresh sage

1. Heat the oven to 350°F. Trim excess skin from the duck legs and discard.

2. Heat a Dutch oven with a tight-fitting lid over medium heat. Add the oil to the pot, and when it begins to shimmer, add 4 of the duck legs, skin side down. Cook until the skin is well browned and the fat has begun to render, 8 to 10 minutes. Turn the legs over and brown the other sides, 5 to 10 minutes more. Remove to a plate to rest and repeat with the remaining 4 duck legs.

3. Pour off all but a few tablespoons of the rendered fat in the pot, then add the celery, carrots, onions, and garlic, and stir to combine. Cook until the onions have softened and have just begun to color, 12 to 15 minutes. Clear a space in the center of the pot and add the anchovies, then swirl them in the fat until they begin to dissolve. Stir to combine. Add the juniper berries, wine, and vinegar, and cook until most of the liquid has evaporated, about 15 minutes.

4. Add the tomato paste and stir to combine, then pile in the duck legs and add enough stock so that the combination takes on a saucelike consistency and just covers the duck. Increase the heat to high and bring to a boil. Put a lid on the pot and place in the oven. Cook

continued on next page

for 1½ hours, or until the meat on the duck legs pulls easily from the bone.

5. Remove the duck from the pot and allow to cool slightly. Remove the skin, dice it, and reserve. Shred the meat off the bones and return to the pot. Place the pot on the stove over medium heat and bring to a bare simmer. Add the reserved duck skin to taste, salt and pepper to taste, then scatter the sage over the sauce and serve with polenta or pasta, as you like.

PASTA *with* PARSNIPS *and* BACON

IBUILT THIS RECIPE OUT OF ONE I found in a Jamie Oliver cookbook years ago and scaled and modified it over the years in the way that each of us ought to scale and modify recipes—by using them often, and watching them change, until they become hardened and pure. Oliver's recipe calls for pancetta, and a relatively fast sauté of pancetta and parsnips makes for an exceptionally clean and fragrant dinner. Me, I mostly use bacon because I don't often have pancetta on hand and anyway prefer guanciale if I'm cooking fancy cured Italian meats. And I cook the mixture of meat and vegetables for a lot longer than Oliver ever did, which gives the sauce a deep, caramelized funkiness that is well suited, I think, to the sort of dinner where you want everyone to devour their food wolfishly, without talking very much.

1 tablespoon extra-virgin olive oil

6 slices thick-cut bacon, guanciale, or pancetta, cut into sticks

3 tablespoons fresh thyme leaves, or a combination of thyme and rosemary

4 cloves garlic, peeled and thinly sliced

8 medium parsnips, peeled and thinly sliced

2 pounds dried fettuccine or any wide-ish flat pasta

3 tablespoons unsalted butter, cut into pats

1 cup grated Parmesan cheese

Kosher salt and freshly ground black pepper

1. Set a large pot of salted water over high heat and allow to come to a boil.

2. Set a large sauté pan over medium-high heat and swirl the oil into it. When the oil shimmers, add the bacon and cook, stirring occasionally, until it is beginning to crisp, 5 to 7 minutes. Remove the bacon to a plate and pour off all but a healthy tablespoon of fat.

3. Add 2 tablespoons of the thyme and the garlic to the pan and fry them, stirring frequently, until they are fragrant and softening, 2 to 3 minutes, then add the parsnips and lower the heat to medium. Cook the parsnips, stirring occasionally, until they are soft and caramelized, about 10 minutes, then return the bacon to the pan and stir. Turn the heat to low and stir occasionally until you're ready to use it.

4. Meanwhile, cook the pasta in the boiling salted water until it is just al dente, probably a minute or so less than the instructions on the packaging, then fish out a cup of the pasta water and drain the rest.

5. Put the pasta in a large, warm serving bowl and add to it the parsnips and bacon, along with the butter and cheese, and toss to combine. Add a few splashes of the reserved pasta water to loosen everything up and give the pasta a sheen. Season to taste with salt and pepper. Sprinkle the remaining 1 tablespoon thyme over the top of the pasta and serve.

PASTA *with* PEAS *and* MINT

IF YOU COOK FOR OTHERS on a regular cadence, you'll discover that not all the meals will be beautifully planned. Sometimes one thing leads to another and you forget to shop, or you forget that you need wood or propane or time to brine the meat. Sometimes you run out of time. Sometimes you run out of energy. Sometimes you just want to cook something simple and eat, toast one another, wash everything up, and take a long walk with the dog.

Pasta with peas and mint can answer that call, provide a bright summer evening on a plate. It's a pantry meal for those who grow mint and always have dried pasta in a cabinet and a few bags of organic peas in the freezer. (It's an easy shop for those who don't.) You can use fettuccine or tagliatelle, though I like how medium shells hold the peas. Could you add some chopped bacon to the pan? Why, yes, you could, and that would be fine.

2 tablespoons extra-virgin
　　olive oil
3 tablespoons unsalted butter
2 cloves garlic, peeled and thinly
　　sliced
2 small shallots or 1 large one,
　　peeled and thinly sliced
2 cups shelled fresh or frozen
　　peas
1 pound dried pasta, such as
　　fettuccine, tagliatelle, or shells
1½ cups grated Parmesan cheese
2 large handfuls of mint leaves,
　　either roughly torn or
　　thinly sliced
Kosher salt and freshly ground
　　black pepper

1.　Set a large pot of salted water over high heat and allow to come to a boil.

2.　Set a large sauté pan over medium-high heat and swirl the oil and 1 tablespoon of the butter into it. When the oil and butter shimmer and foam, add the garlic and shallots to the pan and stir. Cook, stirring, for a few minutes, until the garlic has started to soften and the shallots turn translucent. Add the peas and a splash of water and cook, stirring occasionally, until the peas are cooked through and the water has evaporated, 3 to 5 minutes.

3.　Meanwhile, cook the pasta in the boiling salted water until it is just al dente, probably a minute or so less than the instructions on the packaging, then fish out a cup of the pasta water and drain the rest.

4.　Put the pasta in a large, warm serving bowl and add to it the peas, along with the remaining 2 tablespoons butter, the cheese, and most of the mint, and toss to combine. Add a few splashes of the reserved pasta water to loosen everything up and give the pasta a sheen. Season to taste with salt and pepper. Sprinkle the remaining mint over the top of the pasta and serve.

SPAGHETTI *with* BUTTER *and* SWISS CHEESE

THERE WAS A BEAUTIFUL LITTLE Brooklyn restaurant we used to take the children to when they were small: French and idiosyncratic and not very good save for its children's menu, which was nonpareil. The chef—glowering and intense in his little kitchen—served chicken nuggets and fries that were really marinated chunks of thigh meat roasted crisp, then tossed in a hot, oil-slicked pan to finish, with small crushed red potatoes treated the same. The kids ate that food with relish. But they absolutely demolished the pasta every time: spaghetti tossed with sweet, high-fat European butter and a fair amount of grated Emmental cheese. They ate bowls of it as if it were candy. We did too, thrilling to the sweet, nutty, slightly salty taste. It was cosmopolitan comfort food, I guess, best accompanied by cheap red wine and a cast of Polly Pocket dolls holding court on the table. The chef's offerings of *pissaladière* and *daube* went unordered, and this was apparently no way to run a business. We mourned the restaurant's eventual closing and, when the cast of our weekly meal runs more than 40 percent children—which happens!—I haul out this recipe to recall its joys. Feel free to substitute Norwegian Jarlsberg for the Emmental, or use Raclette, and absolutely serve a big green salad on the side. The children may not touch it. But that's quite all right. This is a Sunday dinner for children and those who love them. Let them eat as they like.

1 pound dried spaghetti

4 tablespoons (½ stick) unsalted butter

2 cups grated Swiss cheese, such as Emmental or Raclette or Norwegian Jarlsberg

Freshly ground black pepper

1. Bring a large pot of salted water to a boil over high heat. Add the pasta to the water and cook it until it is tender but not quite done, approximately 8 to 10 minutes.

2. Meanwhile, place the butter in a skillet or saucepan large enough to hold the cooked pasta and turn the heat to medium, allowing the butter to melt. When the butter foams, turn the heat down to very low.

3. When the pasta is close to finished, scoop out a cup of the cooking water, then drain the pasta and add to the pan with the butter. Raise the heat to medium and stir in the grated cheese. Add about ½ cup of the pasta water and stir. The mixture will be loose, almost soupy. Cook for about a minute as the cheese melts and the water is absorbed, and the pasta is done.

4. Add some pepper to taste, stir to combine, and serve immediately in a warmed bowl.

LASAGNA

L ASAGNA IS NOT A DISH to make on the quick. It's an all-day affair. There's the ragù to cook and the béchamel to stir and stir. There's cheese to grate and a lot of pasta to deal with. You can cut corners if you like, deliciously, by omitting the béchamel and replacing it with a mixture of fresh ricotta, mozzarella, eggs, and chopped fresh parsley. But I wouldn't unless the ricotta you have is sublime. I find the combination of ragù and béchamel to be more elegant and delicious, more in keeping with what I want after a full day's work at the stove. (You can, if you want, make both sauces a day ahead of assembly, then keep them chilled in the refrigerator. Reheat on the stove before making the lasagna. And you can let an unbaked lasagna cool, then cover it with plastic and freeze it for nearly a month. Defrost overnight in the refrigerator before baking.) That said, I make no apologies for cooking with either no-boil sheets of lasagna or the excellent fresh ones you can get from Antica Pasteria and other sources. Boiling dried sheets of lasagna in advance of making lasagna is, I think, a guarantee that you will never make lasagna again. Here, amid my shortcuts and maybe yours, is a dinner that defines old-school Sunday suppering, with a beautiful reveal at the table—and an amazing meal to follow.

FOR THE RAGÙ

2 tablespoons neutral oil, such as
    canola or grapeseed
6 tablespoons unsalted butter
3 medium red onions, peeled and
    diced
3 celery stalks, trimmed and diced
3 carrots, peeled, and diced
1½ pounds ground beef, or
    1 pound ground beef and
    ½ pound ground pork
Kosher salt and freshly ground
    black pepper
3 tablespoons tomato paste
2 cups whole milk

1 nutmeg for grating
2 cups dry red wine
One 28-ounce can peeled whole
    tomatoes, with their juices
½ to ¾ cup chicken or beef stock,
    ideally homemade or low-sodium,
    or water
1 tablespoon red wine vinegar,
    or to taste

FOR THE BÉCHAMEL SAUCE

7 tablespoons unsalted butter
¼ cup plus 3 tablespoons all-purpose flour
6 cups whole milk
1 cup grated Parmesan cheese (about ¼ pound)

continued on next page

Pinch of cayenne pepper

Pinch of ground nutmeg

Kosher salt and freshly ground
black pepper

FOR THE LASAGNA

1 to 2 tablespoons unsalted butter

1¼ pounds no-boil lasagna
noodles or fresh sheets of
lasagna

½ cup grated Parmesan cheese
(about 2 ounces)

1. **Make the ragù.** Place a large, heavy-bottomed, high-sided pot or Dutch oven over medium heat and swirl into it the oil and then the butter. When the butter is foaming, add the onions and cook them, stirring often with a wooden spoon, until they begin to turn translucent, 5 to 7 minutes. Add the celery and carrots and cook for another 5 minutes or so, stirring often to coat them with the fat.

2. Add the meat, along with a healthy spray of salt and pepper, and cook, stirring to break up the meat, until it releases its liquid and is about to brown, 5 to 7 minutes. Use your spoon to create an opening on the bottom of the pot and add to it the tomato paste. Stir this around in small circles until it begins to melt and caramelize, about 2 minutes, then stir the pot to incorporate it into the whole.

3. Add the milk and stir to combine, then cook at a low simmer, stirring occasionally, until it has reduced almost entirely, about 20 minutes. Then grate some nutmeg over the top—six or so strokes on a Microplane, or about ¼ teaspoon—and stir to combine.

4. Add the wine to the pot and stir to combine, then repeat the process of reducing it until it is mostly gone, another 15 minutes or so. Stir in the tomatoes, breaking them up with the spoon, and reduce the heat to the barest of simmers. Add ½ cup of the stock and cook, uncovered, stirring occasionally, for as long as you can stand it: 2 or 3 hours is good. If the sauce threatens to dry out, you can add a few splashes of water or, better yet, more stock. Add some more salt, if needed, then stir in the vinegar and keep warm.

5. **Make the béchamel.** Melt the butter in a medium, heavy saucepan set over medium heat. Whisk in the flour and continue to whisk until the flour just starts to smell nutty, 4 to 5 minutes.

6. Whisk the milk into the flour-and-butter mixture and increase the heat under the pan to medium-high.

Bring the mixture to a bare simmer, whisking all the while, and cook until the béchamel thickens, another 4 minutes or so. Then reduce the heat to low and cook, whisking occasionally, until the sauce is very smooth, about 10 minutes. Remove from the heat and whisk in the cheese, cayenne, and nutmeg, then season to taste with salt and pepper.

7. **Make the lasagna.** Heat the oven to 325°F. Use the butter to grease a 13-by-9-inch glass or ceramic baking dish. Ladle a thin layer of ragù into the dish and spread to the corners. Lay a single layer of noodles over the sauce, breaking or cutting some in half in order to fill the gaps. Then ladle a thin layer of the béchamel over the noodles, using the back of the ladle or a spatula to even it out. Ladle another layer of ragù over the top of the béchamel.

8. Repeat, creating five or six layers of pasta, bringing the lasagna right up to the very top edge of the dish. Finish with a final coating of béchamel.

9. Sprinkle the top of the lasagna with the grated cheese, cover the dish with aluminum foil, and place it on a sheet pan. Bake for 45 minutes or so, until the edges of the dish are bubbling, then remove the foil and cook until the top is browning and the edges are crisp, another 10 to 15 minutes. Let sit for 10 or 15 minutes before serving.

MONICA BYRNE'S MUSHROOM LASAGNA

I FIRST HAD THIS LASAGNA AT A WEDDING held in a loft high up above the West Side docks of Manhattan. Jay-Z and Alicia Keys were singing over the sound system as everyone danced in candlelight, with flowers everywhere and the crowd running middle-aged and well-seasoned. We were aware, the lot of us, that we were experiencing the kind of love and commitment you can't possibly grasp until you've experienced it for a while. We bore witness to a marriage built on the firmest of foundations.

The dinner was served family style, in keeping with the aesthetics of both the couple and the caterers who served them that day, Monica Byrne and Leisah Swenson. Monica's mushroom lasagna was near the beating heart of that meal—luscious and rich and sweet and salty and thrumming with that strange and magical fifth taste the aesthetes call umami. We ate it in happiness and amazement, filled with joy, and when eventually it was time to go home, I buttonholed Monica and asked her if she'd show me how to make it. She did, and the dish has since become the one I turn to when the Sunday supper forecast calls for Epic.

Some will quail at the use of no-boil sheets of lasagna, and if you are one of them, go to: Boil your own and use them instead. Even better are fresh sheets of lasagna, if you can find any. But, jeepers, the no-boil ones work well in this dish. Serve under candlelight, please, with a green salad dressed in a peppery vinaigrette.

½ cup extra-virgin olive oil

6 large shallots, peeled and minced

1½ pounds mixed mushrooms, such as oyster, shiitake, and cremini, trimmed and sliced

1 cup dry white wine

1 softball-sized head of radicchio, halved, cored, and cut into ½-inch slices

Kosher salt and freshly ground black pepper

4 tablespoons (½ stick) unsalted butter

3 large cloves garlic, peeled and minced

¼ cup all-purpose flour

3 cups whole milk

½ teaspoon ground or freshly grated nutmeg

1 cup grated Gruyère cheese

1 cup grated Fontina cheese

Two 9-ounce boxes no-boil lasagna sheets

1 baseball-sized ball smoked mozzarella, sliced

1 cup grated Parmesan cheese

1. Heat the oven to 350°F. Place a large sauté pan over medium-high heat and add ¼ cup of the oil. When the oil begins to shimmer, add half of the shallots and cook, stirring occasionally, until translucent. Add the mushrooms and toss to coat, then cook until they begin to color but are still plump, 12 to 15 minutes. Add the wine to deglaze the pan and allow to cook down into a

syrup, 5 to 7 minutes. Put the mushrooms into a large bowl and reserve.

2. Meanwhile, in another bowl, toss the radicchio with the remaining ¼ cup oil and season well with salt and pepper. Spread the strips out onto a rimmed baking sheet and place in the oven until the strips are lightly browned around the edges, about 15 minutes. Combine with the mushrooms and reserve.

3. Make a béchamel. Place a saucepan over medium heat and melt the butter. When the butter foams, add the rest of the shallots and cook until they begin to turn translucent. Add the garlic and stir to combine, then cook until the garlic has begun to soften. Sprinkle the flour over the top and stir to combine, then cook gently until the mixture has turned light brown and gives off a nutty scent, about 10 minutes. Add the milk to the mixture, whisking as you do, and cook until the sauce is thick and creamy. Add the nutmeg, ¼ cup of the Gruyère, and ¼ cup of the Fontina, then stir to combine. Season to taste with salt and pepper.

4. Reserve 1 cup béchamel. Pour the rest over the mixture of mushrooms and radicchio, and stir to combine.

5. Assemble the lasagna. Spread the plain béchamel across the bottom of a 13-by-9-inch baking dish. Place a layer of lasagna sheets across the sauce, being careful not to overlap. Spread a generous layer of the mushroom mixture on top of the pasta and follow with some grated Gruyère and Fontina. Top with another layer of pasta, then with smoked mozzarella. Repeat until the pasta is gone and the pan is full. Top with the remaining Gruyère, Fontina, and mozzarella, and a generous amount of the grated Parmesan. Cover with a buttered sheet of aluminum foil and place in the oven for 45 minutes. Remove the foil and cook until the top is golden and bubbling. Let rest for 15 minutes or so, then serve with the remaining Parmesan on the side.

SEAFOOD

—

Picture a dozen people wedged around a dinner table, all of them reaching toward a platter piled high with chunks of fried bass or scallops or walleye, dipping the meat into tartar sauce, eating it with slaw. Picture them folding tortillas around grilled fluke. Slurping clams or oysters from the half shell in the yard, fast as you can shuck them. Seafood should be one of the great players in your big-dinner repertory.

Think of whole sides of wild salmon, hot off the grill, scented with miso, mirin, and ginger. Think of grilled shrimp, steamed shrimp, clams. Think of crabs stacked on newsprint, dusted in seasoning salt. Think of lobster, corn, red potatoes to go along with them. Of moist crab cakes, salad on the side. Of grilled swordfish, sprayed with lemon. Think of chowder, of the interplay between the cream and the stock and the clams, as children crumble crackers into their bowls.

Fish for dinner needn't be formal. It can always be great.

Oh, I know. Worriers worry. *Fish for a crowd is a bear,* they say. It is delicate, hard to cook, expensive. Or it is cheap, factory-farmed mystery flesh. Not to mention: You can stink up the house with the stuff. There are a lot of people coming to dinner tonight. Chicken's easier. Fish is confusing. Why bother?

This is a central paradox of our lives in the kitchen. On the one hand, there is no easier thing to cook than seafood. You take a glistening piece of fresh fish and season it simply, apply a blast of heat to it, then serve it accompanied by a wedge of lemon or a spoonful of sauce. The results can be incredible, a taste of natural perfection, the best thing you've had all year.

On the other hand: *Which fish?* Choose wrong and it's a bummer, the opposite of delicious, a violation of the joy that should accompany every Sunday meal. The question is vexing, and worth considering closely.

So to market we go. Look at the fish there. This one's on the brink of extinction and costs a million dollars and probably shouldn't have been harvested in the first place. That one looks very, very dead, its eyes clouded, its flesh slack. Another appears to have been raised in a lab, or a prison. Here's a fine specimen, though it carries an unfamiliar name. Should you buy the snapper, pearlescent and firm? The whiting? The swordfish steaks? The char? The perch? Look at these fillets now. "Sole," says the sign—some of them are creamy in hue, others gray, nearly yellow, vaguely pink. You have a recipe that calls for grouper. There is no grouper. Can you make it with wreckfish? Cobia? Which tuna do you buy? Which salmon? These cockles—are they the same as littleneck clams? Is it Atlantic halibut we're meant to be buying, or Pacific? (The latter—the stock is healthier on the West Coast.)

Shopping for fish can be overwhelming. It needn't be, so long as you have faith in the transaction. Knowing the shop where you buy, and ideally having a relationship with the people who sell, is of greater importance with fish than it is with almost anything else we cook. Looking and touching and smelling are grand: They can tell you a lot. But we need to know, or need to be assured that someone knows: When was this fish caught and where? Where was it farmed and how? What's good today? What's not?

What's best will most likely be locally harvested or farmed. It may be cheap. It may be the opposite.

The game is to play these factors off one another. Local fish trumps all: A fluke from the fishmonger I visit in New York can be among the greatest feeds on the planet, but that doesn't mean a reader in Houston should cook it, not when she's got triggerfish at the market that's as good as my fluke, and better than my fluke if I had to ship it south.

Wild king salmon from a fish shop in Anchorage in July is a bargain; in Washington, D.C., it will cost you loads. In the District, then? Don't get the salmon. Get the crabs instead, or the bluefish trucked in on ice from Chesapeake Bay.

Or say you're in Wisconsin. Nine times out of eleven the state-farmed rainbow trout will answer better than the mahi-mahi brought in from Ecuador. Spot prawns? If you're in Southern California, that's a find. In Des Moines, it's a hefty expense, and may disappoint. Buy some tilapia and make fish tacos instead.

The overall idea is simple: Buy well. Buy fish that looks fresh and clean and glistening and firm. That is the hardest part of cooking fish, right there. Manage to do it and you are well on your way to delicious.

ROASTED FISH

THERE IS NO BETTER INTRODUCTION to the joys of cooking fish for a crowd than to roast a side of bluefish or salmon, cod, bass, or walleye, then serve it alongside a pot of steamed rice and a pile of sautéed greens. This recipe is one you'll find in some form in the kitchens of those who fish for protein from Maine to Florida, across the Gulf Coast, up into the lake-dotted dales of the Midwest, in California, Oregon, Washington, all the way to the fish camps of rural Alaska. It is not fancy—the key ingredients, in addition to the fish, are mustard and mayonnaise—but the results are sublime, with the prepared condiments doing a magnificent job of both keeping the fish moist and giving it a flavorful crust. Some will tell you to make your own mayonnaise for the "paint" that adheres to the exterior of the fish. But that's not at all necessary. Your favorite store-bought mayonnaise and the best mustard you can find are all you need.

¼ cup mayonnaise

3 tablespoons Dijon mustard

½ teaspoon dried thyme

1 large fish fillet (the side of a
    bluefish or cod, say), 1½ to 2
    pounds, or four 6-ounce fish
    fillets, skin and bones removed

Kosher salt and freshly ground
    black pepper

1. Place a large cast-iron griddle or oven-safe skillet under the broiler and heat until very hot, at least 10 minutes.

2. Meanwhile, combine the mayonnaise, mustard, and thyme in a small bowl.

3. Generously season the fish with salt and pepper. Paint one side of the fish thickly with the mustard mixture.

4. Place the fish in the skillet, painted side up, and broil until the coating is brown and bubbling and the interior is just cooked all the way through, 4 to 5 minutes. Serve immediately.

ANOTHER ROASTED FISH

YOU CAN MAKE THIS DINNER ON A GRILL as in the oven, and the recipe should be the subject of experimentation not just with the topping but with the fish. Try roasting salmon, or striped bass, or cobia. Mixing white miso with brown sugar and a dash of soy sauce is excellent as well. Go heavy with the black pepper whatever you cook.

1/4 cup Dijon mustard

2 tablespoons extra-virgin
   olive oil

3 tablespoons light brown sugar

8 salmon fillets, preferably wild,
   about 6 ounces each

Kosher salt and freshly ground
   black pepper

1.   Heat the oven to 400°F. Mix together the mustard, oil, and brown sugar, adjusting the mixture to increase or decrease the sweetness or spiciness, to your taste.

2.   Season the salmon aggressively with salt and pepper.

3.   Place the fillets, skin side down, on a lightly oiled, aluminum foil–lined baking sheet. Slather the tops of the fillets with the mustard and brown sugar glaze and slide them into the top half of your oven. They ought to be done in 12 minutes or so.

HOW TO TELL IF FISH IS "DONE"

PUT YOUR FINGER ON THE TIP of your nose and press down lightly. That's about what a cooked piece of fish feels like, if you cook it to the temperature that the government asks you to, which is 145°F. Insert an instant-read thermometer into the thickest part of the fish you're cooking. If the reading is in the neighborhood of 125° to 130°F, and you like perfect fish, the fish is ready to come off the heat and rest (the government wants us to be safe, but it often errs on the side of overcooking). Slide a spatula under one side of the piece of fish you're cooking and gently lift it above the pan. If it begins to crack along the line where the fillet is unsupported by the spatula, and the interior appears opaque and flaky, it's ready to go, no thermometer or nose required.

Or you can make like a professional. The most perfectly cooked fish I ever ate was at a tiny Los Angeles restaurant called Petit Trois, a dish of sole meunière prepared by the restaurant's superbly mustachioed chef de cuisine at the time, Sydney Hunter III. Petit Trois has an open kitchen, and so I was able to watch as he cooked. Hunter's labor was painstaking, his movements precise. After he had dredged the fish in flour and panfried one side of it in clarified butter so that it was the perfectly honeyed color of a piece of polished fruitwood, he turned it over and stared at it for a while. Then he pulled a small tool from his work station, not quite a skewer and not really a knife, and gently plunged it into the center of the fish. After a few seconds he removed it and placed the edge of the blade along the top of his lip. He nodded. The fish was done.

It will take you only a few tries to learn this method, and you don't need a special tool—a small paring knife or sharp metal skewer will do just fine. Slide it into the fish, let it pick up the heat, and test it on the top of your lip just the way new parents test the temperature of heated milk on the inside of their wrists. You're looking for warmth that is demonstrably north of the body's temperature, but not totally hot, which your friend the instant-read thermometer calls 125° and 130°F. In matters of style, art beats science nearly every time.

GRILLED FISH

GRILLING FISH, PARTICULARLY STEAK-ISH FISH such as tuna, swordfish, shark, or halibut, is relatively easy work, so long as the grill is clean and hot and there's a slick of oil on the fish. You can serve the steaks with salsa, with cut lemons, or beneath a pat of compound butter cut through with herbs. A grilled fist of tuna goes beautifully with a simple sauce of melted butter enlivened by chopped ginger and a hit of soy. A platter of grilled fish steaks served to a large group of friends on a warm night is an amazement, particularly when paired with salsa and rice, or slaw and pilaf and a glass of wine. You'll see.

Thick fish fillets, like tuna, swordfish, shark, or halibut, about 1/2 pound per person
Kosher salt and freshly ground black pepper
Extra-virgin olive oil

1. Build a fire in your grill. If using a gas grill, turn the burners to high.

2. Season the fish aggressively with salt and pepper, then drizzle with oil and lightly massage to make sure the fillets are covered in a thin sheen of oil.

3. When the fire in the grill has died down slightly and you can hold your hand above the coals for 4 or 5 seconds, place the fish over the fire and cook for 4 to 5 minutes, until it is firm enough to turn easily with a spatula. (Thinner fillets will cook more quickly.) Turn the fish over and grill until done, generally another 3 to 5 minutes. (When done, the fish will still be firm and juicy but its interior will be opaque—you can slide a thin-bladed knife through it with ease.) Serve immediately.

A FISH FRY

PEOPLE FRY FISH INDOORS ALL THE TIME. I am not one of them, though I still do it plenty. Better is this recipe for cooking outdoors, either in a gigantic camp skillet set over a propane hob, which calls for equipment many of us do not have, or in a roasting pan set over a gas grill, which does not.

The process seems intimidating, but only the first time you do it. (Make sure to wear shoes, please.) Just set the pan on the grill and turn the burners below it to high. Add enough oil—peanut, grapeseed, safflower, soybean, sunflower, or canola—that it comes up the sides of the pan about one-quarter inch or so, then lower the lid and allow everything to heat. You're looking for an oil temperature of 350° to 375°F on a candy thermometer or, if you don't have a thermometer, for a small scrap of fish to sizzle furiously in the oil.

Stout fish fingers will cook in this environment in five minutes or less, and a very large number of them can be made at once, making it a terrific recipe for a warm-weather dinner for a crowd. Serve with a tartar sauce or lemon, or as the basis for fish tacos. When you're done cooking, just turn off the grill, close its top, and deal with the used oil in the morning. (You can pour it off into an old milk carton and discard.) A similar technique, with a smaller pan and less fish, can of course be exercised indoors, especially if you have a good exhaust fan above your stove.

1 cup all-purpose flour

1 tablespoon kosher salt

1 tablespoon freshly ground
   black pepper

2 tablespoons Old Bay seasoning,
   or to taste (you can omit the
   Old Bay and add a teaspoon
   or so of cayenne pepper,
   and increase the amount
   of salt and black pepper by
   1 tablespoon each)

3 pounds fish fillets, like flounder,
   cod, sea bass, cobia, or halibut,
   3/4 to 1 inch thick, cut into
   chunks about 1½ inches across

3 to 4 cups neutral oil, such as peanut, grapeseed, safflower, soybean, sunflower, or canola

1. In a large sealable plastic bag or paper supermarket sack, combine the flour, salt, pepper, and Old Bay seasoning, and shake to mix. Add 4 or 5 pieces of the fish to the bag and shake to coat. Remove the fish, shaking to remove excess flour, and set aside on a baking sheet or wire rack. Repeat with the remaining fish.

2. Light an outdoor gas grill and turn the burners to high. Place a large roasting pan on the grilling surface and add the oil to the pan. Close the lid and heat until the temperature of the oil reaches 350°F on a candy thermometer or a small scrap of fish added to the oil sizzles furiously.

3. Using kitchen tongs, add the floured fish to the pan. Work in batches so as not to crowd them. The

temperature of the oil will dip then rise as you add the fish and as it cooks. Adjust the heat accordingly, so that the oil bubbles hard but does not burn the fish. Cook until deep golden brown on the first side, 2 to 3 minutes. Then flip over and once again cook until deep golden brown on the other side, a further 2 to 3 minutes. Remove the fish from the oil, drain briefly on paper towels or a wire rack, and serve with Tartar Sauce (recipe follows).

TARTAR SAUCE

Here is an Anglo American take on the classic sauce, incorporating both the British style of adding capers and the American one of using sweet new pickles. It is a terrific accompaniment to fried fish. You can swap in a small, seeded jalapeño pepper in place of the hot sauce if you like, for a high zip of fruity heat that gives the edge to the Americans.

1 cup mayonnaise

3/4 cup chopped sweet pickles

1 small shallot, peeled and finely diced

3 tablespoons chopped fresh flat-leaf parsley

1 tablespoon drained capers

1 tablespoon fresh lemon juice

1/2 tablespoon Worcestershire sauce

1/2 tablespoon Dijon mustard

1 teaspoon hot sauce (optional)

Combine the mayonnaise, pickles, shallot, parsley, capers, lemon juice, Worcestershire, mustard, and hot sauce, if using, in a bowl. Whisk well to combine.

FISH CAKES

I USED TO MAKE FISH CAKES MOSTLY WITH COD, using the first ragged fillets cut after offshore fishing trips for freezer meat. But one day I made them with tautog instead, and it was like opening a door to a new world, one where I ate well without feeling guilty about contributing to the collapse of a once-plentiful species. Truth is, you can make fish cakes out of almost any flaky-fleshed fish. Just poach the meat in lemony water scented with bay leaf and peppercorns, then add it to a New England–style mirepoix of sautéed onions and celery. Use eggs and cracker crumbs to help bind everything together in a drift of spices, then put the resulting patties into the refrigerator for a while to "set." Adding a light smear of mayonnaise to the exterior of the cakes just before you cook them will encourage the most glorious crust. I like them served with a thatch of green salad or a neat pile of slaw. If you're feeling exceptionally grand, make them a little smaller than usual and float them on bowls of chowder.

8 peppercorns

2 bay leaves

2 lemons, cut into eighths

2 pounds cod fillets (or other flaky white fish)

4 tablespoons (½ stick) unsalted butter

4 celery stalks, trimmed, peeled, and diced

2 medium yellow onions, peeled and diced

4 cloves garlic, peeled and minced

2 heaping tablespoons mayonnaise, homemade or store-bought

4 teaspoons Dijon mustard

4 large eggs

1 tablespoon kosher salt

1 teaspoon freshly ground black pepper

4 teaspoons Old Bay seasoning, Lawry's Seasoned Salt, or 2 teaspoons paprika and 2 teaspoons red pepper flakes, or to taste

2 "sleeves" unsalted saltine crackers, crushed, or 2 heaping cups panko bread crumbs

1 bunch fresh flat-leaf parsley, roughly chopped

½ to ¾ cup neutral oil, such as canola or grapeseed

1. Fill a wide, shallow pan with high sides with about 1 inch of water and set it over high heat. Add the peppercorns, bay leaves, and one section of the lemon to the water, and allow to come to a bare simmer. Place the fish into this poaching liquid and cook, barely simmering, until the flesh has just begun to whiten all the way through, 6 to 8 minutes. Using a wide spatula, carefully remove the fish from the water and set aside to cool. You may need to do this in batches.

2. Empty the pan and return it to the stove, over medium-high heat. Add the butter and allow it to melt, swirling it around the pan. When the butter foams, add the celery, onions, and garlic and sauté, stirring often, until the vegetables soften and the onions turn translucent, then transfer the vegetables to a large bowl.

3. In a medium bowl, mix together the mayonnaise, mustard, eggs, kosher salt, pepper, and seasoning salt, then add this mixture to the bowl with the sautéed vegetables. Pour the crushed saltines over them and stir to combine. Add the parsley and stir again.

4. Flake the cooked fish into the binding sauce carefully, keeping the flakes as whole as you can manage, then gather them into small balls and form them into patties, 8 to 10 for a main course. Place them on a sheet pan or platter, cover loosely with plastic wrap, and transfer to the refrigerator for at least 30 minutes to set.

5. Place a large sauté pan over high heat and add to it the oil. When the oil is shimmering, remove the fish cakes from the refrigerator and carefully sauté the patties until they are golden brown, 4 to 5 minutes a side. Work in batches so as not to crowd the pan. (A small smear of mayonnaise on the exterior of the patties will give them a crisp crust.) Remove the patties to a rack and keep warm in a low oven until ready to serve. Serve a cake per person, alone or with greens dressed in a lemony vinaigrette, and with the remaining wedges of lemon.

CRAB CAKES

I LEARNED TO MAKE CRAB CAKES from Marian Burros, a *Times* reporter and old Washington hand who is one of the best recipe writers and home cooks of our or any age. Crabmeat is not cheap, so this is not the sort of recipe you'll want to quadruple for company unless you're flush. But you can easily serve eight people off a pound of meat if you accompany each cake with a big, bright salad and serve a generous dessert.

1 large egg, lightly beaten

½ cup mayonnaise

1 tablespoon Dijon mustard

1 tablespoon Worcestershire sauce

½ teaspoon hot pepper sauce

1 cup crumbled unsalted saltines

1 pound fresh lump crabmeat

Kosher salt (optional)

¼ cup neutral oil, such as canola or grapeseed

1. Mix together the egg, mayonnaise, mustard, Worcestershire, and hot pepper sauce in a bowl large enough to hold all the ingredients.

2. Finely crush the saltines between two pieces of wax paper with a rolling pin. Fold the crushed crackers into the mayonnaise mixture.

3. Pick over the crabmeat to remove bits of shell or cartilage. Fold the crabmeat into the mayonnaise mixture and season with salt, if desired. Gently shape into 8 crab cakes, handling as little as possible. Refrigerate, covered, if desired.

4. When you're ready to cook, heat the oil in a pan large enough to hold the crab cakes (or in two pans) and sauté them over medium heat, 3 to 5 minutes on each side, until golden brown.

FISH CHOWDER

I MAKE THIS FRAGRANT STEW MOST often with cod or fluke, but it's nice with salmon (in which case, you could try smoked salmon in place of the bacon), grouper, medallions of monkfish, even mixtures of whatever fish you caught or bought that day. Omit the cream if you like, for a clear chowder of remarkable delicacy. And absolutely experiment with the stocks you use: A lobster or clam stock, if you have some in the freezer, is an excellent medium for fish chowder, as is a vegetable one, or a mock stock of water and white wine.

1 tablespoon unsalted butter

1/4 pound slab bacon, ideally double smoked

2 leeks, tops removed, halved, and cleaned, then sliced into half-moons

3 large Yukon gold potatoes, peeled if you're feeling fancy and cubed

1/2 cup dry white wine

3 cups fish stock, vegetable stock, or water

3 fresh thyme sprigs

1 bay leaf

2 pounds fresh fish fillets

2 cups heavy cream

Freshly ground black pepper

1/4 cup chopped fresh flat-leaf parsley

1. Put the butter in a large, heavy Dutch oven over medium heat. When the butter foams, add the bacon and cook, stirring occasionally, until the fat has rendered and the bacon has started to brown, 5 to 7 minutes. Use a slotted spoon to remove the bacon from the fat, and set aside.

3. Add the leeks to the fat and cook, stirring frequently, until they are soft but not brown, about 10 minutes. Stir in the potatoes and wine, and continue cooking until the wine has evaporated and the potatoes have just started to soften, about 5 minutes. Add enough stock to just cover the potatoes, then add the thyme and bay leaf. Partly cover the pot and simmer gently until the potatoes are tender, 10 to 15 minutes.

4. While the potatoes cook, cut the fish fillets into fingers. When the potatoes are tender, add the cream, the reserved bacon, and the pieces of fish. Add pepper to taste. Let come to a simmer and cook until the fish is pearlescent and just beginning to flake, then remove from the heat. (Do not let the chowder come to a full boil.) Remove the thyme sprigs and bay leaf, and discard.

5. If you have the time, allow the chowder to sit for a while to cure. Reheat it to a bare simmer before serving, then garnish with the chopped parsley. Serve with oyster crackers.

YUCATÁN SHRIMP

I DON'T BUY FARMED SHRIMP. REPORTS OF environmental depredation and disturbing accounts of working conditions on the Asian farms that grow them leave a bitter taste in my mouth. If I'm cooking at home in New York, I'll get flash-frozen ones from Maine or Florida; I'll look for Pacific shrimp out west. This recipe was adapted from one I discovered at Doc Ford's restaurant on Sanibel Island, Florida. It evokes late afternoon there, the sun falling in the west over the beach, and the feeling that summer will last forever. Resist the urge to peel the shrimp before cooking. Just serve them in a large bowl with an empty discard bowl beside it, and allow everyone to peel and eat at will. Later you can serve an actual meal.

8 tablespoons (1 stick) unsalted
   butter
2 large cloves garlic, peeled and
   minced
Juice of 3 large limes
2 tablespoons Indonesian sambal
   or Sriracha sauce
Kosher salt and freshly ground
   black pepper
3 pounds fresh, large shell-on
   shrimp
1 jalapeño pepper, seeded and
   chopped (optional)
3 tablespoons chopped
   fresh cilantro

1. In a small saucepan set over low heat, melt 2 tablespoons of the butter. Add the garlic and cook, stirring, for 2 minutes.

2. Add the remaining 6 tablespoons butter to the saucepan. When the butter melts and begins to foam, stir in the lime juice, sambal, and salt and pepper to taste. Turn off the heat and allow the sauce to rest.

3. Bring a large pot of well-salted water to a boil. Add the shrimp and cook for 2 minutes, or until they are just firm and pink. Do not overcook. Drain into a colander and shake over the sink to remove excess moisture.

4. In a large bowl, toss the shrimp and sauce. Add the jalapeño, if desired, sprinkle with the cilantro, and toss again.

CARAMELIZED SCALLOPS

THESE DINNERS YOU'RE MAKING NEED not always be giant-platter affairs, with food piled high and guests reaching over one another to get at their share. Occasionally you're going to want to take the delicate approach, and serve composed plates of something awesome, as if your guests had made reservations to eat at your place, and not just dropped in after an afternoon replacing brake pads or shuttling the kids to soccer games. Two giant, golden brown sea scallops on each plate is the way to do that, served with a neat spoonful of rice and a delicate thatch of roasted asparagus, on a table covered with cloth and a few low candles winking off the wineglasses. Fancy! The cooking is too, though it's easily done, at least if you make time to plan and execute. First, make a quick brine for the scallops to firm them up, then use a number of pans to cook them over high heat in neutral oil or, better yet, clarified butter, so that the scallops can get a good sear on them without steaming. Top with beurre blanc, if you have the time, or just a squeeze of lemon.

2 cups kosher salt

16 extra-large sea scallops, preferably dry-packed, the tough muscle on the side removed

4 tablespoons neutral oil, such as canola or grapeseed, or clarified butter

Freshly ground black pepper

Beurre Blanc (recipe follows) or fresh lemon juice

1. Combine the salt and 2 cups boiling water in a large bowl. Stir until the salt dissolves, then add 8 cups cold water. Stir again and allow the brine to sit until it is at room temperature.

2. Add the scallops to the brine and allow to sit for 10 minutes or so. Then rinse under running water, dry well with paper towels, and place on a baking sheet. Cover the scallops with more paper towels and place in the refrigerator for at least an hour but no longer than two, or the scallops will turn salty.

3. Heat two large, stainless-steel sauté pans over high heat, then add 2 tablespoons of the oil to each and swirl to coat the pans. When the oil is shimmering and close to smoking, sprinkle a little pepper on the scallops and place them in the pans, making sure that there is enough room between them that they do not touch. Cook, undisturbed, until the bottoms of the scallops are a dark golden brown, about 3 minutes, then carefully turn each scallop and allow the other side to cook until golden, another 2 minutes or so.

4. Transfer 2 scallops per person to warmed plates, drizzle with Beurre Blanc or a little lemon juice, and serve with whatever side dishes you desire.

BEURRE BLANC

Beurre blanc—"white butter" from the Loire Valley in France—was first popularized in the United States by Julia Child: a reduction of white wine and vinegar,
flavored with shallots, into which a vast amount of cold butter is whisked. The
reaction is magical: a silky emulsion with a bright, clean, and buttery flavor, perfect on fish. (The cream helps stabilize it.) Add a dash or two of hot sauce if
you're feeling frisky. I use it on scallops, or spoon it over roasted fish.

¼ cup dry white wine
¼ cup white wine vinegar
1 medium shallot, peeled and finely minced
   (about 2 tablespoons)
⅓ cup heavy cream
Pinch of kosher salt
Pinch of ground white or black pepper
1 cup (2 sticks) unsalted butter, cut into tablespoon-sized
   bits and kept chilled

1. Combine the wine, vinegar, and shallot in a medium saucepan set over medium-
high heat and allow to come to a boil. Allow the mixture to cook, swirling the pan
occasionally, until the liquid has reduced to a syrup, about 5 minutes.

2. Add the cream, salt, and pepper and allow to bubble away for 1 minute.

3. Turn the heat to low, add a pat of butter, and use a wire whisk to mix it into
the sauce. Repeat with the remaining pats of butter, adding a few at a time, whisking
constantly and removing the pan from the heat occasionally to allow the sauce to
cool. (Too much heat will break the emulsion.) Remove from the heat. For a classic
beurre blanc, strain the sauce before serving and discard the minced shallot. But there
is really no need.

WHY YOU SHOULD SOMETIMES BRINE YOUR FISH

HERE'S A TRUTH ABOUT FRESH FISH: It's sometimes not so fresh. Fisherman
Bobby catches it out at sea and puts it on ice and keeps fishing and fishing and

putting the fish on ice for as long as it takes to fill his hold and return to the dock to sell it. That might be a couple of days. Then the fish goes to a wholesaler, who takes it to market in his refrigerated truck, and a day or so later it's sold whole or broken down into fillets and put on ice in the fish shop for you to buy. You do so and go home and cook it in a pan with some butter and a little thyme . . . and it's amazing—a fresh, wild, perfectly firm piece of protein that has been dead for, like, a week.

There is nothing wrong with that. Indeed, if you've spent any time fishing yourself, you know that there can be such a thing as fish that is *too* fresh. You've killed a nice big weakfish that you caught on a perfectly tied Clouser minnow fly, bled it carefully and laid it on ice, cleaned it and taken it home and put it in a sauté pan within six or eight hours of bringing it over the gunwale and . . . it is a little slack in its musculature, a little bland and squishy, not precisely firm, not entirely delicious. It wants a little time to rest, to firm up, to get ready for the pan.

This is why I sometimes brine fresh-caught fish in a solution of water, salt, and a pinch of sugar: fresh-caught porgies or sea bass, fluke, that weakfish, blue-fish, tautog, the occasional cod. (Those are the target species where I reside.) I do it sometimes even with fish from the market, because the market I frequent runs fish traps not five miles from the store, and an afternoon's porgy might have been swimming hard just that morning. I do it for the same reason people brine tur-keys, lean pork, and chicken. The process heightens the flavor of the meat, to be sure, but it also firms it and improves its texture. Particularly when I'm grilling fish, I brine it so that it holds together well in the direct heat of the flames, and I thrill to the flavor it imparts along the way.

It's a quick process. Fish have muscles built out of short strands of fiber, not the long ones that make up a pork tenderloin or turkey breast. They take on the salt quite quickly. A 15-minute run in a gallon of water into which you've swirled a handful of coarse kosher salt and a teaspoon of sugar yields flesh that cooks up beautifully, whatever the recipe you use. Just make sure to dry the fish well with paper towels before cooking.

GENERAL TSO'S SCALLOPS

Serve a heap of deep-fried scallops in a sticky, sweet, fiery sauce, accompanied by white rice, steamed broccoli, and ten thousand cold beers, and you may find yourself doing it all the time. This recipe is inspired by one used by a long-gone restaurant in Montauk, New York, called Wok N' Roll, where the motto was, "You hook 'em. We cook 'em." At Wok N' Roll, you could get General Tso's striped bass or fluke, porgy or shark, whatever you'd caught on the charter boats that work the rips for paying customers. I found General Tso's fish tough home cooking, though: The fish had a terrible tendency to turn to mush when I tossed it in sauce. Not scallops. They're sturdy and firm, with a clean sweetness beneath their crusts, and hold up well in the saucy environment. The key is frying them three times, at increasing temperatures, to develop the crust; use a candy thermometer to keep track of the heat. Now, the first time you make the recipe, you may curse me. There's a lot going on. The second time, you won't. Soon you'll have your rhythm and can scale the meal up for a crowd. In the meantime, you'll be eating very well indeed.

1 extra-large egg

2 1/2 tablespoons Shaoxing rice wine or dry sherry

3 teaspoons dark soy sauce

1 teaspoon vegetable oil

1 cup cornstarch

1 1/2 pounds sea scallops

1 1/2 tablespoons light soy sauce

3 tablespoons chicken stock, homemade or low-sodium

2 tablespoons sugar

1 teaspoon distilled white vinegar

2 teaspoons potato starch

4 cups plus 3 tablespoons peanut or vegetable oil

4 dried chile peppers, broken into pieces, or to taste

2 cloves garlic, peeled and minced

1 tablespoon diced fresh ginger

3 scallions, both light-green and white parts, chopped

2 teaspoons black vinegar

1 teaspoon sesame oil

1. Make the marinade. In a large bowl, combine the egg, 1 1/2 tablespoons of the rice wine, 1 teaspoon of the dark soy sauce, the vegetable oil, and 1/4 cup of the cornstarch. Remove the tab of flesh attached to each scallop and add the scallops to the bowl. Stir to combine, then cover and refrigerate for 6 to 8 hours.

2. Make the sauce. Combine the remaining 1 tablespoon rice wine, the remaining 2 teaspoons dark soy sauce, the light soy sauce, stock, sugar, and white vinegar in a small bowl. In a separate small bowl, combine the potato starch with 1 1/2 tablespoons water and stir until dissolved.

3. Heat 4 cups peanut oil in a wok until moderately hot (roughly 280°F). Meanwhile, remove the scallops

from the marinade and toss with the remaining ¾ cup cornstarch, shaking off excess. Add the scallops to the peanut oil and, using a slotted spoon, gently stir until the scallops separate and begin to form a crust, about 30 seconds. Using the slotted spoon, remove the scallops and transfer to a strainer suspended over a bowl.

4. Turn the heat to the highest level and let the peanut oil temperature rise to 350°F. Carefully add the scallops and cook for about 20 seconds. Remove to the strainer and drain.

5. When the peanut oil has reached 375°F, add the twice-fried scallops and cook for another 45 seconds, until the pieces develop a golden brown crust and are completely cooked through but still juicy. Remove to the strainer.

6. Carefully pour the hot peanut oil into an empty pot and clean the wok with a paper towel. Return the wok to the stove and place over the highest heat.

7. When the wok is very hot, swirl the remaining 3 tablespoons peanut oil around it to coat the surface. Remove all but 1 teaspoon of the oil from the wok and add the chiles, stirring until they scorch and begin to smoke. Working quickly, add the garlic, ginger, and scallions and stir without browning until they become fragrant, about 10 seconds. Add the sauce, using a spoon to stir constantly. When the sauce boils, stir the dissolved potato starch once more and add it to the sauce in 1-teaspoon increments until the sauce is thickened.

8. Immediately add the scallops to the wok and stir until completely coated, about 15 seconds. Mix in the black vinegar, stir once, and sprinkle with the sesame oil. Serve immediately.

CLAM CHOWDER

CLAM CHOWDER MAY HAVE ORIGINATED in the cauldrons of coastal France and migrated to kitchens across the English Channel in Cornwall. But it grew up in the Plymouth Colony and is one of America's first recipes, a stew of fish or shellfish flavored and thickened with stores brought from Britain aboard colony ships: salt pork, biscuits, the odd potato. "Chowder breathes reassurance," wrote Clementine Paddleford, the great American food journalist. "It steams consolation." My version—essentially the same as my recipe for fish chowder—combines the clams with potatoes and leeks instead of the more commonly used onions (feel free to use those, though!), and is flavored with thyme and bay leaves, along with a splash of white wine. Using bacon adds a marvelous smokiness to the chowder. Using salt pork allows the clams to sing on their own. When I can, I use lobster stock in place of the water. When I feel like it, I omit the cream. Sometimes I add fish to the pot. Other times, mussels. You should do the same.

24 medium quahog clams, usually rated top neck or cherrystone, rinsed

1 tablespoon unsalted butter

1/4 pound slab bacon, ideally double smoked, or salt pork, diced

2 leeks, tops removed, halved, and cleaned, then sliced into half-moons

3 large Yukon gold potatoes, cubed

1/2 cup dry white wine

3 fresh thyme sprigs

1 bay leaf

2 cups heavy cream

Freshly ground black pepper

1/4 cup chopped fresh flat-leaf parsley

1. Put the clams in a large, heavy Dutch oven, add about 4 cups water, then set over medium-high heat. Cover and cook until the clams have opened, 10 to 15 minutes. (Clams that fail to open after 15 to 20 minutes should be discarded.) Strain the clam broth through a sieve lined with cheesecloth or doubled-up paper towels and set aside. Remove the clams from the shells and set aside as well. (Discard the shells.)

2. Rinse out the pot and return it to the stove. Add the butter and turn the heat to medium-low. Add the bacon and cook, stirring occasionally, until the fat has rendered and the bacon has started to brown, 5 to 7 minutes. Use a slotted spoon to remove the bacon from the fat and set aside.

3. Add the leeks to the fat and cook, stirring frequently, until they are soft but not brown, about 10 minutes. Stir in the potatoes and wine, and continue cooking until the wine has evaporated and the potatoes have just started to soften, about 5 minutes. Add enough clam broth to just cover the potatoes, about

3 cups, reserving the rest for another use. Add the thyme and bay leaf. Partly cover the pot and simmer gently until the potatoes are tender, 10 to 15 minutes.

4.   Meanwhile, chop the clams into bits about the size of the bacon dice.

5.   When the potatoes are tender, add the cream and stir in the chopped clams and reserved bacon. Add pepper to taste. Let it come to a simmer, then remove from the heat. (Do not let the chowder come to a full boil.) Fish out the thyme sprigs and bay leaf, and discard.

6.   If you have the time, allow the chowder to sit for a while to cure. Reheat it to a bare simmer before serving, then garnish with the chopped parsley. Serve with oyster crackers.

STEAMED CLAMS

THIS IS A RECIPE FOR A MESS OF CLAMS, which I define as at least a hundred little-necks or cherrystones. You can certainly cook fewer, though it's worth noting that a reasonable human can eat more than a dozen clams at a sitting, mopping up the broth with crusty bread and washing it all down with cold beer or lemonade. You can add herbs or other aromatics to the steaming liquid (thyme or garlic, say, or cilantro, parsley, tarragon), and you need not add sausage or bacon. The point is just to create steam, and to allow the clams to open within it, then to eat them with the liquor that pours from the interior of their shells, and some melted butter.

100 littleneck or cherrystone clams

1 tablespoon unsalted butter

1/4 cup diced chorizo or bacon (optional)

2 cups beer (about 1 can or bottle)

1. Carefully scrub the clams under cold running water to remove sand and grit, then set aside.

2. Melt the butter in a very large pot set over medium heat and, when the butter foams, add the chorizo and allow it to crisp, stirring occasionally, for about 5 minutes.

3. Add the beer to the pot (use just 1 cup if cooking 50 or fewer clams) and allow to heat through, then carefully add the clams in layers. Cover the pot and allow the clams to steam and open, 10 to 12 minutes. Serve in the pot, or use tongs or a slotted spoon to remove the clams to a platter. Serve alongside a bowl of the remaining clam broth, and a bowl of melted butter.

STEAMED MUSSELS

FOLLOW THE SAME PROCEDURE AS WITH steamed clams, but add a cup more liquid. As with the clams, you should save the liquor that results from the cooking, both as a dipping sauce for the mussels and as an ingredient for other dishes. Top a bowl of spaghetti with mussel broth and serve it to a crowd? That is an easy win.

CLAMS *in* BLACK BEAN SAUCE

THIS RECIPE RIFFS OFF AN OLD CHINATOWN STANDBY and is a simple way to deliver immense flavor to a pot or wok filled with clams. The salty pungency of fermented black beans combines beautifully with the sweet salinity of the shellfish, while ginger and dry Chinese rice wine provide cool jolts of flavor above and around them. Served with white rice and a platter of steamed or stir-fried greens, it makes for a dinner of remarkable complexity and ease. Attention: You'll need a large wok or Dutch oven in which to cook the clams.

48 littleneck clams

2 tablespoons neutral oil, such as canola or grapeseed

One 3-inch piece fresh ginger, peeled and cut into thin coins

4 cloves garlic, peeled and crushed

2 scallions, both green and white parts, chopped

1 teaspoon red pepper flakes, or to taste

¼ cup fermented black beans, roughly chopped

3 tablespoons Shaoxing rice wine

3 tablespoons oyster sauce

1 teaspoon soy sauce (optional)

1 teaspoon sugar (optional)

3 tablespoons cornstarch mixed into ¼ cup water to make a slurry

3 tablespoons roughly chopped fresh cilantro

1. Rinse and scrub the clams and set aside.

2. Heat the oil in a large wok or Dutch oven set over medium-high heat. When the oil begins to shimmer, add the ginger, garlic, scallions, and red pepper flakes and stir-fry until the garlic begins to color, about 1 minute.

3. Add the fermented black beans and cook for 15 to 20 seconds, then carefully add the clams to the wok, followed by the rice wine. Cover the wok and allow to cook until the clams begin to open, 5 to 10 minutes, depending on the size of the clams.

4. Once the clams have started to open, give them a stir in the wok, add the oyster sauce, and stir again. Taste the liquid in the bottom of the wok. If it is not salty enough, add the soy sauce; if it is too salty for you, add the sugar.

5. Stir in about half of the cornstarch slurry and allow the sauce to thicken. Add more of the slurry if you want a thicker sauce.

6. Transfer the clams and sauce to a large rimmed platter and sprinkle with the cilantro. Serve immediately.

STEAMED CRABS

T HIS IS PERHAPS A RECIPE for an appetizer, ahead of a summer dinner of fresh corn and a lot of tomatoes, grilled chicken, and plenty of potato salad. If you want it to be more than that, you're going to need a pot from the big-and-tall shop to accommodate the extra crabs. Figure on two per person unless you're eating with people from the Mid-Atlantic region, where a dozen crabs per person is light work, and they'll still want a big dinner afterward.

One 12-ounce can or bottle beer
1 cup cider vinegar
18 to 20 large blue crabs
½ cup Chesapeake-style crab seasoning (I use Old Bay)

1. Place a lobster or crab pot or any large, heavy pot with a tight-fitting lid on the stove. (In the latter case, improvise a rack on the bottom of the pot that will keep the crabs an inch or so from the bottom.) Add the beer, vinegar, and 1 cup water. Bring to a boil over high heat.

2. Put a layer of crabs on the rack in the pot. Sprinkle with a generous amount of seasoning, then repeat with another layer, and another, until all the crabs are in the pot (and well seasoned). Cover and steam over medium-high heat until the crabs are bright red, 25 to 30 minutes. Remove the crabs with tongs. Serve over newspaper, with mallets and picks.

STEAMED LOBSTER

THE SQUEAMISH CAN PLUNGE THE TIP of a heavy knife into the carapace of the lobster, right between its eyes, and end its life before it goes into the pot. I don't do that. I do always cook an extra lobster or two so that there is meat left over for Lobster Bisque (see page 209), and I always make stock with the water left in the pot. It enriches chowders beyond belief. Also, I make Lobster Butter (see page 208). Lobster butter can make an old running shoe taste good.

1 tablespoon kosher salt

Live lobsters, 1¼ to 1½ pounds each

1. Fill a large lobster pot with 1 inch water. Stir in the salt, set a rack or large steamer basket in the bottom of the pot, and bring the water to a boil.

2. Add the lobsters, cover with a tight-fitting lid, and return the water to a boil. Once the water is boiling, lower the heat to a gentle boil and steam the lobsters until they are bright red, about 10 minutes. Check for doneness by pulling an antenna. If it comes off without resistance, the lobster is done. If not, cook for a few more minutes.

HOW TO STRETCH A LOBSTER

LOBSTER IS EXPENSIVE. YOU SHOULD MAKE it last. The least you can do is make things out of the empty shells. Here's how.

LOBSTER STOCK

½ cup olive oil

Shells from cooked lobsters, rinsed

1 onion, peeled and diced

2 bay leaves

10 peppercorns

In a large stockpot, heat the oil over medium-high heat. Add the lobster shells and sauté for 1 minute. Add enough water so that the pot is two-thirds full, then add the onion, bay leaves, and peppercorns. Bring to a boil, reduce the heat to low, and simmer for several hours or overnight, understanding that the longer it simmers, the better the stock. Using tongs, remove and discard the large shells, then strain the stock twice through a fine sieve.

LOBSTER BUTTER

Maybe you're intrigued by this idea of lobster butter. It's great too. This recipe is a cover-band take on one I first tasted at the Montreal restaurant Joe Beef, where it accompanied cold steamed shrimp—a Quebecois version of the classic French recipe for *beurre de homard*, which incorporates cooked lobster meat into a compound butter. The shells are used to impart flavor here, instead of meat; it's basically a lobster stock made with butter instead of water. Make a great deal of this stuff if you can, and freeze it. The butter knows no peer as a dipping sauce for shrimp, or as a topping for sautéed scallops or fish. It also makes for an excellent sauce for spaghetti, with bread crumbs and a shower of Parmesan. Serving Clam Chowder (see page 203)? Make toasts and slather them with lobster butter, then float one on top of each bowl. Oh, man.

Shells of cooked lobsters, broken into pieces

8 tablespoons (1 stick) unsalted butter per lobster

1. Heat the oven to 300°F. Put the lobster shells on the largest sheet pan you can fit into the oven, and allow them to dry and roast for 15 to 20 minutes. Remove from the oven and set aside.

2. Meanwhile, melt 1 stick butter per lobster in a large bowl or double boiler set over simmering water, making sure that the bowl does not touch the surface of the water. Add the lobster shells to the melted butter and allow them to simmer gently, without boiling, for about 20 minutes.

3. Strain the melted butter through a cheesecloth-lined sieve into another bowl then set that bowl into ice to chill. Cover the bowl and refrigerate to set, then skim off the top and discard any liquids. Use within a few days, or freeze for up to a few weeks.

LOBSTER BISQUE

Finally, if you have any leftover lobster at all, and the stock you've made from its shells, try this recipe for lobster bisque, which I picked up from James Sakatos, the executive chef of the Café Carlyle in Manhattan. It's an excellent start to a meal of roast chicken or grilled fish. You'll discover something wonderful when making it, as well: Adding a half cup or so of rice to a soup base, letting it cook soft, then putting the result in a food processor results in a liquid of incredible velvety excellence.

2 tablespoons olive oil

1 carrot, peeled and chopped

2 celery stalks, trimmed and chopped

1 medium onion, peeled and chopped

2 cloves garlic, peeled and crushed

2 fresh thyme sprigs

2 fresh tarragon sprigs

2 tablespoons tomato paste

1 cup medium sherry

continued on next page

3 cups lobster stock (see page 208), or broth left over from cooking the lobsters

½ cup long-grain white rice

1 cup heavy cream

Any leftover lobster meat you may have, chopped

Kosher salt

Cayenne pepper

1. Swirl the oil in a large pot over medium heat, then add the carrot, celery, onion, garlic, thyme, and tarragon. Sweat until the onion is translucent, about 5 minutes, then add the tomato paste and cook for an additional 3 to 4 minutes.

2. Add the sherry, then ignite or cook until the alcohol has evaporated. Add the lobster stock. Bring to a simmer and cook, covered, for 30 minutes, then add the rice and cook for another 30 minutes or so, until the grains are cooked to extreme softness.

3. Blend the bisque in a food processor or blender, then pass through a fine sieve, pressing down hard on what solids remain. Add the cream and bring to a low simmer. Add the chopped lobster meat, let it heat through, then season to taste with salt and cayenne.

TACO
NIGHT

—

"Everything tastes better on a tortilla."

—DON WINSLOW, *The Dawn Patrol*

Discada is a style of cooking that arose alongside the irrigated fields of northwestern Mexico and inevitably made its way to the United States. It takes its name from the instrument in which the food is cooked: a disco, made from a repurposed disk harrow blade, its center hole welded shut and ground smooth, then mounted on legs to sit above a wood fire or propane hob. Some call it a Mexican wok.

You could use one to cook outside, for a Sunday supper with friends under endless skies: beef or pork or chicken or chorizo browned in hot oil, hit hard with cumin and red pepper and chili powder. Add chopped onions and peppers, hot and sweet, then some tomatoes, canned or fresh. Stir-fry until everything has gone soft and crisp at the edges. Add a beer and let it cook down. Top with an immense amount of shredded soft cheese and slide a piece of sheet metal over the top of the pan so as to melt the cheese. Then serve it all with warm tortillas, hot sauce, plenty of salsa, and sour cream. You don't need utensils. Warm the tortillas on the edge of the disco, then use them like gloves to scoop up the food and eat, eat, eat until everything's gone, everyone huddled around the dying fire and the last sweeps of meat and cheese and sauce.

Of course you probably don't have a disco. (It ain't no fooling around.) No matter. (Though if you have a huge camp skillet you could give it a try, over propane or a fire pit.) It is just the idea of discada that you're looking for when you serve tacos: friends and family and a lot of good food, warm tortillas to put it on, arms stretching here and there as everyone eats messily and well.

There might be carne asada, charred on the grill then sliced into bits, or battered fish fried crisp. You could make carnitas, some stewed mushrooms, or a vat of picadillo for that middle-school cafeteria vibe and the understanding that this ancient Mexican style of cooking and eating has become, here in the United States, something bigger and more flexible, more weird and wonderful. Sometimes I cook carne asada in the style of the chef Roy Choi, who rose to fame on the strength of the Korean-ified tacos he sold from a truck that moved restlessly across the east side of Los Angeles. One night one of my kids was eating my take on one of those, standing at the kitchen island amid a crowd of more than a dozen, a Sunday supper for the ages. "Taco night is the best night," she said.

To ensure that this is so, make sure your tortillas are fresh. The authenticity police will tell you that tacos, in the main, should be served on corn tortillas, and that flour ones are a Tex-Mexican abomination, a sop for gringos. That is not true, but I get it. There is little better than a couple steaming-hot small corn tortillas topped with sliced avocado, pico de gallo, and a spray of hot sauce and lime. But a charred flour tortilla wrapped around fried fish is a marvelous rejoinder, and so is a breakfast one made with eggs, cheese, and scallions. Rules are important in the kitchen as in life. But in matters of tacos? No judgments.

Whichever you choose, though, buy your tortillas somewhere that sells a lot of them, looking for bags that show a little condensation within, an indicator that they were recently made. (You could make your own tortillas, but here's a truth: They won't be as good as the ones from the place that sells a lot of them, not for years and years.) Make sure too that you serve your tortillas warm and pliable. You can scorch them in a pan, with or without oil, or on a grill, or wrap them in aluminum foil and put them in a low oven. There are few real purposes for a microwave oven, but heating tortillas is one of them. However you do the heating, they'll stay warm for a while when wrapped in a dish towel, but taco professionals prefer the confines of a tortilla warmer. (I have a couple cheap plastic faux terra-cotta numbers, and each holds more than a dozen tortillas.)

And absolutely make sure you have a lot of bowls. A successful Sunday supper of tacos and fixin's requires a vast spread of them, alongside the central protein on a platter or tray, a mise en place designed as much for serving as for cooking. You'll need them lined up like tubs at the salad bar at work: bowls for salsa, pico de gallo, avocado, chopped cabbage, sliced radishes, diced onions, lime wedges, shredded cheese, cilantro, grilled scallions, as you like, alongside bottles of hot sauce. There will be leftovers of all of this, no doubt. You'll get the hang of how to portion these things over time. But what's left will make for a fine next-day taco bowl for lunch, and that's important too. The best Sunday suppers offer memories that last forever, and a few extra meals besides.

CARNITAS

LITTLE MEATS! THIS IS A RECIPE of endless variation. Traditionally, you simmer chunks of pork shoulder in lard with citrus and herbs, then broil or fry the results until they are crisp, then serve them as part of a taco-night feast. You can certainly do that. But my recipe replaces the lard with a couple bottles of dark Mexican beer, and the results are fantastic. Double the recipe for a crowd.

1 boneless pork shoulder,
    about 4 pounds
Kosher salt and freshly ground
    black pepper
3 tablespoons neutral oil, such
    as canola or grapeseed
Two 12-ounce bottles dark beer
1 orange, cut into quarters
1 lime, cut into quarters
6 cloves garlic, peeled and
    minced
1 teaspoon red pepper flakes
1½ teaspoons fresh oregano
    leaves (or 1 teaspoon dried)
2 cinnamon sticks
1 bay leaf

1. Cut the pork shoulder into 1-to-2-inch chunks, trimming lightly to remove excess fat. Season to taste with salt and pepper.

2. Place a large pot or Dutch oven with a lid on the stove over medium-high heat and swirl 2 tablespoons of the oil into it. When the oil shimmers, add the pork, in batches if necessary, and sear the meat on all sides, removing the meat to a bowl when it browns.

3. When all the meat has been browned, return it to the pot, along with the beer, orange, lime, garlic, red pepper flakes, oregano, cinnamon sticks, and bay leaf. Bring to a boil, then reduce the heat beneath the pot, place the top on it, and simmer steadily until the pork is entirely tender, 1 to 2 hours. (Working ahead? You can stop the recipe at this point and refrigerate the pork in its braising liquid for a day or two before completing the recipe.)

4. When you're ready to cook, either heat the broiler, heat a large cast-iron pan on the stove top, or light a grill. Remove the pork from its braising liquid and pat it dry with paper towels. Brush the meat lightly with the remaining 1 tablespoon oil, season it with salt and pepper, and either broil, fry, or grill until the meat is browned and crisp, 4 to 5 minutes.

5. Serve with warm tortillas, chopped cilantro, onion, lime wedges, Pico de Gallo (recipe follows), and hot sauce.

PICO DE GALLO

Pico de gallo—"the rooster's beak"—is a raw Mexican salsa of deceptive simplicity. It has only six ingredients including salt, but it's rare in my experience that any two versions of the recipe taste the same. That's a good thing. Start with this recipe, but be prepared to add more or less cilantro and salt or lime juice, more or fewer onions or jalapeños or tomatoes, to your taste. That's your pico de gallo recipe, right there.

4 plum tomatoes, diced

1 small to medium white onion, peeled
   and diced

1 or 2 jalapeño peppers, seeded and diced

Juice of 1 lime, or more to taste

Kosher salt

½ cup roughly chopped fresh cilantro
   leaves and stems

1. Combine the tomatoes, onion, half of the jalapeños, the lime juice, and a big pinch of salt in a bowl. Mix to combine and add half the cilantro. Set aside to rest for 30 minutes.

2. Taste and adjust the seasonings, adding more jalapeño or lime juice or salt if you feel you need it. Sprinkle the rest of the cilantro on top and serve.

STEAK TACOS

THERE ARE AS MANY WAYS TO MAKE steak tacos as there are ways to cook steak. But for the purposes of a dinner with a load of people, there is no better method than to grill or sear skirt steak—a long, flat, deeply flavorful cut of meat from the "plate" of the cow, right behind the brisket. Skirt steak takes well to a marinade (see Carne Asada, page 220), but it is terrific as well with just a simple rub of salt and pepper. Cooked quickly over high heat and then sliced against the grain to maximize its tenderness, it goes beautifully with beans, pico de gallo, sliced avocado, diced tomato, grated jack or cheddar cheese, sliced radishes, chopped cilantro, cut limes, sour cream, hot sauce, and warm tortillas made of corn or flour, to your taste. Does the skirt steak at your market cost a bajillion dollars a pound, as it does sometimes at mine? I substitute hanger steak, and it's fantastic. Just make sure before cooking to cut out the seam that runs down the center of each steak.

2 to 3 pounds skirt steak, cut into
    10-to-12-inch sections
2 to 3 tablespoons olive oil
Kosher salt and freshly ground
    black pepper

1. Heat the broiler on high or build a fire in your grill. If using a gas grill, turn all the burners to high.

2. Put the skirt steaks on a large rimmed baking sheet and drizzle with the oil, tossing the meat to coat. Season aggressively with salt and pepper.

3. When the coals are covered with gray ash and the fire is hot (you can hold your hand 6 inches over the grill for only a few seconds), place the steaks on the grill directly over the coals and cook until deeply seared, turning a few times, 8 to 10 minutes overall for medium-rare. If cooking in the broiler, arrange the steaks on the sheet pan in a single layer, with as much space as you can manage between them, and place beneath the broiler. Rotate the pan periodically over the course of 5 minutes or so, then turn the steaks over and repeat on the other side. Remove the steaks from the heat and allow to rest for 10 minutes or so. Slice against the grain into thin strips and serve with warm tortillas and whatever toppings you desire.

CARNE ASADA

This is a slightly more involved version of steak tacos, one I learned from the mystical Los Angeles chef Roy Choi, whose cooking does a lot to bring the flavors of that city alive on the plate. So there is something Mexican about this dish, yes, but something Asian too. That makes the meal deeply American and altogether delicious. Make the marinade and put the steaks in it the day before you're going to cook. The reward the following evening will be worth the time spent.

2 medium jalapeño peppers

1 medium tomato, cored and cut into quarters

1 small yellow onion or ¼ large one, peeled and cut into quarters

5 cloves garlic, peeled and roughly chopped

2 tablespoons sugar

¼ cup ancho chili powder

1 tablespoon freshly ground black pepper

¼ cup kosher salt

½ large bunch fresh cilantro leaves and stems, well rinsed

Juice of 1 orange

Juice of 1 lime

¼ cup mirin

One 12-ounce can beer, whatever you've got

2 to 3 pounds skirt steak, cut into 10-inch sections, or hanger steak with the connective tissue in it removed, or flank steak

2 tablespoons olive oil

1. Make the marinade. Place the jalapeños directly over a burner on the stove and turn the burner to medium-high. Using tongs, turn the jalapeños in the heat until their skins begin to blacken and bubble and begin to soften. Remove the jalapeños from the heat and, when they are cool enough to handle, pull out their stems and skin them, then slice them open and remove their seeds. Put the jalapeños into a food processor or blender. (You can also blacken the jalapeños under a broiler, on a cookie sheet.)

2. Add the tomato, onion, garlic, sugar, chili powder, black pepper, and salt to the bowl of the machine and pulse to combine. Add the cilantro, orange juice, lime juice, mirin, and beer. Process again until smooth.

3. Transfer the marinade to a large nonreactive bowl or baking pan and submerge the steaks in it. Cover and place in the refrigerator for at least 4 hours or overnight.

4. Build a fire in your grill. If using a gas grill, turn all the burners to high. When all the coals are covered with gray ash and the fire is hot (you can hold your hand 6 inches over the grill for only a few seconds), remove the steaks from the marinade, drizzle with oil, and place on the grill directly over the coals. Cook until deeply seared, turning a few times, 8 to 10 minutes overall for medium-rare. Remove the steaks from the grill and allow to rest for 10 minutes or so. Slice against the grain into thin strips and serve with warm tortillas and whatever toppings you desire. Dressing some scallions in olive oil, salt, and pepper and grilling them over the dying flames is an excellent addition to the mix.

FISH TACOS

THE MOTHER RECIPE IS SIMPLE: Cook fish, serve in a taco. You can grill the fish. You can fry it. Whatever method you use can yield fish worth folding into a tortilla. Here, though, is a bespoke fish taco recipe I ginned up after watching a bunch of chefs cook fish fillets for a lot longer on one side than another, and seeing what a marvelous crust they got in return. Fluke works great if you're in the Northeast. But any firm white fish will do up to and including tilapia, the farmed protein fish that many street-corner fish taco joints use really well. Deploy a simple salsa and lime-flecked crema topping to accompany the fish, however you end up cooking it.

FOR THE SALSA

2 medium tomatoes, seeded
    and finely chopped
1 small red onion, peeled and
    diced
1 clove garlic, peeled and minced
1/2 cup roughly chopped fresh
    cilantro
1 jalapeño pepper, halved
    lengthwise, seeded, and cut
    crosswise into half-moons
    (optional)
Kosher salt

FOR THE CREMA

1/4 cup mayonnaise
1/2 cup sour cream
1 lime, cut in half
Kosher salt and freshly ground
    black pepper
1 tablespoon canned chipotle
    pepper, finely chopped
    (optional)

FOR THE FISH

1 cup all-purpose flour
1 tablespoon chili powder
1 1/2 teaspoons kosher salt, plus
    more for finishing
1 1/2 teaspoons freshly ground
    black pepper
1 cup whole milk
2 pounds flounder or any firm
    white-fleshed fish, cut across
    the grain of the flesh into
    strips about 1/2 inch wide
    by 3 inches long
1/2 cup peanut oil, plus a splash
    more for greasing the pan
2 tablespoons unsalted butter
Twenty-four 6-inch fresh
    corn tortillas
2 to 3 cups shredded green
    cabbage

1. **Make the salsa.** In a medium bowl, combine the tomatoes, onion, garlic, cilantro, and jalapeño, if using. Add salt to taste.

continued on page 224

2. **Make the crema.** In a small bowl, whisk the mayonnaise and sour cream until combined. Season to taste with the juice of the halved lime, the salt, the black pepper, and the chipotle, if using.

3. **Prepare the fish.** In a medium bowl, mix together the flour, chili powder, salt, and black pepper. Pour the milk into another medium bowl and place the fish in it.

4. Pour the peanut oil into a 12-inch frying pan and place over medium-high heat until it shimmers and is about to smoke. Remove the fish pieces from the milk bath and dredge them lightly through the flour mixture, shaking to remove excess. Add the butter to the pan. Place some fish pieces in the oil, without crowding them, and cook until deep golden brown on one side, 3 to 4 minutes. Turn carefully and cook for 1 minute more. Remove to a warmed, paper towel–lined plate and sprinkle with salt. Repeat with the remaining fish.

5. Meanwhile, lightly grease a skillet with a drizzle of oil and set over medium heat. Heat the tortillas, one or two at a time, until they are soft and hot. Keep them warm, wrapped in a dish towel if you don't have a tortilla warmer.

6. Fill each tortilla with 3 pieces of fish, browned side up, followed by the tomato salsa and a pinch of cabbage. Drizzle with the crema. Serve 1 or 2 tacos per person, with lime wedges and hot sauce, such as Tapatío or Frank's, on the side.

MUSHROOM *and* CHILE TACOS

PORTOBELLO MUSHROOMS, COOKED FOR A long time over low heat, become a textural marvel, nearly steaklike in their depth of flavor. Paired with mildly hot poblano chiles, chili powder, cumin, and oregano, along with as much hot sauce as you like and a spray of lime juice to provide an acidic zing against the beefiness, they make for a rich and satisfying filling for warm corn tortillas. (Also, for what it's worth, they're an exceptional side dish for a dinner of grilled steak.) Top, as always, exactly as you like. But I like the nutty creaminess of queso fresco and an additional acidic bite from pickled jalapeños.

2 tablespoons plus 2 teaspoons
    neutral oil, such as canola or
    grapeseed
1 tablespoon unsalted butter
1 tablespoon chili powder
2 teaspoons ground cumin
1 teaspoon dried oregano
Pinch of red pepper flakes,
    or to taste
2 fresh poblano chiles, seeded
    and cut into finger-width strips
1 medium red onion, peeled and
    thinly sliced
2 cloves garlic, peeled and minced
1 tablespoon kosher salt,
    or to taste
1 teaspoon freshly ground
    black pepper, or to taste
1 pound portobello mushrooms,
    gently cleaned and cut into
    finger-width strips
12 to 18 corn tortillas
2 medium tomatoes, diced
¼ cup roughly chopped fresh
    cilantro

1 lime, halved
Hot sauce

1. Place a large sauté pan over medium-high heat and add 2 tablespoons of the oil and the butter. When the butter foams and the oil begins to shimmer, sprinkle on the chili powder, cumin, oregano, and red pepper flakes and shake the pan to combine. As soon as the spice mix becomes fragrant, add the chiles, onion, and garlic, along with a teaspoon or so of the salt and the black pepper. Cook, stirring often, until the onion has softened, turned translucent, and started to color, 12 to 15 minutes.

2. Add the mushrooms and the remaining salt, and stir again to combine. Cook, stirring occasionally, until the mushrooms begin to give off their liquid, then turn down the heat and allow to cook gently, stirring occasionally, until they are deeply browned and very tender, about 20 minutes.

3. Meanwhile, set a skillet over medium heat and add to it the remaining 2 teaspoons oil. When the oil shimmers, add the tortillas, one or two at a time, and cook, flipping them a few times, until they are soft and hot. Keep them warm, wrapped in a dish towel if you don't have a tortilla warmer.

4. Remove the pan from the heat and tip the contents into a bowl. Add the diced tomatoes and

continued on next page

cilantro and toss to combine. Season to taste with lime juice, then hot sauce. Serve with the warm tortillas and whatever toppings you desire: crumbled queso fresco, cotija, or feta cheese; pickled jalapeños, sliced radishes, sliced avocado, pico de gallo, salsa, crema, whatever you please.

HARD SHELL TACOS

HERE IS A PLATTER OF FAUX-MEXICAN MADELEINES for those who grew up in the 1980s and a delicious introduction to that era for those who did not. The meat sauce is better than anything a taco kit's stale, premixed spices can provide, and you can trick out all that goes on top of it as you like, substituting the traditional shredded lettuce, industrial cheese, and sour cream with cabbage, radishes, cilantro, cheddar, guacamole, pickled jalapeños, actual jalapeños, whatever you please. (Can't stomach the idea of using prefabricated tortilla sleeves? Make your own. Shape a form out of aluminum foil, fry fresh corn tortillas over medium-high heat in shimmering neutral oil, then allow them to cool into shape on their aluminum saddle.) The result is not true to any culture or cuisine save those built out of memories of the school cafeteria, dinner at someone's mom's house, taco nights before a scheduled viewing of *Magnum P.I.* Authenticity is for the birds. These are delicious tacos.

2 tablespoons neutral oil, such as
    canola, peanut, or grapeseed
1 medium yellow onion, peeled
    and diced
4 cloves garlic, peeled and minced
2 pounds ground beef
2 tablespoons chili powder
1 tablespoon ground cumin
2 teaspoons kosher salt, or to
    taste
2 teaspoons freshly ground black
    pepper, or to taste
2 teaspoons cornstarch
2 teaspoons smoked paprika or
    substitute hot or sweet
1 teaspoon red pepper flakes, or
    to taste
1 cup chicken stock or beef stock,
    homemade, or low-sodium if
    store-bought
12 to 18 hard taco shells

1. Place a large skillet over medium-high heat, and add the oil. When the oil begins to shimmer, add the onion and cook until softened and starting to brown, 5 to 7 minutes.

2. Add the garlic and cook for a minute or so to soften, then the ground beef. Cook until the beef is starting to brown, stirring and chopping with a spoon to break up the meat, 5 to 7 minutes. Pour off excess fat, leaving only a tablespoon or two in the pan.

3. Heat the oven to 325°F. Add the chili powder, cumin, salt, black pepper, cornstarch, paprika, and red pepper flakes to the meat and stir to combine. Add the stock, stir, bring to a simmer, and cook, uncovered, until the sauce has thickened slightly, 4 to 5 minutes.

4. As the sauce cooks, place the taco shells on a sheet pan and toast in the oven until they are crisp and smell nutty. Serve a few tablespoons of meat in each taco and top to please: grated cheese, sliced jalapeños, chopped tomatoes, shredded lettuce, sour cream, guacamole, whatever you like.

CHAPTER

NINE

VEGETABLES

—

Time was, the role of vegetables in any serious Sunday feast was
spare, dutiful, supporting. There was at the center of the table a roast or something
equally impressive, surrounded by pale piles of plants and tubers and grains drenched
in butter, in gravy, in Wish-Bone Italian dressing, in cream. Vegetables were cho-
rines, footmen, maids. (Occasionally they were comic foils.) They did not draw
focus from the star.

That fact is changing, and thankfully so, as plant-based dishes move from the
outskirts of the table to its center. The ritual of a Sunday meal may have been born in
the slaughter of a large animal to feed a village of serfs after church, and it may have
risen high on the pleasures of a vat of sausage-studded meat sauce eaten with extended family. But we come to the table with different needs and interests and tastes
now. Many are worried about our nation's soaring rates of obesity and diabetes, are
concerned with the role that our meat-rich, sugar-enhanced diets are having on our
personal health. Vegetables are low in calories and fat; they contain no cholesterol;
they are high in fiber and vitamins. You better believe we ought to be eating more of
them.

Not to mention, vegetables are inexpensive, relative to the cost of a lot of meat or
fish, even when they're raised organically.

That last fact is an important consideration notwithstanding the positive health benefits of a plant-based diet. Really, it is. The thesis of this book is that you ought to try to serve a big dinner to family and friends as often or as regularly as you can. That sort of recurring expense can add up. It can lead to trepidation. It could get in the way of scheduling the next meal or the one after that. Which is why in this book, as in life, I mostly eschew your veal and prime rib for dinner, your morels and caviar, except in rare circumstances.

And that is why—though not only why!—I champion vegetables. With a large tub of beans to accompany a smaller cut of meat or fish, with a gigantic kale salad studded with blue cheese and pecans and cranberries, with a heap of potatoes or rice, I can keep costs down while also serving food that is good for us and, as much to the point, delicious.

That's the theory, anyway. (Nothing like a lecture before dinner!) The practice may take longer to implement, to enjoy. Start by cooking organic vegetables, if you can. We are in a golden age for that, right now. Take a bite of a raw organic carrot and then another of one grown "conventionally" in California's Central Valley and see. (Time was, conventional farming was organic farming!) Make some mashed potatoes with organic Yukon golds, then repeat with the "regular" ones from the gigantimart. The differences in sweetness, depth of flavor, and general awesomeness are clear. But do not get hung up on that. A non-organic lettuce or cauliflower or eggplant or to-mato can be made sublime.

Start with beans, with grains, with potatoes. Roast vegetables and drizzle them with yogurt or adorn them with spice. Stew some greens. Put those at the center of the table with a side dish of wee little pork chops or a few slices of beef. And eat them together as if this were how we always did it, without a sermon.

ROASTED VEGETABLES

L IGHT WORK TO ACCOMPANY A ROAST: Cut every vegetable in your refrigerator crisper to the same size, then drizzle with olive oil, season with salt and pepper, and place on a sheet pan to cook in a hot oven until everything is crisp at the edges and soft within. A handful of herbs scattered among the vegetables about halfway through the process ties the flavors together nicely, and if the combination provides a perfect side dish, it is also on its own a hearty dinner salad.

3 pounds assorted root vegetables. Say: carrots, parsnips, celeriac, potatoes, and turnips? Some fennel or broccoli? A rutabaga?

¼ cup extra-virgin olive oil

Kosher salt and freshly ground black pepper

1 large handful of chopped fresh rosemary, thyme, or parsley, plus more for garnish

1. Heat the oven to 425°F. Peel the vegetables and cut them into 1-to-2-inch chunks of equal size, then put them onto a sheet or baking pan and toss with the oil and a healthy sprinkling of salt and pepper.

2. Put the vegetables in the oven and roast without stirring for 20 minutes, then check on them. If they look dry or are sticking to the pan, drizzle with more oil. Continue roasting, stirring or turning the vegetables once or twice, for another 20 minutes or so. Stir in about three-quarters of the herbs, then return the pan to the oven for another 20 to 40 minutes, until crisp at the edges and soft.

3. Remove the vegetables from the oven. Garnish with the remaining herbs and serve.

WHOLE ROASTED CAULIFLOWER

THESE BIG AND IMPRESSIVE HEADS can serve as a main dish for vegetarian nights, but they go terrifically well with roast chicken or pork as well. Sometimes I'll top the cauliflower with a coverlet of bread crumbs moistened in olive oil with a couple anchovies minced into the mixture for an extra pow of flavor. The result, bread crumbs or no, is as good at room temperature as it is hot.

2 heads cauliflower, green leaves removed

¼ cup extra-virgin olive oil

2 teaspoons kosher salt

2 tablespoons fresh lemon juice

2 tablespoons capers, rinsed and drained

Freshly ground black pepper

3 tablespoons fresh flat-leaf parsley, roughly chopped

1. Heat the oven to 450°F. Using a chef's knife, cut off the stem of each cauliflower and then use a paring knife to cut around its base to remove the cores of the cauliflower heads, leaving the heads intact. Place the heads on a sheet pan.

2. Drizzle the oil over the cauliflower, turning to coat them well, and season each with ½ teaspoon of the salt. Roast in the oven until tender and golden, about 1 hour.

3. Meanwhile, whisk together the lemon juice, capers, the remaining 1 teaspoon salt, and pepper to taste. When the cauliflower is done, remove to a warmed platter, drizzle the lemon-and-caper sauce over the heads, and top with the parsley.

ROASTED BROCCOLI WITH BALSAMIC AND SOY SAUCE

NO REAL RECIPE NEEDED HERE. Just heat the oven to 450°F. Cut a head or two of broccoli into florets. Trim the stalks and cut them into planks, about the same length as the florets. Toss them all with neutral oil, such as canola or grapeseed, in a bowl, then spread them out onto sheet pans, season with salt and pepper, and roast until they're blistering, about 20 minutes. Then, toss them around and continue cooking the other sides, another 20 minutes or so. When they're done, drizzle a mixture of soy sauce and balsamic vinegar over the top and toss to combine.

ROASTED CAULIFLOWER
with PARMESAN BREAD CRUMBS

I LIKE THE ADDITION OF A LITTLE SUGAR to the oil that coats the cauliflower as it roasts because it helps the florets caramelize. But if you're cooking with fresh and organic cauliflower, from a farm nearby, you may wish to omit it. In any event, tossing crisp-soft-fragrant florets of cauliflower with crisp-soft-fragrant bread crumbs is a marvelous activity, and the result makes for a delicious thing to eat on its own or alongside a roast or casserole.

2 heads cauliflower, green leaves removed

8 to 10 fresh sage leaves, roughly chopped

Zest of 2 lemons

2 teaspoons sugar

¼ cup extra-virgin olive oil

Kosher salt and freshly ground black pepper

3 cloves garlic, peeled and minced

1 medium shallot, peeled and diced

1 cup fresh bread crumbs

¼ cup grated Parmesan cheese

1. Heat the oven to 400°F. Break the cauliflower into florets and toss in a bowl with the sage, lemon zest, sugar, and 2 tablespoons of the oil. Season with salt and pepper and spread out on a large baking sheet.

2. Place in the oven and roast until tender and golden, 20 to 25 minutes.

3. Meanwhile, prepare the bread crumbs. Heat the remaining 2 tablespoons oil in a large sauté pan set over medium heat. When the oil begins to shimmer, add the garlic, shallot, and bread crumbs. Cook, stirring often, until the bread crumbs are golden, 5 to 7 minutes.

4. In a large bowl, toss together the cauliflower and bread crumbs, then top with the cheese. Serve on a warmed platter.

HONEY-ROASTED SWEET POTATOES
with YOGURT SAUCE

THIS IS A RIFF ON A RECIPE THAT the Los Angeles chef Travis Lett made famous at his Gjelina restaurant in Venice and that I hacked around with in a winter kitchen on Long Island in New York for a column for the *Times*. It has since become a regular guest at our table. The trick is to toss the sweet potatoes in honey before roasting them, which encourages and intensifies their caramelization—and as you will see, there is no more intense caramelization than the one kicked off by honey. Its tart, near-bitter zip is a beautiful counterpart to the sweetness of the sweet potatoes, the heat of the pepper flakes, and the creamy pop of the yogurt dabbed onto the dish at the end. Serve a sweet potato per person if you're eating the dish with salad and grains, or what works out to half that if serving alongside a roast of some sort.

6 sweet potatoes

¼ cup honey

2 tablespoons red pepper flakes

⅓ cup extra-virgin olive oil

Kosher salt and freshly ground black pepper

1 cup Greek-style yogurt

⅓ cup fresh lime juice (about 4 limes)

1 bunch scallions, both green and white parts, trimmed and thinly sliced

1. Heat the oven to 425°F. Cut the sweet potatoes lengthwise into 4 wedges each. Put these in a large bowl or bowls and toss them with the honey, 1 tablespoon of the red pepper flakes, and all but 2 tablespoons of the oil. Let that sit for 10 minutes or so, tossing once or twice to coat, as the oven heats.

2. Transfer the sweet potatoes to two aluminum foil–lined rimmed baking sheets, season with salt and black pepper, then roast until they are deeply caramelized around the edges and soft when pierced with a fork at their thickest part, 30 to 35 minutes.

3. As the sweet potatoes roast, combine the yogurt, lime juice, and the remaining 2 tablespoons oil in a bowl, and whisk to combine. Season to taste with salt and black pepper and set aside.

4. When the sweet potatoes are done, transfer them to a large serving platter, drizzle the yogurt over them, and garnish with the remaining 1 tablespoon red pepper flakes, the scallions, and a final sprinkle of salt, if you like.

ROASTED SWEET POTATOES
WITH SPICY SAUCE

FROM THE POINT OF VIEW OF ease of preparation, this is among the simplest dinners to prepare in this book—it doesn't even require a recipe. Just roast one sweet potato per person in a 400°F oven on an aluminum foil–lined pan or pans until the potatoes are soft and bursting, which will take roughly an hour, maybe more if the tubers are huge or you have a ton of them in the oven. While they cook, make rice in the rice cooker I asked you to purchase (see page 8), then chop up a bunch of scallions, cilantro, and jalapeño peppers. Put those aside and make a sauce of oyster sauce thinned out with water and built up again with pats of butter in a pan on the stove. Make that sauce fiery with red pepper flakes or chile paste or a sauce like Sriracha. Experiment with that sauce as you like. You could make it instead with gochujang, soy sauce, and a splash of mirin. Or with soy sauce, white pepper, molasses, and jalapeños. The idea is just to balance salty with a little sweet and a lot of fire, or to balance a lot of sweet with a lot of fire and an underlying salty thrum. You'll taste and taste and come up with what you like. And when the sweet potatoes are done, you can split them open and drizzle some of the sauce into each, followed by the greens and peppers. Serve those with the rice and what remains of the sauce on the side and you'll do so six times a year, mostly on evenings when ten are coming to dinner and the last thing you want to do is work.

ROASTED CARROTS

PEEL A BUNCH OF CARROTS, at least two per person unless they're huge, and put them in a big skillet with a lot of butter. Set over low heat and allow them to cook forever, rolling them around occasionally so they get good and caramelized all over. About 10 minutes before you're ready to serve, drizzle some maple syrup over the pan and roll the softened carrots around in it. Grind some black pepper over the top—or red pepper flakes, if you like the axis of sweet and fiery—then tip the carrots onto a serving platter. Did someone give you some fancy flaky salt at some point and it's sitting on a shelf? Now would be a good time to deploy some, for crunch and a salty pop against the sweet.

ROASTED POTATOES
with ONIONS *and* ROSEMARY

I WAS NINETEEN AND WORKING AS A PREP COOK in a fancy restaurant when the chef asked me to roast some potatoes for a staff meal. I made these and was not fired. I have been making them ever since. The onions will come close to burning but not quite, and the caramelized result plays off the creaminess of the potatoes. Generally speaking, a little rosemary goes a long way. This is not one of those times.

3 pounds potatoes, ideally Yukon
    gold or red-skinned (6 to
    8 large), quartered
2 large Spanish onions, peeled
    and quartered
6 cloves garlic, peeled
1 tablespoon fresh rosemary
    leaves, roughly chopped
1/2 cup extra-virgin olive oil
Kosher salt and freshly ground
    black pepper

1. Heat the oven to 425°F. In a large roasting pan, combine the potatoes, onions, garlic, rosemary, and oil. Stir them around, then spread them evenly across the pan.

2. Place the pan in the oven and roast until the potatoes are golden brown and crisp, 45 to 60 minutes. (The more crowded the pan, the longer the potatoes will take to cook.)

3. Remove the pan from the oven and tip its contents onto a warmed serving platter. Season to taste with salt and pepper and serve.

MASHED POTATOES

D O NOT UNDERESTIMATE THE POWER of a large bowl of hot mashed potatoes, their flavor heightened by butter and salt, their texture smoothed with a little milk. They are an ideal accompaniment to roasted meats, fried chicken, or simply sautéed fish, though you could easily serve them with a giant roasted head of broccoli, if you like, or planks of grilled butternut squash. Adding a few peeled and chopped parsnips to the boiling potatoes is a nice variation, as is doing the same with celery root. Either adds a welcome sweetness. Finish with some chopped fresh parsley or chives for an elegant, continental vibe.

3 pounds potatoes, ideally
    Yukon gold or russet (6 to
    8 large), scrubbed and
    quartered
Kosher salt
5 tablespoons unsalted butter,
    plus extra for dotting at
    the end
½ cup whole milk

1. Place the potatoes in a large pot and cover with water, then add 2 tablespoons salt. Set the pot over high heat and bring to a boil, then turn down the heat slightly and cook until the potatoes are soft and you can slide a fork into them with almost no resistance, about 20 minutes.

2. Meanwhile, combine the butter with the milk in a small saucepan and place over medium heat until the butter has melted and the mixture is very hot. (Do not allow it to boil.)

3. When the potatoes are done, drain them very well and return them to the pot. Using a masher or a ricer, mash the potatoes until they are smooth, then mix in about half of the milk mixture. Taste and add salt and more butter and milk as needed. (If you want the potatoes to be creamier, you can transfer them to the bowl of a stand mixer and beat them until they are very smooth, 30 to 45 seconds.) Put the potatoes in a warmed serving bowl, dot with a little more butter, and either serve or cover tightly until you are ready to serve—they'll stay hot that way for a half hour or so, more if set in a low oven.

CLAIRE'S POTATOES

I HAD A TERRIFIC BREAKFAST ONCE on San Juan Island, north of Seattle, in a dockside coffee shop that served commercial fishermen, hippie farmers, kayak tourists, and boat builders in equal measure. The grated hash brown potatoes there were cooked in thin sheets, then run under the broiler beneath a handful of grated cheese to create crisp pancakes that could be used as a platter on which to serve fried eggs, or as a hat to top them, depending on your mood. When I got home to New York, I started making them for dinner, which was labor-intensive and eventually annoying because one of my children wanted them for dinner all the time. Together we worked out a hack. It is this recipe, and you can easily double it, and serve with just about anything. Omit the bacon if bacon's not your game, and replace it with a couple tablespoons of butter. The point is simply to aim for a thick, caramelized crust of potatoes. The interiors will be soft and sweet.

2 slices bacon, ideally double smoked or slab

1 tablespoon unsalted butter

2 pounds medium Yukon Gold potatoes (about 5), scrubbed and diced

1 medium yellow onion, peeled and diced

Kosher salt and freshly ground black pepper

1½ cups shredded cheddar cheese

2 scallions, green parts only, thinly sliced

1. Put the bacon on a large rimmed baking sheet, put it in the oven, and heat the oven to 400°F. Cook the bacon until it is cooked through, chewy, and going to crisp, 15 to 20 minutes. Remove the bacon from the pan and set aside. There should be a couple tablespoons of bacon fat in the pan. If there is more, remove and discard it.

2. Add the butter to the bacon fat, then put the potatoes and onion onto the pan and stir to coat. Spread the potatoes and onion evenly across the pan and return the pan to the oven for 20 minutes or so. Take the pan out again and use a spatula to turn the potatoes. Return the pan to the oven and cook for another 20 minutes or so, until the potatoes are beginning to crisp, then turn them once more and cook for an additional 10 to 15 minutes.

3. Take the potatoes out of the oven, season with salt and pepper, and top with the shredded cheese. Stir to combine and return the pan to the oven until the cheese has melted, 3 to 5 minutes. Tip onto a warmed serving tray, garnish with the scallions, and serve.

MOCK FRITES

To boil new potatoes, then smash them onto an oiled sheet pan, roast them, and douse the finished numbers with malt vinegar and salt—why, it is one of the great potato treatments of our age, an easy homage to bistro frites. The dish makes an excellent accompaniment to roasted meats and fish.

16 to 24 new, baby, or C-grade
    potatoes
4 tablespoons neutral oil, such
    as canola or grapeseed
Kosher salt and freshly ground
    black pepper

1.   Heat the oven to 450°F. Set a large pot filled with salted water on the stove. Add the potatoes, turn the heat to high, and cook, gently boiling, until they are softened, about 15 minutes. Drain the potatoes and dry them well.

2.   Grease a rimmed sheet pan with half the oil and put the potatoes onto the pan. Using a potato masher or the bottom of a heavy glass, gently smash each potato, pressing it down to a thickness of less than an inch. Drizzle the rest of the oil over the smashed potatoes, place the pan on the top rack in the oven, and roast until the exteriors are golden and crunchy, 20 to 25 minutes.

3.   Remove from the oven, season with salt and a grind of pepper, and serve on a warmed platter, with malt vinegar on the side.

ROASTED BRUSSELS SPROUTS
with BREAD CRUMBS *and* BACON

AT THANKSGIVING I LIKE TO SAUTÉ BRUSSELS sprouts in bacon fat until they are deeply caramelized, then hit them with an enormous amount of cream. That's a fine way to make Brussels sprouts—you can even add some maple syrup to the mix, if you like. But this high-heat oven method is a little less rich and rib-sticking, and delivers excellent textures to the plate as well. If the steps seem too fussy, you can dial back on toasting the bread crumbs in bacon fat and just toast them in butter or olive oil on the stove top. Likewise, if you'd like to omit the bacon entirely, go to. The key to the whole meal is that you coat the sprouts in oil and give them some seasoning before putting them in the devil's crosshairs on that aluminum foil–lined sheet pan. The 500-degree heat blisters them beautifully without roasting their deep interiors into mush, and the result is sweet-salty-soft-crisp, perhaps America's most favored combination of flavor and texture.

¼ **pound thick-cut bacon**
    (about 3 strips)
1½ **cups fresh bread crumbs**
1 **tablespoon fresh thyme leaves**
2 **pounds Brussels sprouts**
¼ **cup olive oil**
Kosher salt and freshly ground
    black pepper
3 **tablespoons balsamic vinegar,**
    or to taste

1. Heat the oven to 400°F. Line a rimmed baking sheet with aluminum foil and place the strips of bacon on it. Roast on the top rack of the oven until the bacon is deep golden brown and crisp, 15 to 20 minutes, though it will depend on the thickness of the bacon. Remove the pan from the oven and set the bacon aside on a plate. When it has cooled slightly, chop the bacon into bits and set aside.

2. Combine the bread crumbs with the thyme leaves in a medium bowl and scatter the mixture across the baking sheet on which you cooked the bacon, tossing lightly to coat with the fat. Set the bowl aside and toast the bread crumbs on the upper rack of the oven, tossing frequently, until they are golden, about 10 minutes. Remove the pan from the oven, scrape the bread crumbs back into the bowl, and set aside.

3. Raise the heat to 500°F. Replace the foil on the sheet pan if it's been banged up by the bacon and the bread crumbs and put the pan back into the oven to heat, again on the highest rack. Trim the ends of the Brussels sprouts, and remove all yellowing exterior

continued on next page

leaves. Cut the larger sprouts in half. Put the Brussels sprouts into a large bowl and toss them with the oil, and salt and pepper to taste. Remove the pan from the oven and pour the Brussels sprouts onto it, working fast to arrange them cut side down. Return the pan to the oven and roast until the sprouts are deeply caramelized and very tender, 20 to 25 minutes. Fifteen or 20 minutes into the cooking, drizzle the balsamic vinegar over them and shake the pan to distribute it.

4.   Taste and add more salt, pepper, or vinegar if you like, then transfer to a warmed bowl or platter and scatter the bread crumbs and bacon bits over the top.

CORN *on the* COB

WHEN CORN IS IN SEASON, there are few better things to serve a crowd than a big platter of corn on the cob with butter and salt or with mayonnaise and a sprinkle of chili powder or cotija cheese, a squeeze of lime. Corn is comically easy to prepare, whether you steam the corn or blanch it, grill the cobs or roast them. You can cook the corn with the husks on. You can strip them partly off, remove all the silks, and then rewrap the ears before cooking. To me, this is a matter of preference, born out of experience; there is no one correct way to cook corn save not to boil it into bland submission. So what follows isn't so much a recipe as a methodology, one you can adapt to the stove, the oven, or the grill.

1 ear of corn per person, or more

Unsalted butter, at room temperature

Kosher salt

1. Prepare the corn. Either strip off the husks and silks entirely, or pull back the husks and remove the silks, then rewrap the corn with the husks.

2. To steam corn: Bring a large pot of water to the boil. Reduce the heat to a simmer. Place the corn in a steamer over the water. Cover and steam until the corn is tender, 10 to 12 minutes. **To roast corn:** Heat the oven to 375°F. Put the corn on a baking sheet and place in the oven until tender, turning it a few times, 30 to 35 minutes. **To blanch corn:** Add it directly to the boiling water, reduce the heat to a simmer, and cook until the corn is tender, 5 to 8 minutes. **To grill corn:** Blanch it for only 3 minutes or so, then remove it from the water and stack on a platter. Apply just a little butter to each ear of corn, then place it on the grill. Cook, turning often, until the corn is tender and some of the kernels are beginning to darken, about 5 minutes.

3. Serve with butter, salt, mayonnaise, crema, cotija cheese, chili powder, lime juice, whatever you like.

CORN PUDDING

THERE IS NOTHING FANCY AT ALL about this pudding, and it pairs excellently with grilled or barbecued chicken or indeed with anything slightly salty and crisp. Add a diced jalapeño pepper to the mix if you like a little extra pop.

4 cups fresh or frozen corn kernels, from about 8 ears of corn or one "family-size" bag of frozen organic corn

4 cups whole milk, warmed slightly

4 large eggs, beaten together

8 tablespoons (1 stick) unsalted butter, melted, plus 1 tablespoon unmelted

A few dashes of hot sauce, such as Frank's, or to taste

2 teaspoons sugar

2 teaspoons kosher salt

1 teaspoon freshly ground black pepper

1. Heat the oven to 350°F. Combine the corn, milk, eggs, melted butter, hot sauce, sugar, salt, and pepper in a large mixing bowl and stir to mix well.

2. Use the remaining 1 tablespoon butter to grease a large, oven-safe casserole dish, then pour the pudding batter into the dish. Place the casserole in a large roasting pan and fill it with enough hot water to come about halfway up the sides of the casserole dish.

3. Carefully place the roasting pan with the casserole in it in the oven and allow the pudding to bake until firm but still shiny with moisture, and a little jiggly at its center, about 45 minutes to an hour. Remove the roasting pan from the oven and the casserole dish from the roasting pan, and allow the pudding to sit for 5 to 10 minutes before serving.

SIMPLE SAUTÉED GREENS

Hot salad, my children used to call this dish when I served it alongside roasted birds or beside a pile of chops. You can add smokiness by dialing back a little on the olive oil and using it to fry a little bacon with the garlic, before adding the greens, or by adding a tablespoon or two of tomato paste and healthy shakes of smoked paprika before the greens go into the pot. At the end, taste and taste and taste again. You may desire a little more vinegar, red pepper flakes, salt, or black pepper. I like making this dish with kale, but it's terrific with mustard greens, Swiss chard, or turnip greens, with any substantial, sturdy leaf.

1/4 cup extra-virgin olive oil

3 cloves garlic, peeled and sliced

2 large bunches kale or other sturdy greens, trimmed, with leaves coarsely chopped and stems cut into 1-inch-long segments

1/2 cup vegetable stock, dry white wine, or water

Kosher salt and freshly ground black pepper

Red pepper flakes

2 tablespoons red wine vinegar

1. Heat the oil in a large, heavy-bottomed pot or Dutch oven with a lid over medium-high heat until it shimmers. Add the garlic and cook, stirring, until fragrant and soft.

2. Add the kale to the pan, turn the heat to high, and add the stock. Use tongs to toss the greens in the oil and stock, then cover and cook for 5 to 7 minutes, until the greens are soft and wilted but still quite green. Remove the lid and continue to cook, stirring occasionally, until all the liquid has evaporated, another 2 to 3 minutes. Season to taste with salt, black pepper, and red pepper flakes. Add the vinegar and toss to combine.

SIMPLE GREEN BEANS

THERE IS NO REAL PERCENTAGE IN TRYING to improve on simplicity. Here the beans are cooked off in boiling water, then tossed with butter and lemon juice. A huge pile of them served next to a tray of roasted chicken or grilled pork chops or sautéed fish is a great pleasure.

3 pounds fresh green beans, tailed
  and topped
4 tablespoons (½ stick) unsalted
  butter, cut into small cubes
1 tablespoon fresh lemon juice or
  dry white wine
Zest of 1 lemon
Kosher salt and freshly ground
  black pepper

1. Bring a large pot filled with salted water to a rolling boil over high heat. Add the green beans and cook for 3 to 4 minutes, until they are bright green and just tender.

2. Drain the beans and toss them in the still-hot pot with the butter, lemon juice, and lemon zest, until the butter has melted. Season to taste with salt and pepper and serve in a warmed bowl.

PEAS WITH BACON *and* MINT

ONE OF THE BEST LARGE-PARTY COOKS of my acquaintance is the painter Tim Lovejoy, who runs his kitchen in Hadlyme, Connecticut, with the flair and precision of Fred Astaire dancing. I once saw him cook, serve, bus, and officiate a dinner party for more than a dozen without once appearing to sweat, save for a brief moment of panic at the notion of having an unlucky thirteen at his table. (As I remember it, he added an extra place setting and put a stuffed animal in the chair to ward off bad luck.) A version of these peas was served as part of that meal, a song to summer. (Frozen organic peas will do almost as well as fresh ones.)

¼ pound bacon, cut into bâtons

2 pounds fresh or frozen peas

1 small bunch fresh mint, the
    leaves stripped from the stalks
    and minced

Kosher salt and freshly ground
    black pepper

1.   In a large sauté pan set over medium heat, cook the bacon until it is crisp. Remove the bacon from the pan and set aside.

2.   Return the pan to the stove and add the peas, sautéing until they are bright green and completely heated through.

3.   Transfer the peas to a warm serving bowl, toss with the mint and reserved bacon, and season to taste with salt and pepper.

GREENS *with* OYSTER SAUCE

THE BEST OYSTER SAUCES ARE MADE with oysters cooked down into a dark and umami-rich slurry. The worst combine various shellfish extracts with sugar, soy, and MSG to approximate the taste of the real thing with less effort and more profit to the manufacturer. You'll need to taste your way to a good one, and that's annoying. I can, though, offer a head start by saying that the condiment is generally recognized to have been invented by a Chinese cook named Lee Kum Sheung, in the late nineteenth century, who had the good sense to make it a business that still stands. Lee Kum Kee oyster sauce is exceptional, if you can find it. Made into a sauce with a little soy sauce and rice wine vinegar, along with a pinch of sugar, it makes for a marvelous drizzle for stir-fried greens, and an exceptional accompaniment to plain steamed rice. Can't find any oyster sauce at all? Swapping in some hoisin sauce instead is no crime, along with perhaps a splash of fish sauce.

2 pounds sturdy greens, such as
    collards or bok choy
1 tablespoon soy sauce
3½ tablespoons best-available
    oyster sauce
Pinch of sugar
2 tablespoons rice wine vinegar
1 tablespoon neutral oil
1 tablespoon finely minced garlic
3 tablespoons chicken stock,
    homemade or low-sodium,
    or water

1. Stem the greens and chop coarsely.
2. Combine the soy sauce, oyster sauce, sugar, and rice vinegar in a bowl and set aside.
3. Place a large skillet or wok over high heat on the stove. Swirl the oil into the pan and when the oil shimmers, add the garlic, then the greens, and stir-fry for 2 to 3 minutes. Add the stock, then cover the skillet and allow to cook for 2 to 3 minutes more, until the greens have softened nicely.
4. Remove the greens from the skillet and place on a warmed platter. Drizzle the reserved sauce over the greens and serve.

BABY BOK CHOY *with* GINGER *and* GARLIC

THIS IS A SIMPLE SAUTÉ, barely a stir-fry, which yields a tangle of greens scented with ginger and garlic. Serve it alongside rice as a main dish, or alongside rice and any protein that's even remotely Asian in its flavors. It is crisp-soft, salty-sweet: a Sondheim song on a plate.

4 heads baby bok choy

2 tablespoons neutral oil, such as canola or grapeseed

4 to 6 cloves garlic, peeled and minced

2 tablespoons minced fresh ginger

Red pepper flakes

4 teaspoons soy sauce

Freshly ground black pepper

1. Cut the baby bok choy in half lengthwise. Cut out the core in the bottom of each cabbage. Remove the stalks, then cut them each in half lengthwise.

2. Heat the oil in a large skillet over medium heat. Add the garlic, ginger, and red pepper flakes to taste, then cook, stirring constantly, for about 45 seconds. Add the bok choy and soy sauce. Stir until evenly coated and sauté for an additional 3 to 4 minutes, until the greens are wilted and the stalks are just beginning to become tender. Season to taste with pepper, adjust the seasonings, and serve on a warmed platter.

COLLARD GREENS *in* POT LIKKER

T HESE LONG-COOKED STURDY GREENS, which you can make with turnip or mustard greens as easily as with collards, look like something you'd get at a steam table meat-and-three restaurant in the American South. They are velvet-textured, soft and pliant, a pale green that belies the immense taste each bite holds. For flavoring the pot likker—the stock that cooks the greens—I generally use a smoked ham hock, available in most large supermarkets, near the lard, and flake the cooked meat into the finished dish. But a smoked turkey leg or wing works brilliantly (same deal with the flaking of the meat) or, if you don't eat meat or can't serve it this evening, you'll certainly cook the meal faster. Just add a few tablespoons of soy or tamari, along with a liberal sprinkling of smoked paprika, to the water you cook the greens in, and it will take you a very long way toward nirvana. Do you save the stock after cooking to use in a subsequent meal? I do!

2 smoked ham hocks or turkey legs or wings, approximately 2 pounds

2 large bunches collard greens or other sturdy greens, such as mustard or turnip

3 tablespoons red wine vinegar

Red pepper flakes

Kosher salt and freshly ground black pepper

1. Fill a large, heavy-bottomed pot with around a gallon of water and set over high heat. Add the smoked meat and allow the water to come almost to a boil, then lower the heat to a simmer and cook, partially covered, for an hour or so, until the meat of the hocks is pulling away from the bones.

2. Remove the hocks from the stock and shred the meat from them, discarding the skin. Reserve. You can make the stock, or pot likker, ahead of time and keep it in the refrigerator or freezer until ready to use.

3. When you're ready to cook the greens, warm the stock in a large, heavy-bottomed pot. As the stock heats, trim the greens of their stalks, then take 3 or 4 of the leaves, stack them on top of one another, and roll them into a cigar. Slice these crosswise into thick strips. Repeat with the remaining leaves.

4. Add the greens to the simmering stock and stir. Allow them to simmer for 20 minutes or so, uncovered, then check their tenderness. They may be beautifully soft and pliant, with a velvet texture. Or they may not. Older greens take longer to cook into submission,

sometimes as long as 90 minutes or so. Patience is a virtue here.

5. As the greens cook, combine the vinegar and red pepper flakes to taste. When the greens are finished, remove them to a warm platter and anoint them with a splash or two of the vinegar, then taste and season with more vinegar if you like, along with salt and pepper to taste.

QUICK-COOKED COLLARD GREENS

FOR SOME THERE IS NO SUBSTITUTION FOR the texture of collard greens cooked forever in the lap of pork-scented liquor until they are silky and soft. But this faster version, which I adapted from a recipe used by the great Alabama chef Frank Stitt, has become a staple of my Sunday suppering—a bright, flavorful take on a classic of southern cuisine. Best, you can cook the collards in the morning, shock them cold in ice water, squeeze them dry, and hold them in the refrigerator until right before you need them. A quick sauté in a hot pan with some olive oil (or butter or bacon grease!) gets them into perfect condition to serve alongside whatever you like, the greens wilted but still holding structure, and phenomenally delicious.

2 large bunches collard greens or other sturdy greens, such as mustard or turnip

2 tablespoons olive oil

4 slices slab or thick-cut bacon, chopped into bâtons

1 large onion, peeled and diced

Red pepper flakes

2 cloves garlic, peeled and smashed

Red wine vinegar

Kosher salt and freshly ground black pepper

1. Trim the greens so you get rid of the stems, then take 3 or 4 of the leaves, stack them on top of one another, and roll them into a cigar. Slice these crosswise into thin strips, slightly thicker than a chiffonade. Repeat with the remaining leaves.

2. Bring a large pot of salted water to boil on the stove and, while it heats, set up a big pot or bowl filled with ice water in your sink. When the water is boiling, add the greens and cook them for 2 to 3 minutes, until they begin to wilt, then drain the pot or fish the greens out of it and put them into the ice bath to stop them from cooking, swirling them around in the ice to cool. Drain the ice bath and squeeze the greens dry, into baseballs you can store on a sheet pan or platter until ready to cook.

3. When you're ready to finish the greens, swirl the oil into a large, wide-bottomed pan or pot set over medium-high heat and, when the oil shimmers, add the bacon. Stir to coat with fat and allow to cook until it sizzles, then add the onion. Cook, stirring, until the onion has started to soften and turn translucent, about 10 minutes. Add red pepper flakes to taste and the garlic and continue to cook until fragrant, another 2 to 3 minutes.

4. Turn the heat to high and add the greens, then cook, stirring and tossing, until they are wilted and glossy with fat, 5 to 7 minutes. Fish out the garlic cloves and mound the greens on a warmed platter, seasoning with salt, black pepper, and a splash or two of vinegar to taste.

FAIRY TALE EGGPLANTS
with GOAT CHEESE *and* MINT

FAIRY TALE EGGPLANTS, PURPLE AND WHITE, the size of a cartoon thumb smashed by a hammer, are to my mind the most beautiful of the eggplant varieties. They are also delicious, less seedy than their big Italian counterparts, and less bitter to boot. Like all eggplants, Fairy Tales take well to the grill, and you can certainly assemble this dish by tossing the eggplants in half of the oil, then grilling them into submission and tossing them lightly with the cheese, before topping them with mint and the Middle Eastern spice blend known as za'atar, if you have any. But knocking them out in a hot oven in a casserole is easy work, and the result makes for an excellent accompaniment to roasted lamb or chicken, or as a main dish to go with rice or couscous. Can't find Fairy Tales at the market? Use Chinese or Japanese eggplants instead, or the Sicilian ones sometimes called Graffiti eggplants. As for the goat cheese, you could substitute a crumbly feta cheese, or a creamy Bulgarian feta, according to your desires.

2 pounds Fairy Tale eggplants, trimmed and halved lengthwise

2 tablespoons kosher salt, or to taste

½ cup olive oil

½ pound fresh goat cheese

¼ cup roughly torn fresh mint leaves

1 or 2 large pinches of za'atar (optional)

1. Heat the oven to 425°F. Put the eggplants onto one or two large rimmed baking sheets and sprinkle with the salt, then drizzle half of the oil over them. Toss to coat and arrange the eggplants, cut side up.

2. Dot the eggplants evenly with the cheese and then drizzle the remaining oil over the dish.

3. Roast in the oven for 35 to 40 minutes, until the eggplants are soft and caramelizing, and the cheese is browned in spots. Top with the mint and, if using, the za'atar.

EGGPLANT PARMESAN

Y OU COULD, IF YOU WANTED TO, dip the eggplant slices in scrambled eggs, then in bread crumbs, and fry them in oil before assembling the casserole. That's a fine way to make eggplant parm. But this method of oven-roasting the eggplant is excellent and a lot easier, and if you let the slices go a little longer than I suggest in the recipe below, you'll get a hard crispness to them that will taste delicious against the soft sweetness of the tomatoes and the creamy mozzarella on top. I like eggplant parm piled on hero rolls for sandwiches, or served alongside a simple bowl of pasta and a salad that's heavy on the red wine vinegar. Scatter red pepper flakes over the top and consume with chilled red wine.

3 medium-large eggplants,
    trimmed at head and tail and
    cut crosswise into 1/2-inch slices
1/4 cup olive oil, plus more for
    brushing eggplant
1 large Spanish onion, peeled and
    cut into small dice
1 large clove garlic, peeled and
    thinly sliced
1 1/2 teaspoons dried oregano
1 teaspoon red pepper flakes,
    or to taste
One 28-ounce can peeled whole
    or crushed tomatoes
1 tablespoon red wine vinegar
1/2 cup fresh basil leaves
Kosher salt and freshly ground
    black pepper
1/2 cup grated Parmesan cheese,
    or to taste
1/2 cup grated mozzarella
1/3 cup dry bread crumbs
1 tablespoon chopped fresh
    oregano leaves (optional)

1. Heat the oven to 450°F. Brush both sides of the eggplant slices with oil and place in a single layer on two or more baking sheets. Roast until the bottoms are golden brown, 10 to 15 minutes, then flip and bake until the other sides are lightly browned. Set aside. Reduce the oven temperature to 375°F.

2. Meanwhile, in a large saucepan set over medium heat, heat 2 tablespoons of the remaining oil until it shimmers, then add the onion to the pan. Sauté until softened and starting to turn translucent, about 10 minutes, then add the garlic, dried oregano, and red pepper flakes and cook for another minute or so. Add the tomatoes and their juices, breaking up whole tomatoes with a spoon. Cover the pan, reduce the heat to low, and simmer for 15 to 20 minutes.

3. Add the vinegar to the tomato mixture along with the basil, and salt and black pepper to taste. Spoon a few tablespoons of the sauce into a medium baking pan or casserole and scatter some Parmesan over it. Put a layer of eggplant over the sauce and cheese. Spread some more sauce and Parmesan over the eggplant, then top with another layer of eggplant. Repeat until you've run out of eggplant, and top with the remaining sauce and Parmesan. Scatter the mozzarella over the top of the casserole.

continued on page 261

4. Put the bread crumbs in a small bowl and moisten them with 1 to 2 tablespoons of the remaining oil, then sprinkle the mixture over the top of the shredded mozzarella, eggplant, and sauce. Bake until the casserole is bubbling and heated all the way through, 30 to 40 minutes, depending on the size of the pan. Allow to rest for 5 to 10 minutes before serving, and shower with fresh oregano if you'd like.

CREAMED MUSHROOMS

HERE IS A DISH TO BUILD OUT of the common mushrooms of the supermarket produce aisle, your buttons and baby bellas, that makes an impressive accompaniment to grilled and roasted meats. Its flavor packs a punch. Double the recipe and you can serve these mushrooms as a main dish with rice or noodles or toast. It is filling, awesome fare.

3 tablespoons neutral oil, such as canola or grapeseed

3 tablespoons unsalted butter

1½ pounds best-quality common mushrooms, ideally cremini or baby bellas, cleaned and sliced

½ teaspoon fresh thyme leaves

Kosher salt and freshly ground black pepper

2 small shallots, peeled and minced

3 tablespoons sherry vinegar

½ cup heavy cream

1. Heat a heavy-bottomed pan over high heat. Once the pan is hot, add the oil. Once the oil shimmers, add the butter. When the butter foams, add the mushrooms and cook, stirring occasionally, until the mushrooms have released their liquid and are golden brown, 15 to 20 minutes.

2. Reduce the heat to medium-low and, using a spoon, create a well in the middle of the mushrooms. Add the thyme, salt and pepper to taste, and the shallots, then sweat them until the shallots have cooked through and become translucent, 3 to 5 minutes.

3. Return the heat to high and add the vinegar to deglaze the pan, then add the cream and reduce the heat so that the cream comes to a very low boil.

4. Check for seasoning. The mushrooms can be reserved until you need to serve them, then reheated over a medium flame. Add a splash of extra cream to loosen, if needed.

MUSHROOMS *with* BUTTER *and* SOY

BUTTER AND SOY IS A DELICIOUS COMBINATION. Try it on warm white rice, a steaming pile of greens, or an old laptop case—regardless, the taste is a sublime velvet of sweet and salty, along with a pop of umami, that fifth taste beyond sweet, sour, bitter, and salty. Serve these mushrooms beside any grilled or roasted meat or, having doubled the recipe, alone on polenta or rice.

½ ounce dried porcini
    mushrooms
5 tablespoons unsalted butter,
    cold, cut into pats
1 clove garlic, peeled and minced
8 to 12 ounces fresh mushrooms,
    wild or cultivated,
    thinly sliced
1 teaspoon fresh thyme leaves
1 tablespoon soy sauce
1 tablespoon heavy cream
1 tablespoon extra-virgin olive oil
Freshly ground black pepper

1. Put the dried mushrooms in a small bowl and cover with about ½ cup boiling water. Allow to steep for 20 minutes. Remove the mushrooms and pat dry, then chop roughly. Strain and reserve the mushroom stock.

2. Melt 2 tablespoons of the butter in a sauté pan set over high heat until it has started to foam. Add the garlic and cook until it starts to sizzle, about 30 seconds. Do not let the garlic brown.

3. Add the fresh and reconstituted mushrooms and the thyme to the pan, and sauté for 3 to 4 minutes, turning until browned. Add about ¼ cup of the mushroom stock to deglaze the surface, using a spoon to scrape at the browned bits. Allow the stock to reduce by half, then turn the heat to medium-low and add the remaining 3 tablespoons butter, whisking to combine, followed by the soy sauce, cream, and oil. Allow the mixture to cook until it thickens a little, then remove from the heat. Taste for seasoning, adding pepper to taste.

A FEW WORDS ABOUT SALAD

—

These meals that you are cooking celebrate something, even if one falls on a Tuesday of no particular significance save the fact that you happen to cook on Tuesdays. The occasion, the dinner itself, is by your definition, if no one else's, *special*. You asked friends and family to come to dinner and to share in a meal unlike the others you generally eat. The food you serve will reflect the distinction: protein and sides assembled with care and served as if at a miniature Thanksgiving, a rehearsal for Christmas or Easter, a weekly Passover, a run-through for a Ramadan feast. Light the candles, dear. I'll carve and we'll get started.

For the most part, salad will play a supporting role in this endeavor: light astringency against the rich luxuriousness of a main course of roasted haunch or slippery, meat-flecked pasta. You might serve salad at the beginning of a Sunday supper, in the American tradition, or at its end, as the Europeans do. (Eating salad first increases vegetable consumption a great deal, for what it's worth, particularly among children.) At Actual Thanksgiving with its copious vegetables and sweetly acidic cranberry sauce, you probably won't serve salad at all. Either way, salad should never be an afterthought. Still, its job in the corporation of Sunday suppers is not in the executive suite.

That is not always the case, of course. While many of the recipes that follow here are auxiliary numbers—crunch to offset softness, acid to counterbalance fat—it is worth pointing out that a single salad can be an outstanding Sunday supper meal. You don't even need a recipe to make one, only an understanding of ratio, balance, and weight, along with full commitment to the service: "Just this!"

The ratio to know is 1:3, acid to oil, a proportion that will deliver excellent emulsification practically no matter the acid or oil you use. Adjust the flavors to your personal preference—sharp lemon juice or mellow sherry vinegar against a neutral oil or fruity olive oil, for instance—and amp up the creaminess or pungency with thickeners such as mustard, cheese, or, in my house, more often than not, mayonnaise. Taste and adjust once you've started, adding a splash of oil if the dressing feels too acidic, or an additional splash of lemon or vinegar it it's overwhelmed.

As for balance, the factors to consider are the usual ones in the flavor game: sweetness, saltiness, sourness, bitterness, and the savory essence of umami, a Japanese neologism derived from the word for "delicious." It is the taste of glutamate, mother's milk, dried mushrooms, soy sauce, Parmesan. For a main course salad to remember, you want a dressing, and a salad beneath it, that combines all five of the basic flavors, practically in every bite.

Weight matters, as well: A heavy velvet dressing wants sturdy greens to coat, not tender little shoots. A light emulsification of lemon juice and oil dresses mesclun beautifully. It is no match for potatoes, beets, or mustard greens. Whisk accordingly.

For a main course salad, I like heavy greens—kale, that beleaguered pop star of the early twenty-first century, is still well loved in my kitchen—matched with dried fruit: crumbled, creamy, tart blue cheese; maybe croutons or salty toasted nuts; bits of bacon; and a thickish dressing of olive oil and salt and garlic and shallots cut through with red wine vinegar, Dijon mustard, and a pinch of red pepper flakes.

That salad turns out slightly differently each time I make it, depending on what's in the larder or store. I might poach a few eggs to plop on top of the finished number, just before serving (use a little less dressing if you follow that lead, as the yolks will help cloak the greens). Or I might omit the meat if I don't have any, or don't want to serve any. I might add some lemon zest to the dressing or swap out the olive oil for neutral grapeseed. So long as the ratio remains, you can't screw it up too badly.

I serve the resulting bowl, a bowl as large as I can make it, a standing rib roast of greens, with a warm baguette or two on the side, some cold salted butter, and carafes of chilled red wine. It is a good meal to follow with a walk to town for chocolate. Look at that character among us who blanched at the sight of the salad when he arrived, before eating it and asking for more. Come on now. Aren't you glad you came to supper?

A BIG KALE SALAD

ONE OF THE MORE FASCINATING ARRIVALS in the supermarkets of early twenty-first-century America was the plastic box of "super greens"—a fresh, triple-washed mixture of dark green baby kale, chard, arugula, spinach, and, occasionally, bok choy. Super greens can form the basis of a terrific Sunday dinner salad, though I generally prefer the heftier approach of using chopped adult kale, which holds up mightily against the dressing for about five minutes, then relaxes into fantastic flavor and texture combined. For mix-ins, to borrow a term of art used in the ice cream industry, I like crumbled blue cheese, though dabs of creamy goat cheese work well if blue cheese is anathema to your family's taste, along with dried cranberries and sometimes croutons and always sliced almonds. Bits of bacon add a dinnertime heft and contribute to the idea that this salad isn't some sort of after-dinner afterthought but a meal in itself.

6 ounces thick-cut bacon,
    cut into bâtons
1 cup sliced almonds
⅓ cup fresh lemon juice
    (from 2 to 4 lemons)
1 heaping teaspoon kosher salt,
    plus more to taste
1 cup extra-virgin olive oil
2 cloves garlic, crushed with the
    flat side of a knife, peeled,
    and minced
16 ounces washed and dried kale
    leaves, thick stems removed
    (weight before trimming)
4 to 6 ounces crumbled
    blue cheese
1 cup dried cranberries
1 tablespoon Dijon mustard
Freshly ground black pepper

1. In a skillet set over medium-high heat, cook the bacon until crisp, 8 to 10 minutes. Using a slotted spoon, remove the bacon to a plate.

2. Wipe out the skillet and set it over medium-low heat. Add the almonds and toast, tossing frequently, until golden brown and fragrant. Dump them onto another plate to cool.

3. In a bowl, combine the lemon juice and salt. Slowly whisk in the oil. Add the garlic, whisk again, and set aside to steep.

4. Working in batches, gather handfuls of the kale and cut it into ribbons about ½ inch thick, and put the kale into a very large bowl. Top with the reserved almonds, the bacon, blue cheese, and cranberries.

5. Whisk the mustard into the oil and lemon juice mixture and continue whisking until it begins to emulsify. Add pepper to taste and, perhaps, a little more salt.

6. Pour half the dressing over the salad and toss. Taste for dressing and salt and add more as needed, tossing to coat thoroughly. The salad can sit for 30 minutes or so, but for no longer than an hour. Toss again right before serving.

HOUSE SALAD DRESSING

IT IS GOOD TO HAVE A HOUSE VINAIGRETTE, a salad dressing that can live in your refrigerator until you need it, or that can be assembled by rote in advance of Sunday dinner by anyone who knows the house well. What follows is mine, though we often change it on the fly by adding herbs, or a little more olive oil, or a different vinegar. Attend to the ratios and seize on the combination of ingredients you like the best. Then use it on well-washed salad greens of whatever combination appeals, always attending to the balance between them, perhaps with some nuts or cheese or dried fruit or shallots or olives or capers strewn about as well. With this vinaigrette you'll be more confident about experimentation, more ready to branch out according to what's available at the market or what's in your refrigerator when it comes time to cook.

1 small clove garlic, peeled, smashed, and minced
2 tablespoons red wine vinegar
1/2 small shallot, peeled and minced
2 teaspoons Dijon mustard
1/2 cup extra-virgin olive oil
Kosher salt and freshly ground black pepper

1. Combine the garlic, vinegar, shallot, and mustard in a small bowl.

2. Slowly whisk in the oil until the dressing emulsifies. Add salt and pepper to taste. Whisk again before using to dress a salad lightly.

LUCALI SALAD

HERE IS SALAD MAKING AS AN ALCHEMICAL ART, a way to take really the cheapest store-bought produce and turn it into something phenomenally delicious to eat—especially off a plate on which you've eaten Sunday gravy (see page 164) or an eggplant parm (see page 259). It is an American-Italian salad to remind some of Grandma, and others of the red-sauce joint by the bay; the secret weapons are red wine vinegar and the spice blend known as lemon pepper. I learned how to make it from Mark Iacono, the laconic pizza chef who runs Lucali restaurant in Carroll Gardens, Brooklyn, who serves it only when he remembers to make it in the afternoon, which is not often. "You can't rush this one," he told me. "The tomatoes need time to bleed out." You'll have plenty of leftover dressing. That's a good thing.

FOR THE SALAD

5 smallish tomatoes, halved and cut into fifths

½ smallish red onion, peeled and thinly sliced

1 celery stalk with leaves, ideally from the heart, chopped

18 canned, pitted black olives, plus 2 tablespoons olive brine

2 teaspoons kosher salt

1 teaspoon coarsely ground black pepper

1 teaspoon lemon pepper

⅓ cup olive oil

1 teaspoon red wine vinegar

1 head iceberg lettuce, outer leaves and brown bits removed, roughly torn

FOR THE DRESSING

1 cup plus 2 tablespoons olive oil

½ cup red wine vinegar

½ teaspoon kosher salt

½ teaspoon coarsely ground black pepper

½ teaspoon lemon pepper

1. **Make the salad.** Combine the tomatoes, onion, and celery in a large bowl. Add the olives, bruising each slightly between your index finger and thumb, and the olive brine.

2. Add the salt, black pepper, lemon pepper, oil, and vinegar to the bowl, and mix gently with your hands or a wooden spoon. Cover with plastic wrap and place in the refrigerator for a minimum of 20 minutes and up to 2 hours.

3. Wash and dry the lettuce, then put it into a bowl, cover, and place in the refrigerator until ready to assemble the salad.

4. **Make the dressing.** (There will be a lot left over, which you can cover and store in the refrigerator for up to a few weeks.) Combine the oil, vinegar, salt, black

pepper, and lemon pepper in a jar or large bowl. Cover the jar and shake until emulsified, or use a whisk to achieve the same result in the bowl. Set aside.

5. Assemble the salad. Spoon onto a large platter enough of the tomato mixture and accumulated juices to cover its bottom. Arrange some of the iceberg across the top of the tomatoes and drizzle a little dressing over it. Add some more of the tomato mixture, then another round of the iceberg. Drizzle with some more of the dressing and then repeat. Serve immediately, so the lettuce does not wilt, with Italian bread, perhaps alongside or after spaghetti or eggplant parm.

COUNTRY SALAD

I HAD A VERSION OF THIS SALAD at the lunch my father took me to after I graduated from high school, at the restaurant Odeon in downtown Manhattan, and I've had it a zillion times since—there and elsewhere, most often at home. Adding a few poached eggs to the top of the salad just before serving adds warmth and a delicious slickness to the dressing once the yolks are pierced. Serve in advance of grilled meats, or serve on its own for a lighter night of eating—with baguettes to be torn open and passed around at the table.

⅓ pound slab bacon, cut into
    lardons
½ cup fresh bread crumbs
1 tablespoon fresh lemon juice
2 tablespoons red wine vinegar
1 clove garlic, peeled and minced
1 tablespoon Dijon mustard
½ cup extra-virgin olive oil
⅓ cup good-quality blue cheese,
    crumbled
Kosher salt and freshly ground
    black pepper
2 heads romaine lettuce

1. Fry the bacon over medium heat until almost crisp. Remove with a slotted spoon and set aside. Reserve a splash of bacon fat.

2. Return the bacon pan to the heat and add the bread crumbs, tossing until just golden. Remove from the pan and reserve.

3. Combine the lemon juice, vinegar, garlic, and mustard in a small bowl. Slowly whisk in the oil and the reserved bacon fat until the dressing emulsifies. Add a tablespoon of blue cheese and whisk again. Season to taste with salt and pepper.

4. Roughly chop the lettuce and put it into a salad bowl. Add the bread crumbs, the reserved bacon, and the remaining cheese, then the dressing. Toss to mix. Serve immediately.

CAESAR SALAD

THEY KILLED CAESAR WITH A CHICKEN BREAST. They grilled a fist of it dry and cut and fanned out its slices over romaine slicked in watery dressing and served it for dinner, and that was when this once-mighty American salad fell lifeless to the dining room floor. Caesar salad topped with salmon. With chickpeas. With steak. You can make a Caesar salad that way if you want to, and make it the entirety of your Sunday meal, but really it's better as a starter or side dish, a classic old-school salad of the sort that you might see prepared tableside in an old-school steak house. As at that steak house, the most important thing about the salad is its dressing: anchovy-salty, really quite thick, so it cloaks the lettuce fully. Attend to that well.

4 to 6 salted anchovy fillets, rinsed, dried, and minced, or to taste, plus more for serving
2 tablespoons fresh lemon juice
1 clove garlic, peeled and minced
1/3 cup grated Parmesan cheese, plus more Parmesan for serving
1 teaspoon Dijon mustard
1 egg yolk or 1 tablespoon mayonnaise
1 tablespoon Worcestershire sauce
Kosher salt and freshly ground black pepper
2/3 cup plus 3 tablespoons extra-virgin olive oil
2 cups 1-inch cubes Italian bread
2 heads romaine lettuce, roughly cut, well rinsed and dried

1. Heat the oven to 350°F. In a food processor, combine the anchovies, lemon juice, garlic, cheese, mustard, egg yolk, Worcestershire, and a sprinkle of salt and pepper. Slowly drizzle 2/3 cup of the oil into the mixture as the processor works, emulsifying the dressing. (You may not need all the oil.) When the dressing has achieved the consistency of a loose mayonnaise, remove it from the food processor and set aside.

2. Arrange the pieces of bread on a baking sheet and drizzle with the remaining 3 tablespoons oil. Place in the oven until the croutons begin to turn golden, about 10 minutes, then remove and set aside.

3. In a large bowl, toss the lettuce and the croutons with just enough dressing to cover the romaine as a sauce would pasta. Place in a serving bowl and grate Parmesan over the top. Add extra anchovies to taste.

GRILLED CAESAR SALAD

T HIS IS A COOL TRICK for a salad to accompany steaks. If you set yourself up properly, you can cook it as the meat rests. I learned how to make it from the same guy who taught me to make dry-rubbed steaks (see page 93), the chef Alan Ashkinaze, who spent years working for Laurent Manrique before setting out on his own as the executive chef of the Manhattan steak house Gallagher's. The lime zest and white balsamic in the vinaigrette are particularly excellent additions to what otherwise is a fairly typical take on a Caesar, albeit one prepared above glowing coals. They're fancy. Sometimes we're fancy. If you want an easier version, make grilled lettuce (see page 276).

FOR THE CAESAR DRESSING
1 clove garlic, peeled and minced
4 anchovy fillets, rinsed and
   minced
3 large egg yolks
2 teaspoons Dijon mustard
3/4 cup extra-virgin olive oil
1 tablespoon Worcestershire sauce
1 tablespoon red wine vinegar
Kosher salt and freshly ground
   black pepper

FOR THE VINAIGRETTE
1 tablespoon lime zest
Juice of 1 lime (about
   2 tablespoons)
1 tablespoon white balsamic
   vinegar
1/2 cup extra-virgin olive oil
Kosher salt and freshly ground
   black pepper

FOR THE SALAD
2 tablespoons extra-virgin olive oil
2 heads romaine lettuce, tops and bottoms
   trimmed neatly and the heads cut lengthwise
   into quarters
1/2 cup grated Parmesan cheese

1. **Make the Caesar dressing.** Put the minced garlic into a medium bowl and add the minced anchovies. Using a whisk, mix and mash these ingredients together until they form a paste. Add the egg yolks and mustard, and begin to whisk them with the paste. Add a small stream of oil while continuing to whisk. Add more oil, whisking all the while, until the dressing begins to emulsify. (You can do this in a food processor, and I often do.) Add the Worcestershire and continue to whisk until the dressing achieves a mayonnaise-like consistency. Add the red wine vinegar, whisk to combine, then season to taste with salt and pepper. Set aside.

2. **Make the vinaigrette.** Combine the lime zest, lime juice, balsamic vinegar, and oil in a small bowl, and whisk to combine. Season to taste with salt and pepper. Set aside.

3. **Make the salad.** Drizzle the oil over the quartered heads of lettuce. Lightly grill the lettuce over a dying

charcoal fire or a gas burner set on low, for 15 to 20 seconds on each side, until they have a light goldenness; remove to a platter. Using a pastry brush or a small spoon, paint the Caesar dressing over the lettuce, making sure to get dressing between the leaves. Return the lettuces to the edges of the grill, sprinkle with the cheese, and cover for 30 seconds to allow the cheese to soften and toast. Remove the lettuce to a platter and drizzle with the lime vinaigrette. Serve a piece alongside each serving of whatever else it is you've grilled.

GRILLED LETTUCE

ETTUCES OF ALL SORTS DO nicely on the grill, softening slightly at their centers and charring beautifully at their tips. Their bitterness is a fine counterpart to the sweet spiciness of a lot of grilled foods. Mustard and mayonnaise serve as emulsifiers for the dressing here, while anchovies, garlic, and vinegar provide a welcome kick. Make sure to paint the dressing into the crevices between the leaves, so that while the lettuce caramelizes slightly on the exterior, there is still warm creaminess within.

FOR THE DRESSING

1 clove garlic, peeled and minced

6 anchovy fillets, rinsed and minced

2 teaspoons mayonnaise (store-bought is fine)

2 teaspoons Dijon mustard

1/2 cup extra-virgin olive oil

2 tablespoons cider vinegar

Kosher salt and freshly ground black pepper

FOR THE SALAD

2 tablespoons extra-virgin olive oil

2 heads lettuce, tops and bottoms trimmed and the heads cut lengthwise into quarters

1/2 cup grated Parmesan cheese

1.   Build a fire in your grill, leaving one side free of coals. When the coals are covered with gray ash and the temperature is medium (you can hold your hand 5 inches above the coals for 5 to 7 seconds), you are ready to cook. (For a gas grill, turn all the burners to high, lower the cover, and heat for 15 minutes, then turn the burners to medium.)

2.   Meanwhile, **make the dressing.** Put the minced garlic into a bowl and add the minced anchovies. Using a whisk, mix and mash these ingredients together until they form a paste. Add the mayonnaise and mustard and whisk. Add the oil, whisking all the while, then the vinegar. Season to taste with salt and pepper. Set aside.

3.   **Make the salad.** Drizzle the oil over the quartered heads of lettuce. Lightly grill these directly over the hot coals for 15 to 20 seconds on each side, until lightly golden, then remove to the cool side of the grill. Using a pastry brush if you have one or a small spoon if you do not, paint the dressing over the lettuce, making sure to get dressing between the leaves. Sprinkle the lettuce with the cheese and cover the grill for 1 or 2 minutes to allow the cheese to melt and the lettuce to soften further. Remove the lettuce to a platter and serve.

TOMATO SALAD

NOT REALLY A RECIPE SO much as a late-summer exhortation: When there are good tomatoes in the market, fat and yielding, get a lot of them, of different colors and sizes, to serve for dinner. Slice them thick and fan them across a platter. Add some rounds of red onion as well, if you like, or get some fresh mozzarella in there, and join it with soft basil leaves. A healthy spray of salt across the top, a lashing of good olive oil, and a splash of balsamic vinegar and you're done. Add plenty of bread to mop up the juices, then serve corn on the cob (see page 245). Was there meant to be grilled chicken as well? No one will miss it.

TOMATO *and* WATERMELON SALAD

IN A RESTAURANT, AT THIS POINT IN HISTORY, tomatoes and watermelon can seem a dated preparation, the salad-station equivalent of fried calamari with lemon aioli. But we're not running a restaurant here, and this is still one of the best summertime salads in existence. It makes a fine accompaniment to any warm-weather family feast; it makes a terrific centerpiece if it's very, very hot, before a dinner of sweet potatoes. Get the best tomatoes you can find, and go lighter on the dressing than you might think. If you can find Bulgarian feta, which imparts an amazing creaminess along with its salty bite, so much the better. But the feta you can find will still be great.

4 to 6 large tomatoes, ideally heirloom varieties, cut into 1¼-inch cubes

1 small seedless watermelon, cut into 1¼-inch cubes

1 teaspoon kosher salt, plus more to taste

¼ cup extra-virgin olive oil

2 tablespoons sherry vinegar

Freshly ground black pepper

1 cup crumbled feta cheese

1. Combine the cubed tomatoes and watermelon in a large nonreactive bowl and toss gently to combine. Add the salt and let stand for 5 to 10 minutes while you prepare the dressing.

2. Whisk together the oil and vinegar in a small bowl and season to taste with salt and pepper.

3. Add the cheese to the tomatoes and watermelon, then the dressing, and toss gently to combine.

POTATO SALAD

I HARDLY EVER PEEL POTATOES, BELIEVING both that there are a lot of nutrients in the skin and that the time spent peeling them is better used for making other dishes. But you certainly could do so here if you'd like the salad to be what restaurant cooks call soigné— elegant in the extreme.

3 pounds Yukon gold or
    red potatoes, scrubbed and
    cut into eighths
2 tablespoons kosher salt, plus
    more to taste
1 cup mayonnaise, homemade
    or store-bought
2 tablespoons cider vinegar
3 tablespoons Dijon mustard
Freshly ground black pepper
2 celery stalks, trimmed and diced
1 small red onion, peeled
    and diced
2 slices bacon, cooked crisp and
    crumbled (optional)
2 scallions, both green and white
    parts, thinly sliced

1. Place the potatoes in a large pot and cover with water, then add 2 tablespoons salt. Set the pot over high heat and bring to a boil, then turn down the heat slightly and cook until the potatoes are just barely tender when pierced with a fork, 10 to 15 minutes. Save about 1/2 cup of the potato cooking water, then drain the potatoes well and return to the pot. Cover the pot with a clean kitchen towel and allow the potatoes to steam for an additional 15 to 20 minutes.

2. Meanwhile, combine the mayonnaise, vinegar, mustard, and pepper to taste, and whisk to combine. Thin the mixture slightly with a little of the reserved potato cooking water, then taste it and adjust the seasonings to your liking. (If you're well and truly American, you may want to add a little more mayonnaise.)

3. Put the warm potatoes into a large bowl along with the celery and onion, and add the dressing to the bowl, folding everything together carefully with a rubber spatula. Add the crumbled bacon, if using, and toss. Taste and adjust the seasonings again.

4. Cover the bowl and place in the refrigerator for an hour or so to allow the flavors to meld, then remove and serve at or a little below room temperature, garnished with the scallions.

GRILLED FINGERLING POTATOES *with* CHIPOTLE

A VINEGARY POTATO SALAD WITH BACON is one of the great Germanish summertime traditions. Here I've added a Mexican accent in the form of the canned smoked jalapeño known as chipotle chile en adobo. (A small can, well covered, will keep for months in the refrigerator.) Its smokiness echoes the bacon, and the spiciness is a welcome addition to the mix.

2 pounds fingerling potatoes

1 tablespoon kosher salt, plus more to taste

4 slices slab or thick-cut bacon

2 medium red onions, peeled and thinly sliced

5 tablespoons extra-virgin olive oil

Freshly ground black pepper

4 tablespoons red wine vinegar

1 chipotle chile en adobo, or to taste, mashed and minced

1. Put the potatoes in a large pot and cover with 2 inches of water and the salt, then set over high heat until it comes to a boil. Cook for 5 to 7 minutes. Drain the potatoes, place on a baking sheet, and allow to cool slightly, then cut the potatoes in half lengthwise. (You can do this ahead of time, if you like, up to a day ahead. Just store, covered, in the refrigerator.)

2. Meanwhile, cook the bacon in a sauté pan set over medium-high heat until crisp. Reserve the bacon and, in a small bowl, a few tablespoons of the rendered fat.

3. Light a fire in a charcoal grill, or set a gas grill to high. If you have a strong vent in your kitchen, you may use a grill pan set on your stove over high heat. If using live fire or a gas grill, cook over medium heat.

4. Put the potatoes and the sliced onions in a large bowl and toss gently with 2 tablespoons of the oil, and salt and pepper to taste. Working in batches, grill the potatoes, cut side down, on the grill until they have developed a light char, 2 to 3 minutes. Grill the onions until they are charred, 4 to 6 minutes per side. Return the potatoes and onions to the bowl.

5. For the dressing, combine the remaining 3 tablespoons oil, a tablespoon or more of the bacon fat to taste, the vinegar, and the chipotle in a small bowl, then whisk to emulsify. Add salt and pepper to taste. Add the dressing to the potato-and-onion mixture and toss gently to combine. Let sit for 20 minutes to allow the flavors to penetrate the potatoes. Crumble the bacon over the top and serve.

CHICKEN SALAD

I SPENT MY COLLEGE YEARS WORKING in a restaurant and in the small take-out shop the kitchen ran alongside the dining room. The clientele ran to professors and actors from the repertory theater down the street, local professionals with little time on their hands for cooking. One of the best dishes I made there was for the shop: chicken salad, a righteous, old-line WASP version of it, down to the use of grapes, jarred mayonnaise, and roasted walnuts. It was and remains a perfect summertime picnic dinner. What differentiates it from the chicken salad most of us make (apart perhaps from the grapes and walnuts) is that it is a purpose-made chicken salad. It contains no leftovers. Instead, you poach a whole chicken—poach two if it's to be dinner for more than six, and double the dressing—then strip the cooled bird down to the bone: moist, flavorful meat from breast to thigh. The poached meat reduces the need for mayonnaise and allows the chicken flavor to sing. Discard the skin and save the poaching liquid as stock. (You can omit the Bibb lettuce serving cups if that feels too fancy, and just make a raft of sandwiches instead.)

FOR THE CHICKEN

1 whole chicken, 3 to 4 pounds
1 bay leaf
1 carrot, peeled and cut in half
1 celery stalk, trimmed and
    cut in half
10 to 12 black peppercorns

FOR THE SALAD

2 celery stalks, trimmed and finely
    chopped
1 small bunch green or red grapes,
    rinsed and cut in half
1 handful roasted walnuts, roughly
    chopped
1 cup mayonnaise (store-bought
    is fine), or to taste

2 tablespoons fresh lemon juice (juice
    of 1/2 lemon)
Kosher salt and freshly ground
    black pepper
Bibb lettuce leaves
1 tablespoon chopped fresh
    tarragon leaves

1.   **Make the chicken.** Combine the chicken, bay leaf, carrot, celery, and peppercorns in a heavy pot with a lid and just cover with water. Cover the pot and bring to a boil, then reduce the heat to low and simmer for 30 to 35 minutes. Remove the chicken to cool, then strain the stock and reserve for another use.

2.   When the chicken has cooled sufficiently to touch, remove the skin and discard, then tear the meat from the carcass. Roughly chop the meat into chunks and place it in a large bowl. Cover and place in the

continued on next page

refrigerator to cool some more, or until you're ready to prepare the salad.

3. **Make the salad.** To the chicken in the bowl, add the celery, grapes, and walnuts, then the mayonnaise and lemon juice and stir well to combine. Add salt and pepper to taste (and a touch more mayonnaise, if necessary). Serve in cups of lettuce leaves, garnished with tarragon, or in sandwiches.

MAYONNAISE

You can certainly make your own mayonnaise—homemade mayonnaise is excellent, and here is a recipe for it. But my chicken salad relies on the jarred stuff from the supermarket, by which I mean Hellmann's, which is labeled as Best Foods west of the Rocky Mountains. In southern states you will find devotees of Duke's. Elsewhere you may find people who cook with Miracle Whip, a salad dressing condiment developed by Kraft as a less expensive alternative to mayonnaise. But Miracle Whip is not mayonnaise. It is, in my opinion, a terrible addition to chicken salad.

1 large egg yolk

1 heaping teaspoon Dijon mustard

1 tablespoon fresh lemon juice

1/4 teaspoon kosher salt

3/4 to 1 cup neutral oil, such as canola or grapeseed

Put the egg yolk, mustard, lemon juice, salt, and 1 teaspoon cold water into a medium bowl and whisk until frothy. Continue whisking while you add the oil, drip by drip, until the mixture begins to emulsify and turn thick and mayonnaise-like, at which point you can begin to add the oil in a thin stream until the mixture has achieved the consistency of actual mayonnaise.

COLESLAW

WHAT FOLLOWS IS A RECIPE for a basic coleslaw, which means different things to different people. Mine has a mayonnaise-based dressing. For a lighter version, you could reduce the amount of mayonnaise by half and bring in a half cup of buttermilk or sour cream to replace it. Those who enjoy a tarter slaw might increase the amount of cider vinegar. To shred the vegetables, you can use a food processor or have at them with a sharp knife. I love this salad with fried fish and chicken, and on sandwiches of all kinds. What, no celery seeds? You can add a spray of them if you wish.

2 large carrots, trimmed and
   shredded
1 head green cabbage (about
   2 pounds), outer leaves
   discarded, cored and shredded
1 cup mayonnaise (store-bought
   is fine)
¼ cup cider vinegar
1 tablespoon sugar
2 teaspoons kosher salt, or
   to taste

1. Toss the shredded carrots and cabbage together in a large bowl.

2. Combine the mayonnaise, vinegar, sugar, and salt in a small bowl and whisk to combine. Taste and adjust the seasonings.

3. Pour most of the dressing over the carrots and cabbage and toss gently to spread the coating throughout the slaw. Add the rest of the dressing and toss again. Refrigerate for an hour or so before serving.

PICKLEBACK SLAW

Finished with those great pickles you got at the farmers' market or specialty store? Don't throw out the brine when you're done! It keeps for a good long time in the refrigerator, and will come to good ends. The liquid in which great pickles come, sweet and vinegary, with a pop of spice, is a great secret ingredient—useful for braising chicken or pork, for enlivening Bloody Marys, even as a simple shot to accompany a cold beer and an ounce or so of cheap bourbon. (It's less amazing when you're using the commercial stuff, sweetened with high-fructose corn syrup.) Here, it delivers a thrum of flavor in the dressing to accompany a simple coleslaw, and you can use it alongside most grilled or roasted meats, fried fish, or as a fine side dish for a sandwich. Pickleback slaw made with the vinegar that accompanies pickled jalapeños is particularly fine.

1 small head green cabbage

1 small head red cabbage

2 carrots, peeled and julienned

2 tart apples, such as Granny
   Smith, peeled and julienned

½ cup mayonnaise (store-bought
   is fine)

3 tablespoons juice from a jar of
   good pickles or good pickle
   relish

1 tablespoon Dijon mustard

1 tablespoon cider vinegar

2 teaspoons hot pepper sauce,
   such as Frank's, or to taste

Kosher salt and freshly ground
   black pepper

1. Remove the tough or damaged leaves from the cabbages, then cut them in half and remove the core from each side. Cut each half in half and slice each resulting quarter into thin ribbons. Mix with the carrots and apples in a large nonreactive bowl.

2. In a separate bowl, whisk together the mayonnaise, pickle juice, mustard, vinegar, hot pepper sauce, and salt and black pepper to taste.

3. Pour the dressing over the cabbage and toss. Season to taste. The coleslaw may be covered with plastic wrap and refrigerated. Toss again before serving.

A NICE PARTY

—

N ot all these dinners I'm writing about need be taken around a table, indoors. It would be nice, for instance, to have one on a beach: a clambake at sunset. It would be nice to have one in a field, under live oak and Spanish moss, with lanterns hanging from low branches, everyone picking at barbecued hog. How about lamb roasted over an open fire, somewhere in a snowfield in Patagonia, everyone bundled in colorful blankets, stamping around in fur-lined boots? You've seen the spreads in glossy magazines: beautiful people in beautiful clothes eating beautiful food in beautiful places. It would be nice, occasionally, to be like them. Wouldn't it?

It would. It's nice out there. I once helped Quealy Watson, a chef in San Antonio, smoke a goat and a couple of ducks in the garden of a grand home in the city's King William neighborhood, for a meal he served to more than a dozen friends. And even if all we were doing was cooking up some food pornography for a magazine spread (and that's exactly what we were doing), there was still something astonishing about how the evening came together in a combination of laughter and deliciousness. We stood on the lawn drinking margaritas and dipping chips into his Tex-Asian version of queso, wrapping bits of goat in warm corn tortillas and adorning them with salsa and crema, and even those of us with male-pattern baldness and rumpled khakis felt beautiful, part of something at once magical and real.

Of course most of us don't have access to a beach, to a field, to a redoubt in Argentina. Not all of us have friends with grand homes in old neighborhoods. But there might be a park nearby. You might have a yard of some sort, or an alleyway running beside the house, a sidewalk, a porch. Take advantage of these, every once in a while. Cooking something delicious and serving it under the sky can confer beauty on all who are present, even when there's a sodium-vapor streetlight playing the part of the moon and the stars.

A bold menu helps. It makes a statement: that goat, for example; that lamb; those clams and lobsters and potatoes wrapped in canvas under the sand. Manny Howard, my oldest kitchen companion, came up with a great one, a fever dream of a meal for families and friends, first knocked out in a postage-stamp concrete yard in south Brooklyn, later in driveways and gardens: a simple supper of oysters and fries.

It was in some ways the simplest of endeavors. Manny opened oysters, regular as a metronome; served them with lemon, horseradish, and glasses of wine: a bushel of oysters, two bushels of oysters, more. I stood next to him and fried potatoes in a pot filled with gallons of peanut oil: pound after pound of them, each serving salted and doused with malt vinegar, then tonged into a small paper boat of the sort you can get at the restaurant supply shop, ten dollars a case. One year someone brought along a dozen hot dogs for the kids. I fried those too, and the following year I fried a lot more: rippers, some call them, for the way the heat breaks open the casings on the sausages, leaving them fragrant and crisp.

And that was that. We served no salad, no side dishes, no dessert. And it soon became a tradition for the two of us, sporadically to serve this project meal with an eccentric menu that just so happens to be fantastically delicious. One year Manny got some hay bales for people to sit on. You could always add a keg of beer. (We sure did.) String some Christmas lights in a tree. Invite that family with the instruments and the beautiful voices. Sunday suppers aren't really parties, I know. Their intent is simply communion with family and friends. But sometimes a party is great. And oysters, fries, and fried hot dogs make for a nice party indeed.

Of course it's a project. And project cooking demands forethought. It requires planning. It asks for special equipment: a propane hob, for instance, and the big pot and the implements you'll need to fish the fries and hot dogs out of the oil. (I like what the professionals call a spider, a sort of mesh skimmer, but I've used a wire basket as well.) It may well invite you to learn new skills—how to open oysters chief among them (see page 292).

But that is okay. Sunday suppering should welcome ambition. The challenge of the new and the different can be key to keeping a tradition alive and exciting, not just for the cook but also for all those who take part in the exercise. So start small, if you like. But start. Pop open some oysters. Or clams! Cut a few potatoes and make mock frites (see page 242), then fry a couple hot dogs in oil when you're done. Do it again a few months later. Soon enough maybe you'll find yourself wanting to scale up the operation, outside. That's the plan.

FRENCH FRIES

THIS IS ONE OF THOSE RECIPES THAT YOU can absolutely scale down to cook inside, in a heavy-bottomed pot with high sides, but if you're cooking for a crowd, it is far easier to do outside on a propane hob, with a worktable set up beside it to hold your fries in stages as you cook them, serially, over time—just as if you worked at a dodgy burger stand down by the bad part of town. The double frying of the potatoes gives them a fantastic crispness and a sweet, luscious interior. You'll want a lot of potatoes and a lot of oil— probably close to 4 gallons for one of those deep turkey-frying pots that so often come with the propane hobs, though if you're just practicing with a half dozen potatoes, 6 or 8 cups of oil will do. You'll want as well: a couple deep stainless-steel bowls; a candy thermometer so you can keep track of the temperature of the oil; a wire basket or one of those wire-mesh skimmers, called spiders, to fish the fries out when they're finished; and a few baking sheets equipped with wire-mesh racks, on which you can drain the potatoes of excess oil. Finally, buying some paper food trays of the sort that that dodgy burger stand would use (they're available at restaurant supply shops and, as always, online) helps to serve them to a crowd. Serve the fries as they're finished, with malt vinegar or bowls of ketchup, mustard, and mayonnaise as condiments, alongside a lot of grilled sausages and a giant kale salad or, as we do, with raw oysters and fried hot dogs.

Cook this recipe only once and you'll hate me. Knock it down three or four times over the course of a season and you'll feel confident and proud of our relationship. Party hard, but party fair.

Large, long Idaho potatoes

Peanut or vegetable oil

Kosher salt

1. Fill a large bowl with ice water. Peel the potatoes and cut them into ½-inch sticks. Place the potato sticks into the water and allow to soak for from 30 minutes to overnight, then rinse them well with cold water.

2. Heat the oil in a heavy-bottomed pot set over medium heat, using a candy thermometer to mark when the temperature registers 280° to 290°F. Cook the potatoes in batches for 5 to 9 minutes, until their color has paled and they've started almost to be semitranslucent. Remove the fries from the oil with a skimmer or wire basket and place on a sheet pan to rest for 15 to 20 minutes.

3. Heat the oil to 375°F. Fry the oil-blanched potatoes, in batches, for 2 to 5 minutes, until crisp and golden brown. Remove from the oil, shaking to remove excess oil, and dump into a large bowl. Repeat in batches until there are no more potatoes. Add salt to taste, toss, and serve with malt vinegar and condiments.

HOW TO FRY HOT DOGS

YOU HAVE NO DOUBT MADE HOT DOGS in a skillet on a stove. Even those whose cooking experience comes down to just boxed mac and cheese and mixing granola and jam into yogurt have probably at some point tipped a few franks into a pan and sizzled them tight in butter or oil. The dogs are done when the dogs are done—either just heated through or blistered and dark, nearly burned. Children and adults alike thrill to the result, whether they eat the dog solo or encase it in a bun with mustard or ketchup.

Frying hot dogs is simply a more aggressive run at the same recipe. You can do it on a stove top with a deep-sided heavy pot with an inch or two of neutral oil in it—peanut oil is great, but any neutral oil with a high smoke point, such as canola or grapeseed, will do. But frying outside, in a big pot set over a propane hob with three or four inches of oil in it (see page 74), is the way to do it for a crowd. Heat the oil as you would for fried chicken, using a candy thermometer to track its progress, aiming for a temperature of 350° to 375°F. Then slide a few hot dogs into the fat and watch as they sizzle and pop until their casings burst, creating a torn and beautiful exterior. Tong the dogs onto a rack to drain briefly, then serve on toasted buns. Want more rips, more texture? Create more surface area on the franks by slashing them lightly with a chef's knife before frying, and watch as they tighten and flex in response. They are done when you say they are.

HOW TO OPEN OYSTERS

OPENING OYSTERS IS NOT SOMETHING YOU want to do for the very first time at a Sunday supper. People will tell you it's easy work, and it is. But it's not easy the first time you do it, nor the second and maybe not the third. Opening oysters rewards practice, same as in tennis and target shooting, playing music and driving in snow. You should do it a lot until you can do it well, and then perhaps you will do it all the time.

You'll need an oyster knife. Regional differences in oysters lead to regional differences in the sort of knives used to open them, but in general they are stout little fellows with wide, dulled blades that come to a sharpened point at the tip. Don't buy one blind off the Internet. Ask your fishmonger which sort is best to use for the oysters he or she generally sells and get a similar one, or do the same with the fellows at the raw bar near the train station or in the chic little seafood place downtown. They'll show you.

You'll also need a couple of dish towels, to help hold the shells and, perchance, to protect the hand that holds them tight to your cutting board. (If you're nervous, wear a heavy work glove on that hand. You can spend a lot of money on a fancy chain-mail glove, or get a decent cut-resistant set from the hardware store for around ten dollars.)

Now consider the oysters before you. You should have a dozen, at least, for this first exercise. Each has a top and a bottom shell. The bottom shell is the one that is more deeply cupped than the other, and it is where the flesh of the oyster resides.

Place the oyster before you with the cupped side down, and with the narrow, hinged end facing in your direction. Grip the shell with your nondominant hand and use your other hand to work the tip of the oyster knife into the hinge. Push gently at the hinge while moving the handle of the knife down and up, to the left and right, as if inserting a key into a sticky lock and turning it. The combination of light force and torque should break the hinge and allow you to insert the knife into the oyster. Success! It is this action that you should pay attention to most, for it is the one you will repeat again and again, opening oysters. Learn the intricacies of the "lock" in each oyster's shell and opening an oyster will be no different from entering your home at the end of a long workday.

The rest is cleanup and service. Slide the knife around the outside of the shell, loosening the top from the bottom. (Try not to lose too much of the liquor that surrounds the flesh!) Use the knife to scrape the oyster from the top shell and allow it to drop into the bottom cup. Discard the top shell, flat and luminous.

Now separate the flesh of the oyster from the bottom cup. Scrape the knife along the inside of the shell, under the meat. Once it has separated, the oyster is ready. Use the tip of the knife to remove any spare bits of shell, and either place it gently on ice or eat it straight from the shell. People serve oysters with mignonette, cocktail sauce, lemon juice, hot sauce. But you're practicing here. Just eat the thing raw and repeat, eleven more times, until you're through those first dozen oysters.

And here's a serious proposition: Do it every night for a week, a dozen oysters each night. You'll think me ridiculous at some point, no doubt. But at the end of the exercise, you'll have what the academics call a core competency. You'll know how to open oysters.

ON COCKTAIL SAUCE AND MIGNONETTE

I LIKE MY OYSTERS RAW. I don't truck with cocktail sauce or mignonette, with lemon juice or hot sauce or shaved horseradish. I like the pure saline sweetness of a cold oyster that tastes only of the water in which it was raised, and I thrill to the differences that each variety brings, from the soft almost brackish quality of the ones from shallow bay water and the firm intensity of the ones that come from cold ocean water sweeping in across Block Island Sound. Here the creaminess of a deep-cupped West Coast oyster raised in Pacific cold; there the coppery funk of a plate-shaped Belon from a warmer subtidal cove in Maine. Why try to augment this perfection? Why get in its way?

It is an unpopular opinion, among most of my acquaintance. Many feel a drizzle of acidity is necessary to oyster enjoyment, a zing of hot pepper or lash of horseradish fire. They love the interplay of tomato and salt liquor, the sweetness of shallot against the briny slipperiness of the oyster itself. And so I serve cocktail sauce with my oysters, even if I use it only to daub on oyster crackers between runs of raw flesh. I make a mignonette, as well, and if I sip at it only sometimes, off the edge of a teaspoon, to taste its balance of acid and sweet, I recognize that for some it makes oysters taste even better than mine do raw. There will be cut lemons at my raw bar, and a snowy pile of grated fresh horseradish, as well.

I won't put them on my oysters. But others will. And I'm happy to serve them. That is the point of the game.

COCKTAIL SAUCE

YOU CAN MAKE THIS COCKTAIL sauce with straight ketchup and a lot of horseradish, lemon juice, and Worcestershire sauce, but I think the combination of ketchup and what the Kraft Heinz company calls chili sauce makes for the most recognizably excellent version of the dip. If you're not interested in cooking with processed food, omit the ketchup products entirely, put a pint of cherry tomatoes into a food processor and add the rest of the ingredients, then pulse until you've achieved a rough puree.

1/2 cup chili sauce

1/2 cup ketchup

1 tablespoon freshly grated horseradish or
    prepared horseradish, drained, or to taste

Kosher salt

1 1/2 teaspoons hot pepper sauce, such as Frank's, or to taste

1 tablespoon fresh lemon juice, or to taste

1 tablespoon chopped fresh flat-leaf parsley

Freshly ground black pepper

In a medium bowl, combine the chili sauce, ketchup, horseradish, salt, hot pepper sauce, lemon juice, and parsley and stir to combine. Season with black pepper and add more salt, horseradish, hot pepper sauce, and lemon juice to taste. Cover and refrigerate until you're ready to serve.

MIGNONETTE SAUCE

THIS SIMPLE SAUCE CAN BE MADE with red or white wine vinegar, but I like the gentleness of the champagne version. Shallots used to be small and are now enormous—you're looking to create around 2 tablespoons of mince. And please, please, use freshly ground black pepper, coarse as can be. The stuff in tins simply won't answer. Mix it all up, and it's good to go after a rest of about 20 minutes. Storing it, covered, in the refrigerator for a week or two, though, will yield an incomparable brew. Dab it on oysters as you like!

   ½ cup champagne or white wine vinegar
   2 tablespoons minced shallots
   1 tablespoon coarsely ground black pepper
   1½ teaspoons kosher salt, or to taste

In a medium bowl, whisk together the vinegar, shallots, pepper, and salt to taste. Let stand for 20 minutes or so before serving, or pour into a jar, cover it, and store in the refrigerator for a week or two.

PIZZA

—

A disclosure it pains me to make: It is a fiction that you're always going to want to cook Sunday supper. There are days when the skies are low and black dogs stalk your thoughts, and the last thing you want to do is to welcome people into your home for small talk and a lusty dinner. That happens to me enough that I think about it often, usually in the last hour before people arrive. But cooking anyway is part of the score. It is something to embrace. Sunday suppers are not, after all, always about you.

The work is a balm. There is the planning of the meal, and the provisioning of the kitchen, the mindless prepping of ingredients, the serial labor of putting them together, the craft of cooking itself. So what if you'd rather stay in the kitchen while everyone feeds—cleaning up, putting together a dessert? I've been that guy. I am that guy more often than I'd care to admit. You too, perhaps. It doesn't make you a misanthrope. It's just, it makes you feel better, to be the person working, providing, making people feel better through food. That makes you a cook. Feed people. That is the whole deal, right there. You don't always need to talk.

For that kind of night, I find there is nothing better to cook than pizza. To be sure, I feel that way on plenty of bluebird days, as well, when all is seashells and balloons. But making pizza is an amazing prescription for the eradication of gloom. You take an hour to put together some dough, and then some night soon you can spend all evening cranking out pies for family and friends, one after another to slide onto a cutting board, working while everyone eats. You will grab a slice or two, absolutely, along the way. But the real satisfaction in a pizza meal comes from the service itself, of giving gifts to others in exchange for nothing more than their company. It is a marvelous way to make a Sunday supper, regardless of your mood.

Plus, it's pizza. No one doesn't love pizza.

To make a lot of pizzas, you will need to assemble both ingredients and tools. There is the dough. You will need a surface in the oven on which to cook it. And you will need a tool to transfer the uncooked pizza from your countertop to that surface, and to remove it when it has cooked.

These are all easily obtained. To work backward off the list, you should get yourself a pizza peel, because the people who tell you that you can use the back of a sheet pan to slide your pizza into the oven and a couple of spatulas to retrieve it are not precisely telling the truth. (It doesn't make them bad people. They're just optimists.) You can create a cooking surface out of unglazed quarry tiles placed on the middle rack of your oven, or you can buy a baking stone, or, even better because it doesn't ever crack and reheats like a dream, a baking steel.

You can get dough at the supermarket or buy some from a local pizzeria. Good pizza can result from both, but never great. Great pizza starts with dough you've made yourself: flour, water, yeast, and salt. I've experimented with recipes for years, altering the ratios, the sorts of flour, the kinds of yeast. But for a long time now, I've been using the one developed by the lifestyle wizards at Roberta's in Brooklyn, which comprises a mix of all-purpose flour and a finely milled Italian flour marked "00," along with salt, yeast, and a splash of olive oil. That recipe follows here.

Pay close attention too to your mise en place: your sauces and toppings arranged just so on the counter, near a space where you can work the dough in advance of topping it. You can make a series of pies that are exactly the same, or a couple different varieties. But if you're making more than four or five pies in an evening, I would not suggest too many different varieties, at least until you've pulled off one or two of these evenings already, and rate your confidence level as high.

Finally, you may wish to prepare your guests for what's going to happen, explaining that you'll be working throughout the meal, to deliver nothing but hot pies and deep satisfaction. You don't want to argue that point while you're cooking. You'll be in the zone then, in service, taking your sustenance from the work itself.

THE BEST PIZZA DOUGH

THE THEORY OF PIZZA COGNITION holds that the first pizza a child consumes will become on some level what he or she considers to be the ideal form of pizza, and that all other pizzas will be judged, somehow, against this childhood ideal. Thus the continuing popularity of French bread pizza, and chain-restaurant pizza, and Chicago's mystifying deep-dish pies. The theory of pizza cognition does not hold, however, when it comes to making your own pizzas, or to making your own dough. I made dozens of different pizza dough recipes over the years, some very good, none of them purely satisfying, before alighting on this one, which was taught to me by Anthony Falco, then the pizza czar at Roberta's restaurant in Brooklyn. I left all previous attempts behind, forever. It combines all-purpose flour with the finely milled Italian variety marked "oo" on its packaging, allows it to rest comfortably in the refrigerator to proof, and yields a superlative thin crust that is ideal for use in a home oven, on top of a baking stone or steel.

Some notes. First, you'll see that the recipe calls for kneading. This can easily be done in the bowl of an electric mixer with a dough hook, and indeed it is probably best done in an electric mixer with a dough hook. This recipe yields four pizzas, which can feed eight to ten people. But you may wish to double it and either freeze the leftovers for later, or use them the following night or to make a dessert calzone. (Shape a pizza round. Put a few slices of cheesecake from the pastry place onto one half of the circle and top with strawberries and confectioners' sugar. Fold the empty half of the dough over the cheesecake and crimp the calzone closed with a fork. Bake that for ten minutes or so and serve with some chocolate sauce or a few smears of Nutella. Would I lie to you?)

Second, I've had the good fortune to cook a lot of pizzas in a wood-fired outdoor pizza oven that my friends Jamie Larkin and Nick Rubicco built up in the Catskills, for use when they're not floating the Delaware River for trout. Jamie's dough is pure "oo" flour and works beautifully in the high heat of their oven. I tried that at home, though, and it was too fragile for the lower heat of a residential gas oven. Maintain the flour ratio I've got going here unless you're cooking in temperatures that exceed 700°F.

Third, this dough ages beautifully. For dough I'm going to use all at once, or over the course of a few days, I invested in some stackable dough pans for around six dollars a throw and use them in the refrigerator to hold six or more balls of dough at a time. They make storage and use a breeze. To freeze dough, I place the balls in separate plastic storage bags and place them carefully in the freezer. Thaw in the refrigerator over the course of a day, then put them on the countertop while the oven heats up. It's not quite as awesome, but it works.

Finally, do all of this a lot. "Keep your hands in the dough" is what Falco told me, and what I've tried to do since. Practice is as important in pizza making as it is in competitive darts or concert piano playing. If you do it a lot, you'll do it quite well. And with this recipe, you'll do it well from the start.

306 grams "00" flour (about 2 cups plus 2 tablespoons)

306 grams all-purpose flour (about 2 cups plus 3 tablespoons), plus more for dusting

16 grams kosher salt (about 2 teaspoons)

4 grams active dry yeast (about 1½ teaspoons)

8 grams extra-virgin olive oil (about 2 teaspoons)

1. In a large mixing bowl, combine the "00" flour, all-purpose flour, and salt.

2. In a small mixing bowl, stir together 400 grams (a little less than 2 cups) lukewarm tap water, the yeast, and the oil, then pour it into the flour mixture. Knead with your hands until well combined, about 3 minutes, then let the mixture rest for 15 minutes.

3. Knead the rested dough for 3 minutes. Cut into 4 equal pieces and shape each into a ball. Place on a heavily floured surface, cover with a dampened cloth, and allow to rest and rise for 3 to 4 hours at room temperature or for 8 to 24 hours in the refrigerator. (If you refrigerate the dough, remove it 30 to 45 minutes before you begin to shape it for pizza.)

4. To make pizza, place each dough ball on a heavily floured surface and use your fingers to stretch it, then your hands to shape it into rounds or squares. Top and bake.

A SIMPLE PIZZA SAUCE

EMPTY A 28-OUNCE CAN OF good tomatoes into a food processor or blender. Add a splash of olive oil and a sprinkle of salt. Whiz that together and use about 3 tablespoons per pie. Leftover sauce can be kept, covered, in the refrigerator and used for more pizzas later, or as a simple pasta sauce.

HOW TO STRETCH PIZZA DOUGH

IT WOULD BE NICE IF ALL your pizzas were round and beautiful, thin circles with a raised edge around the circumference. That won't happen at first, no doubt, but that's perfectly fine. The practice is its own reward, and pizzas shaped like quadrangles taste just as delicious.

1. Working on a floured surface, with floured hands, softly pat down the risen ball of dough into a circle, rotating it as you do.
2. Using the tips of your fingers, push down gently around the perimeter of the pie, rotating it as you do, to create the edge.
3. Pick up the dough and lightly pass it back and forth between your palms, trying to rotate it each time you do, using gravity to help the dough stretch. At about 12 inches in diameter, the pizza is ready to go.
4. Return the pizza to the floured surface, making sure that the side that you first pressed down on remains facing upward, and gently slide the pie back and forth a few times to make sure that it does not stick. Add a little more flour to the surface beneath the pie if it does.
5. Gently slide a lightly floured pizza peel beneath the pie, or place it carefully on a floured cutting board or the back of a baking pan. Make sure again that the dough can slide back and forth. If it does, the pie is certified for topping.

PLAIN PIZZA

T HE CLASSIC. GET ON IT. Or add toppings just as they do down at the pie shop in town: cooked crumbled Italian sausage or ground beef; pitted black olives; sautéed mushrooms, onions, or peppers; pepperoni; anchovies; whatever you like. Just use a light hand so you don't overwhelm the pie, then shower the finished pizza with grated Parmesan cheese.

1 round pizza dough
   (see page 299)
3 tablespoons pizza sauce
   (see page 301)
Extra-virgin olive oil
2¾ ounces fresh mozzarella
4 to 5 fresh basil leaves,
   roughly torn

1. Place a pizza stone or tiles on the middle rack of your oven and turn the heat to its highest setting. Let the oven heat for at least an hour.

2. Stretch the dough (see page 301) and use a spoon to apply the sauce to its center. Use the back of the spoon to spread the sauce evenly across the surface, stopping about 1/2 inch from the edges.

3. Drizzle a little oil over the pie. Break the cheese into large pieces and place these gently on the sauce. Add other toppings, if using any, to taste. Scatter the basil leaves over the top.

4. Using a pizza peel, pick up the pie and slide it onto the heated stone in the oven. Bake until the crust is golden brown and the cheese is bubbling, 4 to 8 minutes.

HOW TO TOP PIZZAS

THE NOVICE HOME PIZZAIOLA INEVITABLY OVERTOPS. This can prove disastrous when it comes to sliding the pizza off the peel and onto the surface on which it bakes. And it makes for a sodden pie to boot, with less of the crunch-pliancy that marks the best homemade pizza. You really don't need more than a couple tablespoons of sauce on each pie, a modest allotment of cheese. You need fewer coins of sausage or pepperoni than you think you do, fewer clams or shrimp, fewer everything. Top your pie lightly, in equal proportions, testing your ability to slide the pie around on the peel each time you add an ingredient. Then bake the pie and make another, also topped lightly, and another, and another, into the night.

PIZZA *with* CARAMELIZED ONIONS, BACON, GORGONZOLA, *and* FIGS

I SUPPOSE THIS IS A TAKE on the classic *pissaladière* of southern France, which combines caramelized onions with anchovies on a thickish pizza dough. But I like this version a little better, with its sweet-saltiness, as if a devil on horseback rode into a pizzeria and got lost in the oven. You could use fresh figs, if you have any to hand, or fig preserves in a pinch.

2 tablespoons unsalted butter

1 large Spanish onion, peeled and
    thinly sliced

2 teaspoons fresh thyme leaves

2 bay leaves

Kosher salt and freshly ground
    black pepper

4 thick slices bacon, cut into
    ¼-inch-thick bâtons

1 round pizza dough
    (see page 299), stretched

12 dried mission figs, stems
    trimmed, cut into quarters
    or small pieces

¾ cup crumbled Gorgonzola
    cheese

Extra-virgin olive oil, to drizzle

1. Place a pizza stone or tiles on the middle rack of your oven and turn the heat to its highest setting. Let the oven heat for at least an hour.

2. Melt the butter in a large sauté pan over high heat. When the butter begins to foam, add the onion, thyme, and bay leaves. Cook for 5 minutes, stirring often, until the onion begins to wilt. Reduce the heat to medium-low and cook, stirring occasionally, until the onion has softened and turned a deep golden brown, about 35 minutes. Season to taste with salt and pepper. Remove the bay leaves and transfer the onion to a small bowl. (You can do this well in advance of making the pizza. It's a terrific morning task, while reading the newspaper and drinking coffee.)

3. Place the bacon in the pan and set over medium-high heat. Cook, stirring occasionally, until brown and crispy. Using a slotted spoon, transfer the bacon to a small bowl.

4. Put your stretched dough on a lightly floured pizza peel or rimless baking sheet. Cover with the toppings, being careful not to press on the dough and weigh it down: the caramelized onions first, then the figs and bacon, and finally the cheese, leaving roughly a ½-inch border. Shake the pizza peel slightly to make sure the dough is not sticking. Carefully slide the pizza directly onto the baking stone in one quick, forward-and-back motion. Cook until the crust has browned on the bottom and the top is bubbling and browning in spots, 4 to 8 minutes. Drizzle with a little oil and pepper to taste.

HOT HAWAIIAN PIZZA

THIS IS A PIZZA THAT HITS the flavor trifecta that practically defines American cuisine: salty-sweet-spicy. There are those who decry the combination of ham and pineapple, but I've found they are generally lying to themselves. You can substitute crisped bacon for the ham, or coins of cooked Italian sausage, even a few tablespoons of ground beef. Fresh jalapeños work in place of the pickled ones, but I like the pickled acidity as a counterbalance to the richness of the cheese and the sweetness of the pineapple.

1 round pizza dough (see page 299)

3 tablespoons pizza sauce (see page 301)

2³/4 ounces fresh mozzarella

1/4 cup pineapple chunks, fresh or canned

2 slices ham, cut into ribbons

10 to 12 sliced pickled jalapeño rounds

Extra-virgin olive oil

1. Place a pizza stone or tiles on the middle rack of your oven and turn the heat to its highest setting. Let the oven heat for at least an hour.

2. Stretch the dough and use a spoon to apply the sauce to its center. Use the back of the spoon to spread it evenly across the surface, stopping about 1/2 inch from the edges.

3. Break the cheese into large pieces and place them gently on the sauce. Do the same with the pineapple, ham, and pickled jalapeño. Drizzle a little oil over the top of the pie.

4. Using a pizza peel, pick up the pie and slide it onto the heated stone in the oven. Bake until the crust is golden brown and the cheese is bubbling, 4 to 8 minutes.

GRANDMA PIZZA

Pizza doesn't have to be a show. You can make like somebody's nonna and stretch the dough across a sheet pan, then cook it slowly in the oven, no peel or stone required. And depending on the size of your oven and the number of sheet pans you own, you can make quite a few of them at once, which can be very helpful in the timely execution of dinner for more than your family. The recipe that follows is for a plain pie in the tradition of the Sicilian ones made at L&B Spumoni Gardens, in the Bensonhurst neighborhood of Brooklyn, the pizza covered with a little cheese and then the sauce, instead of the other way around. Add toppings at will (I like provolone and black olives; my children, a combination of Monterey Jack and browned ground beef). Then serve under a shower of grated Parmesan and a few shakes of dried oregano.

3 tablespoons extra-virgin olive oil

1 round pizza dough (see page 299)

6 ounces fresh mozzarella

6 tablespoons pizza sauce (see page 301)

Toppings you desire, though not too many of them!

1. Use the oil to coat an 18-by-13-inch rimmed sheet pan.

2. Working on a floured surface, with floured hands, softly pat down the risen ball of dough, rotating it as you do, and begin to make it into a roughly rectangular shape. Then pick up the dough and lightly pass it back and forth between your palms, using gravity to help the dough stretch. Place the dough on the oiled sheet pan and gently and slowly continue to stretch it until it reaches the edges. If it springs back, allow to rest a few moments before continuing. Put the dough aside and allow to rest for 30 minutes or so.

3. Heat the oven to 500°F. Rip the cheese into shreds and scatter it across the top of the rested dough, then dot with the sauce and any toppings, if using. Bake the pie until it is golden brown at the edges and crisp, about 25 minutes.

CLAM PIZZA

YOU CAN MAKE A CLAM PIZZA SIMPLY, with just a little cheese and a bunch of chopped fresh clams scattered over the top, and I encourage you to do so. But this somewhat more involved preparation, which essentially puts a thick, syrupy clam chowder onto the pie, is astonishingly flavorful, and a showstopper to boot. Make the chowder sauce ahead of time, bake a few plain pizzas to get everyone comfortable, then slide this big fella onto the table to end your meal with cheers.

12 medium quahog clams, such as top neck or cherrystone, rinsed

1½ cups dry white wine

1 tablespoon unsalted butter

¼ pound slab bacon, diced

2 leeks, tops removed, halved, and cleaned, then thinly sliced into half-moons

3 cloves garlic, peeled and minced

3 tablespoons roughly chopped fresh flat-leaf parsley

½ cup heavy cream

Freshly ground black pepper

1 round pizza dough (see page 299)

2¾ ounces fresh mozzarella, roughly torn

1 teaspoon fresh lemon zest

Red pepper flakes

1. Place a pizza stone or tiles on the middle rack of your oven and turn the heat to its highest setting. Let the oven heat for at least an hour.

2. Meanwhile, put the clams in a large, heavy Dutch oven, add about 2 cups water and ¾ cup of the wine, then set over medium-high heat. Cover and cook until the clams have opened, 10 to 15 minutes. (Clams that fail to open after 15 to 20 minutes should be discarded.) Strain the clam stock through a sieve lined with cheesecloth or doubled-up paper towels, and set aside. Remove the clams from their shells, chop roughly, and set aside.

3. Rinse out the pot and return it to the stove. Add the butter and turn the heat to medium-low. Add the bacon and cook, stirring occasionally, until the fat has rendered and the bacon has started to brown, 5 to 7 minutes. Use a slotted spoon to remove the bacon from the fat and set aside.

4. Add the leeks to the fat and cook, stirring frequently, for about 5 minutes, then add the garlic and half of the parsley. Continue cooking and stirring until the leeks are soft but not brown, about 5 minutes more.

5. Stir in the remaining ¾ cup wine and about 1 cup of the reserved clam stock (save the rest for another use), and continue cooking until the liquids have reduced almost to a syrup.

6. Add the cream and black pepper to taste. Let the mixture come to a bare simmer, then allow to reduce and thicken. Add the reserved clams and

remove from the heat. (You can do all this the day before you make the pizza, then refrigerate it until you're ready to use.)

7. Make the pizza. Stretch the dough and place on a lightly floured pizza peel or rimless baking sheet. Using a pastry brush or a spoon, lightly paint the surface of the dough with some of the cream from the clams, leaving a 1/2-inch border all around. Then top the pizza with the chopped clams, bacon and leeks, and the cheese. (If there is any remaining liquid, you can lightly—lightly!—drizzle the pie with it.)

8. Shake the pizza peel slightly to make sure the dough is not sticking. If it is, you can place a sheet of parchment paper beneath the dough. Carefully slide the pizza directly onto the baking stone in one quick, forward-and-back motion. Cook until the crust has browned on the bottom and the top is bubbling and browning in spots, about 7 minutes. Sprinkle with the remaining parsley, the lemon zest, and red pepper flakes to taste, then serve.

SHRIMP PIZZA *with* BACON *and* ARTICHOKE HEARTS

THIS IS A GOOD RECIPE TO QUADRUPLE, cooking a full pound of shrimp and a lot of bacon, and using a full jar of artichoke hearts and a big hunk of Asiago cheese. One of these pies won't do it, not for a crowd, even if you're making other varieties. Experience allows: People love this pizza.

1 tablespoon unsalted butter

4 ounces fresh medium shrimp, peeled and deveined

1 clove garlic, peeled and minced

Kosher salt

2 thick slices bacon, cut into ¼-inch bâtons

1 round pizza dough (see page 299)

3 cooked artichoke hearts, quartered

3 ounces sliced semisoft Asiago cheese

1 tablespoon roughly chopped fresh oregano

Extra-virgin olive oil

Freshly ground black pepper

1. Place a pizza stone or tiles on the middle rack of your oven and turn the heat to its highest setting. Let the oven heat for at least an hour.

2. Melt the butter in a small sauté pan over high heat until it foams. Add the shrimp and garlic, season with salt, and cook for about 1 minute, shaking the pan, until the shrimp just start to color. Transfer to a bowl.

3. Place the bacon in the pan and set over high heat. Cook, stirring occasionally, until brown and crispy. Using a slotted spoon, transfer the bacon to a small bowl.

4. Stretch the dough and cover it with the toppings, being careful not to press on the dough and weigh it down: the bacon first, then the artichoke hearts, the shrimp, the cheese, and finally, the oregano, leaving roughly a ½-inch border.

5. Using a pizza peel, pick up the pie and slide it onto the heated stone in the oven. Bake until the crust is golden brown and the cheese is bubbling, 4 to 8 minutes. Drizzle the pie with a little olive oil and some pepper to taste.

CALZONE

A CALZONE IS SOMETIMES JUST A failed pizza, made in haste when the dough sticks to the peel while you're sliding it into the oven, and you're forced to flip it onto itself to create a kind of envelope of deliciousness. Even if the eating is sublime, you'll serve it with some chagrin. That won't be the case with this purpose-built one, stuffed with ricotta and mozzarella, and served with tomato sauce for dipping. It's a magnificent thing. For a variation, spoon half the cheese mixture onto the dough, then lay down a few slices of deli ham on top of it before adding the rest. For another, saute ½ pound ground beef until it begins to grow crisp, then add a few tablespoons of tomato sauce to it. Stir to combine and use the mixture to top the cheese. You could add some sautéed greens, if you'd like, or mushrooms, or black olives. Your calzone can be what you want it to be.

1 cup fresh ricotta

4 ounces fresh mozzarella, grated (about 1 cup)

1 ounce Parmesan cheese, grated (about ¼ cup)

2 tablespoons chopped fresh basil

¼ teaspoon freshly ground black pepper

1 round pizza dough (see page 299)

Extra-virgin olive oil

1. Place a pizza stone or tiles on the middle rack of your oven and turn the heat to its highest setting. Let the oven heat for at least an hour.

2. In a bowl, stir together the ricotta, mozzarella, Parmesan, basil, and pepper.

3. Lightly flour a work surface, and stretch or roll the dough into a 12-inch round. Spread the cheese mixture on half the dough, leaving a ½-inch border all around. Brush the edges of the dough with water and fold the dough in half over the filling, then pinch the edges of the dough together to seal.

4. Transfer the calzone to a lightly floured pizza peel. Brush the top with a little oil. Slide onto the pizza stone and bake until the crust is golden brown, 15 to 20 minutes. Let cool for 5 minutes, and serve with a bowl of pizza sauce on the side.

JUST US

—

It can be tiring, cooking all these dinners, for all these people. If you cook dinners regularly enough that you're getting phone calls about them, about whether one's happening this week or real soon, it can sometimes lead you to look on the cooking more as an obligation than as an enjoyable activity. And when that happens, the whole business can start to resemble a chore. That's a danger.

My advice: Be careful if you end up in that boat. For when Sunday suppers become a chore rather than a gift made and delivered with real affection and generosity, the person cooking them will inevitably begin to avoid cooking them regularly—and then not really at all. Which is a drag, and not simply because the act of cooking the meal and the act of consuming it are something that lifts nearly all moods and improves almost all situations. Your guests would probably not ever say it aloud, but they might feel it on some deep level where it is only a low hum of bummer and mild anxiety: They depend on the meal. You do too, or may come to. What they will say aloud, wistfully: "Remember when we used to have those big dinners all the time?" That question makes me sad.

Taking some time off to cook and eat with your immediate family can help. Sunday suppers, after all, are just a metaphor for family meals. And if life has put you in a position where you don't feel like making a weekly or monthly meal for a lot of people, where it makes you crabby just to think about it, please don't cease cooking;

don't stop making a table where ideas can be shared as easily as the salt or the hot sauce, where deliciousness reigns. But scale things back a little, for a time, to just us.

A roast chicken is just the thing for such a meal, to eat with potatoes and onions, a green salad, and a baguette and salted butter to drag through the drippings in the pan (see page 22). So is pan-seared steak, basted in butter, with oven-roasted fries and a thatch of watercress. Smothered pork chops that leave everyone gnawing on the bones, with gravy to drizzle on mashed potatoes? A honking big salad dressed with blue cheese and nuts, little nuggets of dried cranberry, some croutons cooked in the oven until crisp and lovely? Any of those would be a fine family meal on a Sunday or any night, and to it you could bring all the trappings of the big dinners you once loved so much: some candles, cloth napkins, the table assembled with care.

Watch what happens when you do. I am the self-styled king of Sunday suppers, the Napoleon of big pots, but I have stumbled too. I have asked, thinking about how everyone will jet after dinner, leaving me with a dozen plates to wash along with the pots and pans, the pile of soiled napkins and dish towels: *Again with gumbo for the neighborhood? Really?* I have retreated from all I stand for to cook only for sustenance or to order from the Italian place with the really good fried calzone. I have taken a break. And enjoyed it. And then made roast chicken on a Friday night and served it like a sacrament only to realize, along with my children and wife, that there is something missing, some people missing. *Maybe we should make chili on Sunday? Or a big paella over the fire? We could go for ribs, or clams, or both.* Call a few someones and see what they're hankering for, and ask if perhaps they could bring a pie. It will be right back on then, again, in theory and practice alike: See you on Sunday?

Here are some recipes, though, for the restoration. They'll get you back on track.

PAN-ROASTED FISH

THE BEST TECHNIQUE FOR PAN-ROASTING fish is one I learned from my colleague Julia Moskin at the *Times*: to cook one side of the fillet for longer than you'll cook the other, allowing the fish to build a substantial crust before flipping it over, then giving it a quick baste in a lot of butter before putting it on a plate. It is a recipe that, if you're cooking for a crowd, rewards the use of a number of pans. You can set three up on the stove to make up to a dozen fillets at a time, though you'll need to work fast and clean while doing it. This is a recipe for the practice round—a small dinner for four, in one pan. Swap out the thyme or other herbs for a bunch of minced, seeded jalapeño pepper, if you like. On fillets of wild salmon, in particular, this makes for fine eating.

Four 5-to-6-ounce fish fillets, such
as cod, haddock, tilefish,
snapper, black bass, grouper,
fluke, swordfish, shark, or
salmon, ½ to 1 inch thick
Kosher salt and freshly ground
black pepper
3 to 4 tablespoons neutral oil,
such as canola or grapeseed
4 tablespoons (½ stick) unsalted
butter
3 fresh thyme sprigs, or whatever
herb you have to hand
4 lemon wedges
2 tablespoons chopped fresh
flat-leaf parsley

1. Pat the fillets dry with a paper towel. Season to taste on both sides with salt and pepper.

2. Heat a large, heavy skillet over high heat, or use two if your pans aren't large enough to fit the fillets comfortably. When the pan is hot, add the oil. Place the fillets in the pan, skin side down if they have skin. (If they do have skin, use a spatula to press down on them gently for 15 to 20 seconds to keep them from curling.)

3. Reduce the heat to medium and let sizzle until the fish is deeply golden and crusted around the edges, which will take from 2 to 5 minutes, depending on the thickness of the fish. Carefully turn the fillets over and add the butter and thyme. Tilt the pan to let the melted butter pool at one end. Use a spoon to baste the fish with the pooled butter. Continue basting until the fish is golden all over and cooked through, a minute or more, again depending on the fish. Serve immediately, garnished with lemon wedges and chopped parsley.

PAN-ROASTED CHICKEN
with MINT SAUCE

THIS IS MY HACK OF A RECIPE the chef Bobby Flay used to serve at Bolo, his elegant little jewel box of a restaurant in Manhattan, long gone. He made it with chicken breasts and it was very fancy, and I ate it a million times. To make it at home, though, I use chicken thighs, and over time I've streamlined some of the folderol in it that is necessary to sell chicken in fancy restaurants at high prices. It's still pretty great. I like it for a small family meal, though truth be told the recipe scales up nicely. You could make a double or triple batch of the rub, use it to season a sheet pan's worth of chicken thighs, then hit it all with a big batch of the sauce at the end and serve a big crowd.

8 bone-in, skin-on chicken thighs

Kosher salt

2 tablespoons Spanish paprika

2 teaspoons ground cumin

2 teaspoons dry mustard powder

2 teaspoons ground fennel seed

1 teaspoon black pepper, plus more to taste

½ cup plus 3 tablespoons extra-virgin olive oil

1 cup fresh mint leaves

½ cup fresh flat-leaf parsley leaves

4 cloves garlic, peeled and minced

1 serrano chile, stems and seeds removed

1 tablespoon honey

1 tablespoon Dijon mustard

1. Heat the oven to 425°F. Pat the chicken thighs dry with paper towels. Season aggressively with salt. Combine the paprika, cumin, mustard powder, fennel, and black pepper in a small bowl, then rub the mixture all over the thighs.

2. Heat 3 tablespoons of the oil in a large, oven-safe skillet set over medium heat. When the oil is shimmering, put the thighs into the pan, skin side down, and cook, unattended, until the skin is golden brown, 6 to 8 minutes. Using tongs, turn the chicken thighs over and place the pan in the oven. Roast until the chicken is golden brown all over and the meat cooked entirely through, 12 to 15 minutes. Remove the chicken to a warmed platter and allow to rest.

3. Meanwhile, put the mint, parsley, garlic, and serrano into a food processor and pulse into a paste. Add the honey and Dijon mustard, and pulse again until combined. With the motor running, slowly add the remaining ½ cup oil until the mixture has become emulsified. Transfer the mixture to a bowl and, if necessary, whisk in a few tablespoons water to thin the sauce. Season to taste with salt and black pepper.

4. Spoon some of the sauce over the chicken and serve with the remaining sauce on the side. Roasted potatoes make a fine accompaniment, along with sautéed greens.

BISTRO STEAK

ONE BIG BONE-IN RIB-EYE STEAK will feed a family of four with ease, if you accompany the protein with a lot of fat in the form of maître d'hôtel butter, a nice portion of watercress, and a big serving of potatoes. Yes, you could make French fries from scratch (see page 290). But you might twice as easily just get a big bag of the frozen variety and cook them crisp in a hot oven. This is perfectly acceptable! (Alternatively, you can take small new potatoes and give them a 10-minute bath in boiling salted water, then use the bottom of a glass or measuring cup to crush them lightly onto an oiled sheet pan. Roast these at 425°F until golden running to something darker than that, and very crisp.) It's all very fancy while at the same time not at all: meat and taties, same as it ever was around the American table.

6 tablespoons unsalted butter

2 teaspoons thyme leaves, minced

1 small shallot, peeled and minced

1 teaspoon fresh lemon juice

½ teaspoon white wine vinegar

1 bone-in rib-eye steak, as thick as you can find, 2 to 2½ pounds

Kosher salt and freshly ground black pepper

1 tablespoon neutral oil, such as canola or grapeseed

1. Put the butter on a cutting board and, using a fork, cut the thyme and shallots into it. Sprinkle with the lemon juice and vinegar and continue to beat it with the fork until the butter is creamy and smooth. Scrape the butter together with a chef's knife and form it into a rough log. If making the maître d'hôtel butter ahead of time, you can roll it tight in a sheet of plastic wrap and refrigerate until you're ready to use.

2. Set a large cast-iron or other heavy skillet over high heat, and let it sit for a few minutes. Shower the steak with an aggressive amount of salt and pepper. Add the oil to the pan and shake to distribute. It will almost immediately begin to smoke. Place the steak in the pan and sear, unattended, for 4 minutes, until it has developed a serious crust.

3. Turn the steak over and cook for an additional 4 to 6 minutes for medium-rare. During the last minute or so of cooking, turn off the heat, add 2 tablespoons of the maître d'hôtel butter to the pan, and tip the pan so that the butter collects at the far side. Use a spoon to baste the steak with the butter, then remove the meat to a cutting board to rest for 5 to 10 minutes. Slice the steak from the bone, then against the grain into thick slices. Top each portion with a pat of the remaining butter and serve with thatches of watercress and whatever potatoes you choose to make.

CHICKEN LIVER PÂTÉ

SOME WILL SERVE THIS DISH as an appetizer at a dinner party, but I think it makes a perfect small family meal, best served with salad on one of those evenings when you want to break out candles and wine and maintain a casual vibe, or used as the base of a sauce for store-bought ravioli (just mix with a little pasta water and top with grated Parmesan cheese). The recipe is my adaptation of the one used at the restaurant Fort Defiance in Brooklyn, where Javier Huerta has made it for years. It takes less than a half-hour to prepare, and it will firm up in the refrigerator in a few hours. Simply pack the mixture into a bowl or glass jar, cover, and refrigerate. Bacon-Onion Jam (see page 324) makes a fine accompaniment, along with toast of the best quality.

8 tablespoons (1 stick) unsalted butter, cut into cubes

2 medium shallots, peeled and minced

1 pint fresh chicken livers (about 1 pound), trimmed of sinew with a small knife

1 tablespoon fresh thyme leaves, chopped

1/3 cup Madeira or port

3 tablespoons heavy cream, plus more as needed

Kosher salt

1. Put a large, heavy sauté pan over medium heat, and melt 4 tablespoons of the butter until it begins to foam. Add the shallots and sauté them until translucent, being careful not to allow to brown. Add the livers, thyme, and Madeira, and bring the heat to high. Cook, occasionally stirring the livers around in the pan with a spoon, until the wine has reduced and the livers are lightly browned but still very soft and pink on the inside, about 5 minutes.

2. Remove the pan from the stove and put its contents into a blender or food processor, along with the cream and the remaining 4 tablespoons butter. Puree until smooth, adding a little more cream, if necessary. Taste and adjust the seasoning, adding salt, if necessary.

3. Pack the pâté into a glass jar or bowl, then smooth the top with a spatula. Cover with plastic wrap and refrigerate until firm, about 2 hours or up to 5 days. Serve with bacon-onion jam and copious amounts of toast.

BACON-ONION JAM

THIS PARTNER FOR THE CHICKEN LIVER PÂTÉ (see page 322) comes from Fort Defiance in Brooklyn. It's a recipe I learned as the line cooks there do, interpreting the scratched accounting of Steve Linares, who was a cook there and who came up with it. You can use it here with the pâté, or as a topping for pizza (see page 306), with crumbled blue cheese.

3/4 pound slab bacon, diced
    into cubes
4 medium white or Spanish
    onions, peeled and diced
1½ teaspoons mustard seeds
2½ tablespoons dark brown
    sugar
¼ cup balsamic vinegar
Kosher salt and freshly ground
    black pepper

1. Set a Dutch oven or heavy pot over medium heat and add the bacon. Cook, stirring occasionally, until the fat is completely rendered and the bacon has started to crisp, 12 to 15 minutes.

2. Drain all but 1 tablespoon of the fat from the pot and add the onions, mustard seeds, brown sugar, balsamic vinegar, and 3 tablespoons water. Stir to combine, then cover the pot, lower the heat, and allow the mixture to cook, undisturbed, for 15 to 20 minutes. Remove the top, stir again, then partly cover the pot. Allow the mixture to cook until most of the liquid is gone and the onions have achieved a dark brown jamminess, 1 hour to 1 hour and 10 minutes. (Add a little more water as needed.)

3. Taste the jam, and add salt and pepper to taste.

4. Remove the mixture from the heat and allow to cool slightly. Spoon the jam into a jar or bowl, then allow to cool completely. Store, covered, in the refrigerator for up to 1 week.

A FAMILY SALAD

I MAKE A LARGE VERSION OF this salad with almonds and blue cheese for company sometimes, but as my children don't like blue cheese, and prefer pecans, and always ask for croutons, this is the version we make for ourselves. The leaves hold up beautifully to the creamy saltiness of the goat cheese dressing, which itself is intensified by the sweetness of dried cranberries. The croutons and toasted nuts add further texture and taste, and if you want to throw some lardons of bacon into the mix as well, go to: The point is not to create a side dish but a meal in itself. As an added benefit, this is the rare salad that improves over the course of thirty minutes or so, as the acidity of the dressing softens the kale while turning it a brighter, more vibrant green.

1 cup shelled pecans

1/4 pound slab or thick-cut bacon (optional)

1 cup extra-virgin olive oil

4 slices good country bread, cubed

1 cup loose dabs of creamy goat cheese

2 cloves garlic, peeled and minced

1/3 cup red wine vinegar

Kosher salt and freshly ground black pepper

2 bunches kale, washed, stems removed, and cut first into ribbons, then squares (10 to 12 ounces); if using precut washed kale in a bag, use 2 bags

2/3 cup dried cranberries

1. In a toaster oven or skillet, toast the pecans until they begin to brown and grow fragrant. Set aside to cool.

2. If using, cut the bacon into 1/4-inch strips, or lardons (if using slab bacon, cut slices first, then the strips). Set a large sauté pan over medium-high heat and add the bacon to it. Cook, stirring occasionally, until the lardons are crisp at the edges, 5 to 7 minutes, then remove and set aside.

3. Drain off all but 2 tablespoons of the bacon fat or, if not using bacon, add 2 tablespoons of the oil to the pan. Return it to the stove and allow the fat or oil to heat, then add the bread cubes to the pan. Sauté them until they are toasted and crisp, tossing often, 5 to 7 minutes. Remove the croutons and set aside.

4. Put 1/3 cup of the goat cheese in a large salad bowl, then add the garlic and the remaining oil. Use a fork to mash the cheese into the oil and whisk the mixture around to combine. Drizzle the vinegar slowly into the cheese and oil and use the fork to whisk it together. Add salt and pepper to taste and set aside.

5. Add the kale to the salad bowl and use tongs or your hands to toss it with the dressing, massaging the leaves lightly as you do. Add the cranberries to the salad bowl, the croutons, and, if using, the lardons of bacon. Toss the salad again and serve, dabbed with the remaining goat cheese, or allow to sit for 30 minutes and up to an hour.

GENERAL TSO'S CHICKEN

FOR A LONG TIME, I felt I could eat General Tso's chicken daily, bad-great food purchased from storefronts on the edge of town with bulletproof glass over the counter, alongside pork fried rice and an eggroll. My brother Toby had a better idea, though. He has, over the years, worked out an adaptation of Fuchsia Dunlop's recipe for General Tso's chicken in her *Revolutionary Chinese Cookbook*, a recipe that is far more pungent than the purely American take-out variety, with a salty-fiery flavor that is nothing less than addictive. He makes it with staples from his local health-food store—liquid aminos instead of soy sauce and barley instead of potato flour—but these substitutions are by no means necessary. The dish is, at any rate, now fully part of our family dinner repertoire: takeout made better, and just as cheaply.

FOR THE SAUCE

2 tablespoons tomato paste,
   mixed with 1 tablespoon water
1 teaspoon barley flour, potato
   flour, or cornstarch
4 tablespoons Bragg liquid
   aminos or low-sodium soy
   sauce
2 tablespoons cider vinegar
1/2 cup chicken stock, homemade
   or low-sodium, or water

FOR THE CHICKEN

8 to 10 chicken thighs,
   bones removed
2 tablespoons Bragg liquid
   aminos or low-sodium soy
   sauce
2 large egg yolks
4 tablespoons barley flour or
   potato flour, or 1 tablespoon
   cornstarch

3 1/2 cups plus 3 tablespoons and
   an extra splash peanut oil
10 to 15 dried red chiles
1 tablespoon finely chopped
   fresh ginger
2 cloves garlic, peeled and minced
1 tablespoon sesame oil
4 scallions, green parts only,
   thinly sliced

1. **Make the sauce.** Mix the tomato paste, barley flour, liquid aminos, vinegar, and stock in a small bowl, whisking to combine. Set aside.

2. **Prepare the chicken.** Pat the chicken dry with paper towels. Lay the thighs on a cutting board and, using a small knife, remove the skin. Slice shallow crosshatches into the meat, then cut each thigh into thin strips, about 1/4 inch thick. Put the chicken in a bowl and add the liquid aminos and egg yolks and stir to combine. Stir in the barley flour, along with a splash of peanut oil, and set aside.

3. Using scissors, cut the chiles into pieces, discarding the seeds. Set aside.

4. Pour 3½ cups of the peanut oil into a large wok, or enough oil to rise 1½ inches from the bottom of a heavy sauté pan. Set over high heat until the oil is nearly smoking, 350° to 400°F. Add about a quarter of the chicken and fry until crisp and brown, 3 to 4 minutes. Using a slotted spoon, transfer the chicken to a plate. Repeat with the rest of the chicken, frying in batches. Pour the oil into a heatproof container and wipe the wok clean.

5. Return the wok to high heat. Add the remaining 3 tablespoons peanut oil. When the oil is hot, add the chiles and stir-fry for just a few seconds, until they begin to color. Add the ginger and garlic and stir-fry for a few seconds, until fragrant. Add the sauce and stir as it thickens. Return the chicken to the wok and stir again to coat. Remove from the heat, stir in the sesame oil, and top with the scallions. Serve with rice.

SMOTHERED PORK CHOPS

S MOTHERED PORK CHOPS ARE A DISH of the American South, but this is a version that comes out of central Texas, where the Austin chef Jesse Griffiths stalks wild boar in the brush, then brings the meat back to town for a brine and a browning before cooking it slowly in a heady sweet-onion gravy. I interviewed Griffiths for the *Times* about the star anise he uses in the brine. It's neither southern nor Texan. "I don't know where I came up with that," he told me. "But that anise sure works." That it does, perhaps especially in the recipe I adapted from his, replacing the tannic funkiness of wild boar with thick pork chops from the local butcher. The recipe is easily doubled, though if you do that, smother the meat in a large roasting pan and cover it tightly with aluminum foil. Don't have time to brine? Use a pressure cooker instead: Make the recipe as written, but use only about half the stock, then add a pod of star anise to the situation and cook the whole thing under high pressure for about 45 minutes, fast-release. Fish out the pork chops and reduce the sauce. Dinner!

FOR THE BRINE

1 cup kosher salt

1 cup packed dark brown sugar

2 star anise pods

4 bay leaves

FOR THE PORK

8 thick, bone-in pork chops (more
    if using smaller chops)

4 tablespoons neutral oil, such as
    canola or grapeseed

1 cup all-purpose flour

8 medium yellow onions, peeled
    and thinly sliced

1 bay leaf

Kosher salt and freshly ground
    black pepper

2 quarts stock, ideally pork, but
    chicken will do (use the low-sodium
    variety if you're buying
    it from the store)

1 tablespoon finely chopped fresh
    flat-leaf parsley

1. **Make the brine.** Combine 1 gallon water with the salt, brown sugar, star anise pods, and bay leaves in a large pot set over high heat. Heat until the mixture is just about to boil and the salt and sugar have dissolved. Remove from the heat and allow to cool completely before using.

2. **Prepare the pork.** In the pot or in another container, submerge the pork in the brine and place it in the refrigerator for at least 10 or 12 hours, then remove the chops and dry well with paper towels.

3. Heat the oven to 325°F. Heat the oil in a large, oven-safe pot or Dutch oven set over medium heat. Dredge the chops in some of the flour, shaking off the excess. Reserve the leftover flour.

4. Cook the chops in the oil, about 4 minutes per side, until brown and crisp on the exterior, and transfer to a plate. Reduce the heat to medium-low. Add the onions and bay leaf and cook, stirring often, until the onions are softened, about 15 minutes. Season well with salt and pepper to taste.

5. Add 6 tablespoons of the flour to the onions, stir well, and allow to cook for an additional 5 or 6 minutes. Slowly add the stock, stirring and scraping the pan well, until it is incorporated and the mixture is slightly thickened.

6. Return the chops to the pot and bring to a simmer, then cover tightly and cook in the oven until very tender, 2 or more hours. Transfer the chops to a plate and place the pot on the stove top over medium heat. Reduce the sauce until it is thick enough to resemble gravy, skimming excess oil and foam, if necessary. Return the chops to the pot to reheat, then serve with their gravy over rice or mashed potatoes. Garnish with the parsley.

CHICKEN *in* MILK

ORK IN MILK IS A TRADITIONAL BOLOGNESE RECIPE, and the wise will turn to Marcella Hazan's recipe to make it. But many years ago a young Jamie Oliver turned up with a chicken version that to my mind called for making right away, and soon it became my family's own. The result is easily stretchable for crowds because of the richness of the sauce. Note: Fresh sage is a must, as is lemon zest. And don't stint on the garlic. The frugal will squawk at the wastefulness of pouring off the butter used to brown the bird—save it, if you like, and allow it to firm up in the refrigerator while the dish cooks. You can use it on bread with the meal.

1 whole chicken, 3 to 4 pounds, trimmed of excess fat

Kosher salt and freshly ground black pepper

2 tablespoons extra-virgin olive oil

6 tablespoons unsalted butter

1 small cinnamon stick

1 bunch fresh sage, the leaves picked off and roughly chopped

Zest of 2 lemons

10 to 12 cloves garlic, unpeeled

2 cups whole milk

1. Heat the oven to 375°F. Pat the chicken dry with paper towels. Season the chicken aggressively with salt and pepper, inside and out.

2. Set a large Dutch oven over medium-high heat and place the oil and butter in it to melt. When the butter foams, place the chicken in the fat and brown it, turning the chicken to get an even, golden color, 10 to 15 minutes. Remove the chicken from the pot and set aside, then drain off the fat.

3. Return the chicken to the pot, along with the cinnamon, sage, lemon zest, and garlic, then pour the milk over it. Slide the pot into the oven and cook for about 1½ hours, basting occasionally, until the meat is cooked through and the sauce has broken into curds. Serve in pieces with plenty of sauce, rice or mashed potatoes, some greens, and plenty of bread with which to mop up the sauce.

DESSERTS

—

I had a perfect dessert one night at a Chinese New Year celebration on a leafy street in Flushing, Queens, at the home of Jerry Tang, a son of a great restaurateur named Shorty Tang. We had eaten an enormous amount of food over a lot of hours—dumplings and ribs, noodles, fish, greens, repeat—and as always seems to happen at terrific meals in the homes of good people, everyone ended up in the kitchen at the end, gabbing and picking at leftovers. The talk was of school buses, martial arts, the benefits of sitting, the impossibility of restaurant life in lower Manhattan.

Then Jerry called the children to him. There were a lot of them. He had a huge knife in one hand and a watermelon in the other. He raised his eyebrows, mischievously. The children looked at one another, nervously. *Whack* went the blade into the meat of the melon, and I thought he might slice open his palm. He didn't. The blade had gone only to the center of the fruit. *Whack* again, and there was a wedge of watermelon, and *whack* again, another. The eyes of the children went wide. What was once whole was now becoming slices, thick and juicy, and Jerry stabbed each one with the end of the knife and handed it dripping to little hands, and then to the rest of us. We ate watermelon standing in that kitchen in Queens, and the room was silent but for the slurp and crunch. It was theater, but also delicious, and after a multicourse meal of real complexity, it was the perfect capstone: a simple watermelon, cold and sweet, shared among friends. I thought about it for months, still do.

Dessert need not be complicated. It can be, of course. It is always nice to have a pie. But pie is a project, same as roasting a haunch or assembling a gumbo, and you may have time for one but not the other. No matter. Have watermelon in the Tang tradition instead, or sliced oranges in season, peaches, a quart of berries to serve under whipped cream. These are each a sort of perfection, in and of themselves. Cut fruit is nothing to be embarrassed about if you're cooking a big dinner for friends.

I tell myself that, anyway. I give myself permission not to bake. And I grant it to you unreservedly, as well.

That said, a pie for dessert after a meal of fried chicken or roasted pork is a marvelous thing. You should try one on for size sometime, see how it goes, even if you don't consider yourself a baker. You might make the meal you serve before it fairly basic—a simple pot of something hot to serve over rice—and then follow it with something fantastic, just because. You could make a pound cake. You could make some pudding. You could make a crumble. (If the something hot you've cooked is gumbo, there is no finer end to the meal than a bunch of bananas sautéed in butter and flamed in rum, with vanilla ice cream.) These are marvelous things to eat.

But I know the world of home cooks often divides into those with a passion for the creation of savory food and those with an ardor for pastry. And if you're in the first camp, you're in the first camp. Your first thought when it comes to a Sunday supper is not going to be dessert, and that is perfectly fine. That is what store-bought ice cream of high quality is for, and why I sometimes serve frozen Mallomars with champagne flutes filled with ice-cold milk.

Yet take heed of a corollary: Give permission to others to bake. There is no better gift to the host of a Sunday supper than dessert, homemade, ready for consumption. Indeed, making dessert and bringing it to a Sunday supper is an outstanding way to begin to make Sunday suppers yourself, or to make Sunday desserts for the delectation of others, to the (probable) relief of your host. Bake enough pies and soon, I'd wager, you'll be making lasagna as well. Dessert is a street that runs both ways.

FRUIT COBBLER

I HAVE BEEN EATING A VERSION of this cobbler since I was very small, when my mother made it out of what wild fruits she could harvest from the fields near my grandparents' home: strawberries, blueberries, raspberries, blackberries, each in turn, maybe in mixture. Now one of my children makes the dish, doing the same, carrying on the tradition, making it her own. I might add rhubarb or apples, to fill out the bill of fare. You could use peaches if you have them, or plums, or apricots. You can make a cobbler with pears. And a cherry cobbler? That is one of the world's great pleasures. If your filling is very sweet, you may wish to add more lemon juice, less sugar. If it is sour, add sugar as you go, tasting all along. Does it seem as if it's going to be watery? That can happen with cherries, those rogues. Add cornstarch or arrowroot. And spices as you like. A cobbler is deeply forgiving. That makes it a welcome guest at any good Sunday supper.

FOR THE TOPPING
1 3/4 cups all-purpose flour, plus
    more for dusting
1/4 cup granulated sugar
1 tablespoon baking powder
1/2 teaspoon baking soda
1/8 teaspoon kosher salt
5 tablespoons unsalted butter,
    cold, cubed
1 cup heavy cream

FOR THE FILLING
8 cups sliced fruit
1/2 to 1 cup granulated sugar or
    packed dark brown sugar
    (taste as you go)
1 tablespoon fresh lemon juice
    (optional), for acidity
2 tablespoons cornstarch
    (optional), for body

1 to 2 teaspoons ground
    cinnamon (optional)
1 tablespoon unsalted butter

1. **Make the topping.** In a food processor, pulse together the flour, granulated sugar, baking powder, baking soda, and salt. Add the cubed butter in batches and pulse until the mixture looks like a bunch of floury beans. Drizzle in the cream and pulse just to combine.

2. Transfer the dough to a lightly floured surface and pat it all together into a mound. Using a spoon or ice cream scoop, take off heaping-tablespoon-sized pieces of dough and roll them into balls—you'll probably end up with somewhere north of a dozen. Put the balls on a sheet pan and press them down into biscuits that are about 3/4 inch thick, then cover the pan with plastic wrap and put in the refrigerator for 30 minutes or so, up to the better part of a day.

3. When you're ready to bake, heat the oven to 350°F. Then **make the filling.** In a large bowl, toss together the fruit, sugar to taste, a little lemon juice if you like the acidity, the cornstarch if you'd like the

continued on page 337

filling to have some body to it, and the cinnamon if that feels right.

4. Use the butter to grease a 13-by-9-inch baking pan, or a similar-sized gratin dish, then add the fruit to it, so that it comes somewhere between halfway and three-quarters of the way up the sides of the pan. Top with the biscuits, place the pan on a sheet pan, and bake until the tops are golden and the fruit is bubbling beneath them, about 1 hour. Serve drizzled with more cream, if you like, or plain, or with ice cream alongside.

ANY FRUIT CRUMBLE

HERE'S ANOTHER FREEWHEELING, IMPROVISATORY DESSERT that you can make with almost whatever fruit you have on hand (though I wouldn't recommend citrus). It is rustic and rich, and perhaps the very opposite of something you'd photograph and put on Instagram. It looks and maybe tastes best when served in low candlelight, the windows dark behind it, everyone dressed in sweaters and already full from the lamb or pork, pasta or cauliflower, a treat no one expected, one that's all the more welcome for that.

12 tablespoons (1½ sticks) unsalted butter, melted, plus more for buttering the pan

1½ cups all-purpose flour

1½ cups packed dark brown sugar, plus more if you need it

1 cup old-fashioned rolled oats

1 cup slivered almonds (optional)

1 teaspoon kosher salt

8 cups fruit, sliced if larger than a berry

1 tablespoon ground cinnamon

2 tablespoons fresh lemon juice, plus more if you need it

1. Heat the oven to 350°F. Butter a 13-by-9-inch baking pan or gratin dish. Combine the flour, 1 cup of the brown sugar, the oats, slivered almonds, if using, and salt. Add the melted butter to the mixture and stir with a fork until everything is evenly moist. Use your fingers to draw the mixture together into rough little crumbles.

2. Add the fruit to the buttered baking pan and toss with the remaining ½ cup brown sugar, along with the cinnamon and lemon juice. Taste and see if you need more sugar or lemon juice.

3. Spread the fruit into an even layer, then top it with the clumps of crumb mixture, almost totally covering the fruit but not quite. Put the baking pan onto a sheet pan and transfer to the oven. Bake until the crumb topping is crisp and deep golden brown, and the fruit is bubbling beneath it, 50 to 60 minutes. Allow the crumble to sit for 20 minutes or so before serving, or serve at room temperature, with ice cream or heavy cream drizzled over the top.

APPLE PIE

THIS IS A TASTE OF my Thanksgiving table, though it's terrific anytime you'd like a taste of America at the end of your meal. I learned how to make it while on assignment for the *Times*, talking to the pastry chef Kierin Baldwin. She taught me how to make a crust that will neither shatter nor wilt, but taste of flake and butter and salt, and how to match it with a filling that is thick without being starchy, intense without being gooey. It is a pie to offer the comfort of a family movie's heartwarming third act. Serve it with whipped cream or vanilla ice cream, slices of cheddar cheese, a glass of milk or low tumbler of brandy, depending on your taste and relationship to beverage alcohol.

2 tablespoons unsalted butter

2½ pounds apples, peeled and cored, then cut into wedges (5 large Honeycrisps will do it)

¼ teaspoon ground allspice

½ teaspoon ground cinnamon

¼ teaspoon kosher salt

¾ cup plus 1 tablespoon sugar

2 tablespoons all-purpose flour, plus more for dusting

2 teaspoons cornstarch

1 tablespoon cider vinegar

All-Purpose Pie Dough (recipe follows), well chilled

1 large egg, lightly beaten

1. Melt the butter in a large sauté pan set over medium-high heat and add the apples to the pan. Stir to coat the fruit with butter and cook, stirring occasionally. Meanwhile, whisk together the allspice, cinnamon, salt, and ¾ cup of the sugar, and sprinkle this over the pan, stirring to combine. Reduce the heat and cook until the apples have started to soften, 5 to 7 minutes. Sprinkle the flour and cornstarch over the apples and continue to cook, stirring occasionally, for another 3 to 5 minutes. Remove the pan from the heat, add the vinegar, stir, then scrape the fruit mixture into a bowl or onto a sheet pan to allow to cool completely.

2. Place a large baking sheet on the middle rack of the oven and heat the oven to 425°F. Remove one of the two disks of dough you've made from the refrigerator and, using a rolling pin, roll it out on a lightly floured surface until it is roughly 12 inches in diameter. Fit this crust into a 9-inch pie plate, trimming it to leave a ½-inch overhang. Place this plate, with the dough, in the freezer.

3. Roll out the remaining dough on a lightly floured surface until it is roughly 10 or 11 inches in diameter.

4. Remove the piecrust from the freezer and put the cooled pie filling into it. Cover with the remaining dough. Press the edges together, trim the excess, then crimp the edges with the tines of a fork. Using a sharp

continued on next page

knife, cut three or four steam vents in the top crust. Lightly brush the top of the pie with the egg wash and sprinkle with the remaining 1 tablespoon sugar.

5. Place the pie in the oven on the hot baking sheet and bake for 20 minutes, then reduce the heat to 375°F. Continue to cook until the interior is bubbling and the crust is golden brown, 30 to 40 minutes more. Remove from the oven and allow to cool on a windowsill or cooling rack, about 2 hours.

ALL-PURPOSE PIE DOUGH

Pie dough is simply flour and fat, brought together by water. I add a little salt and a splash of acidity for flavor. This recipe calls for cold butter as the fat. Some will prefer leaf lard, or a combination of it and butter. You can work yourself in that direction eventually, but start here, in a cool kitchen at the start of the day, before the house heats up with bubbling gumbo or pasta sauce, so that the dough can come together nicely, and not get gummed up by heat and humidity. The result is two disks of dough, enough for a single topped pie or two open ones.

2½ cups all-purpose flour, plus more for dusting

6 tablespoons unsalted butter, cold, cut into ½-inch cubes

2 tablespoons vegetable shortening, cold

¼ teaspoon kosher salt

1 egg yolk, beaten

1 teaspoon cider vinegar

¼ cup to ½ cup ice water

1. Using your fingertips or the pulse function of a food processor, blend together the flour, butter, shortening, and salt until the mixture resembles a coarse meal. There should be pebbles of butter throughout the mixture.

2. Add the egg yolk and vinegar to ¼ cup ice water and stir to combine. Drizzle 4 tablespoons of this mixture over the dough and gently stir or pulse to combine. Gather a golf ball–sized bit of dough and squeeze to combine. If it does not hold together, add a little more of the liquid or additional ice water and stir or pulse, then check again. Repeat as necessary.

3. Turn the dough out onto a lightly floured surface and gather it together into a rough ball. You want to be careful not to overwork the flour, but not too careful; the dough should hold together. Divide the ball in half with a knife or a pastry scraper, then divide each portion in half again, and again, to create 8 portions. Using the heel of your hand, flatten each portion of dough once or twice to expand the pebbles of butter, then gather the dough together again into one ball. Divide this ball in half.

4. Flatten each ball into a 5- or 6-inch disk and dust lightly with flour. Wrap the disks in plastic wrap and place in the refrigerator for at least 1 hour.

PEACH PIE

Here is a recipe to deliver all the pleasure accorded to those who can recall the taste of a perfectly ripe peach eaten in summer heat, soft and warm, slick beneath its fuzz, almost impossibly sweet and creamy, with a slight acidic tang. You get approximately one of those each year, I've found, sometimes two, rarely more. All others fall short in one area or another. But here the oven sets off some crazy alchemical reaction, delivering the magical flavor of a perfect peach even if the fruit you start out with has some flaws. If what you have are very ripe peaches, the peeling's made easy by submerging them in boiling water for 30 seconds or so, then placing them gently into a bowl of ice water. The skins will slip from the flesh with ease. Then you can score each peeled peach into eighths lengthwise with a paring knife and squeeze it so that the flesh falls from the stone within. That's for perfect peaches, though. If you're dealing with merely good ones, not quite as soft as you'd like, you can set at them with a paring knife or peeler, trying hard not to cut off too much flesh from the fruit as you do. Then proceed as above. Make your pie in the morning, or the day before your supper—it sits nicely on the countertop awaiting consumption, with or without ice cream, as you like.

1 recipe All-Purpose Pie Dough
   (see page 340)
¼ cup all-purpose flour, plus
   more for dusting
6 or 7 ripe peaches, peeled and
   sliced (about 5 cups)
2 tablespoons fresh lemon juice
1 cup sugar, plus a pinch for
   sprinkling
Pinch of ground nutmeg
1 large egg, lightly beaten

1. Heat the oven to 425°F. Remove one of the two disks of dough you've made from the refrigerator and, using a rolling pin, roll it out on a lightly floured surface until it is roughly 12 inches in diameter. Fit this crust into a 9-inch pie plate, trimming it to leave a ½-inch overhang. Place this plate, with the dough, in the freezer.

2. Make the filling for the pie. Combine the sliced peaches, lemon juice, sugar, and flour in a large bowl, and gently mix. Remove the pie plate from the freezer and add to it the peach filling. Sprinkle with the ground nutmeg.

3. Remove the second disk of dough from the refrigerator and roll it out on a lightly floured surface until it is roughly 10 or 11 inches in diameter. Gently place the dough on top of the filling. Press the edges together with your fingertips, trim the excess, then crimp the edges with the tines of a fork. Using a sharp

knife, cut three or four steam vents in the top crust. Lightly brush the top of the pie with the egg wash and sprinkle with a pinch of sugar.

4. Place the pie on a sheet pan and bake in the oven for 15 minutes, then reduce the heat to 375°F. Cook until the peaches bubble and the pastry is golden, 45 minutes to 1 hour. Remove from the oven and allow to cool on a windowsill or cooling rack, about 2 hours.

BANANAS FOSTER

HIS ISN'T A PROPER RECIPE, REALLY, but instead a few words of encouragement. Peel as many bananas as you have people at the table, then sauté the fruit in a lot of foaming unsalted butter in a large pan on the stove top, working in batches if you must. Sprinkle ground cinnamon and a tablespoon or so of dark brown sugar over them as they grow golden and crisp. This won't take much more than 5 or 6 minutes, with you shaking the pan a lot and perhaps basting the fruit a little with the butter. The result will astonish, particularly if you add a few ounces of dark rum to the pan at the end, then tip the pan slightly so the alcohol ignites and the flames rise high and everyone gasps. When the flames subside, simply place a banana on each plate with a little drizzle of the butter, and serve with vanilla ice cream. It's like a magic trick. You can't go wrong, though if you're worried about the fire from the rum, keep a lid for the pan on hand so you can quickly extinguish the flames.

TIP: Figure a tablespoon of unsalted butter per banana, and a tablespoon of brown sugar per two. Add cinnamon to taste and no more than a couple tablespoons of rum each time you flame.

BANANA PUDDING

MY FRIEND RAHSAAN BETTS TAUGHT me to make banana pudding, telling me I didn't need a recipe, just milk and eggs and a little cornstarch and sugar. Heat that through to make a custard, he said, and pour over Nilla wafers and a lot of sliced bananas. That worked and was delicious, and I thought maybe banana pudding was a great freestyle affair. But many subsequent attempts at improvisatory pudding did not work and were not delicious, so I went back to the kitchen with notebook and pen, measuring implements and timers, and nailed down a proper set of directions. They follow here, along with a beautiful meringue for the top. (If you'd like to make the dish a slightly more adult affair, add a shot of bourbon or dark rum to the custard.) If you can't find Nilla wafers or don't want to use them because they're processed junk cookies and you're not the sort of person who cooks with that sort of ingredient, fairly crisp vanilla-scented shortbread cookies would work in their place. That makes the dish fancy. Which is sometimes just what you want.

1¼ cups sugar

⅓ cup cornstarch

4 cups whole milk

4 large eggs, separated

1 teaspoon pure vanilla extract

¼ teaspoon salt

2 tablespoons unsalted butter

¼ teaspoon cream of tartar

One 11-ounce box Nilla wafers

3 or 4 bananas, depending on
    size, sliced into coins

1. Heat the oven to 350°F. To make the custard, whisk ¾ cup of the sugar, the cornstarch, milk, and egg yolks in a pot set over medium heat and cook, stirring constantly, until it just begins to bubble, 10 to 15 minutes. Turn down the heat slightly, allow the mixture to simmer, still stirring constantly, for 1 minute, then remove the mixture from the heat. Whisk in the vanilla, salt, and butter.

2. Make a meringue. Put the egg whites, cream of tartar, and the remaining ½ cup sugar in the heatproof bowl of a stand mixer, and set over a medium saucepan of simmering water, making sure that the bottom of the bowl does not touch the water. Whisk until the sugar is dissolved and the mixture is hot to the touch, about 3 minutes. Transfer to the stand mixer fitted with the whisk, and beat until stiff, 5 to 7 minutes.

3. Line a 13-by-9-inch oven-safe casserole dish with one layer of Nilla wafers and one layer of banana slices.

4. Pour the custard over the bananas and cookies, then use a spatula to spread the meringue. Bake for 10 to 15 minutes, until the peaks are the color of a toasted marshmallow. Allow to rest until you're ready to serve.

GRILLED PEACHES *with* MOLASSES *and* RUM

THIS IS A RECIPE TO MAKE OVER the dying embers of the grill you used for steaks or chops or burgers or brats, a simple and elegant dessert that is simultaneously wild and untucked. What follows serves eight, but you can easily ramp up production by making more sauce. All you need is a few teaspoons per peach. Or, failing peaches, per slice of pineapple. Or, failing pineapple, per peeled banana. The idea is simply to apply a little smoke and caramelization and a warming bite of rum to the fruit you have on hand.

2 tablespoons unsalted butter

½ cup molasses

1 tablespoon dark rum

4 ripe peaches, cut in half
    and pitted

2 teaspoons neutral oil, such as
    canola or grapeseed

Ground cinnamon, for dusting

1. Melt the butter in a small pot set over medium heat, then add the molasses and rum and stir to combine. Cook for a few minutes, then turn off the heat and set aside.

2. Put the cut peaches on a sheet pan and drizzle the oil over them.

3. On a charcoal grill with coals that are medium-low heat and falling, or on a gas grill heated to medium-low, place the peaches, cut side down, and allow to cook for 3 to 4 minutes, until browned. Turn them over and spoon a teaspoon or two of the molasses mixture onto the fruit, then cook for an additional 3 to 4 minutes. Carefully remove the peaches to a sheet pan. Dust with cinnamon. Serve after a few minutes, or at room temperature, with ice cream.

POUND CAKE *and* STRAWBERRIES

I F YOU ARE JAMMED FOR TIME, this is a recipe that works extremely well with a store-bought pound cake cut into cubes. But it is markedly more delicious when the cake is homemade, and the recipe is simple enough that it can be handed off to interested children to make, should you have any of those standing by. Enlisting another generation to help with the preparation of a Sunday supper is a smart way to ensure the continuation of the franchise for years to come. If strawberries are out of season, omit the topping and serve with ice cream.

1 pound (4 sticks) unsalted butter, softened and cubed, plus more for greasing the pan(s)

2½ cups sugar

8 large eggs

½ teaspoon salt

1 pound (4 cups) all-purpose flour, plus more for flouring the pan(s)

1½ teaspoons pure vanilla extract

Zest of 1 large lemon

Juice of 1 large lemon

1 quart strawberries, rinsed, hulled, and sliced

1. Heat the oven to 325°F. In a large bowl or the bowl of a stand mixer, beat the butter until it is creamed, then add 2 cups of the sugar, beating until it is well mixed. Beat the eggs in a bowl and add them to the mixture. Add the salt. Add the flour, a little bit at a time, then the vanilla, lemon zest, and lemon juice, mixing to incorporate.

2. Grease and flour a Bundt pan or two 8-inch loaf pans. Pour in the batter. Bake for about 1¼ hours, until a knife inserted into the center of the cake comes out clean. Take the cake out of the oven, allow to cool for a few minutes, then turn it out of the pan onto a rack.

3. Combine the strawberries with the remaining ½ cup sugar in a bowl and allow to sit for 20 to 30 minutes. Cut the cake into large cubes and place on a serving platter or in a bowl. Put the strawberries on top of the cake. Top with whipped cream.

MALLOMARS AND MILK

WHEN MY WIFE AND I WERE MARRIED, we received a bunch of fine champagne flutes because we registered for them as gifts, and we used them as regularly as one uses champagne flutes when one is not a British peer, which is to say rarely. I'd look at them in the cupboard occasionally and wonder about that, about what had compelled us to ask friends and family to pony up for these things at the start of our married lives together, these signals of, what—our position in the social order? Our sophistication? We hardly ever drank champagne, anyway—mostly prosecco, and then as often in jelly jars or tooth glasses as in our fancy flutes. They grew dusty on the shelf.

Then we had children. The children had many needs and one of them was milk. I bought them organic whole milk and tasted it and it was as if I'd never had milk before, so rich and delicious and pure was the taste. And this got me to thinking that, for those of us who grew up on industrial milk in plastic jugs, organic whole milk might be a revelation, as special and rare as, well, a glass of champagne.

I put the flutes into rotation then: a few ounces of cold whole milk for dessert, alongside a Mallomar cookie just because I liked how its shape mirrored the small opening on the glass. You could easily and perhaps more deliciously pair the milk with chocolate chip cookies or a warm brownie. Perhaps that would be more urbane. I'm not sure it matters, though. I concentrate on the milk. It delivers a childlike joy.

A REALLY RICH CHEESECAKE

THIS IS A CRAIG CLAIBORNE RECIPE, luxurious and rich, that has become a close friend. Claiborne published it in *The New York Times* in 1963, when he had the same job at the newspaper that I have now. It is absolutely a New York cheesecake, with none of the savory elements of a ricotta-based Italian-style one, and I can hardly improve on its excellence, except when I use the cake, not as a showstopper dessert in and of itself but as an *ingredient* in a showstopper dessert, as the filling for an after-dinner calzone.

And that too is not my recipe, but one I picked up from the great pizza chef Mark Iacono. One night I was in his restaurant, Lucali, in Brooklyn, and he put slices of cheesecake onto half of a stretched round of pizza dough, then topped the cake with macerated strawberries and folded the rest of the dough over their top to form a turnover. He baked it in the oven, then served it under a dusting of confectioners' sugar. It was crazy making in its deliciousness, and I started to cook a similar calzone at home to provide the capstone to pizza-night Sunday suppers. This cake provides the best filling.

FOR THE CRUST

1 cup all-purpose flour

¼ teaspoon sugar

1 teaspoon lemon zest

8 tablespoons (1 stick) unsalted
    butter, plus more for greasing
    the pan

1 large egg yolk, lightly beaten

¼ teaspoon pure vanilla extract

FOR THE FILLING

Five 8-ounce packages
    cream cheese

¼ teaspoon pure vanilla extract

1 teaspoon lemon zest

1¾ cups sugar

3 tablespoons all-purpose flour

¼ teaspoon kosher salt

5 large eggs

2 large egg yolks

¼ cup heavy cream

1. Heat the oven to 400°F. To **prepare the crust,** combine the flour, sugar, and lemon zest in a large bowl. Cut in the butter until the mixture is crumbly. Add the egg yolk and vanilla. Mix again to combine.

2. Pat one-third of the dough over the bottom of a 9-inch springform pan with the sides removed. Bake in the oven for about 6 minutes, until golden. Cool.

3. Butter the sides of the pan and attach to the bottom. Pat the remaining dough around the sides to a height of 2 inches.

4. Increase the heat to 475°F. To **prepare the filling,** beat the cream cheese in the bowl of a stand mixer until fluffy. Add the vanilla and lemon zest.

5. In another bowl, combine the sugar, flour, and salt, then gradually blend the mixture into the cream cheese mixture. Beat in the eggs and egg yolks, one at a time, then the cream. Beat well.

6. Pour the batter into the prepared pan and place the pan on a sheet pan. Bake the cake for 8 to 10 minutes.

7. Reduce the heat to 200°F. Bake for 1 hour longer, or until the cake is set. Turn off the heat and allow the cake to remain for 30 minutes in the oven with the door ajar.

8. Cool in the pan on a rack for an hour or so, then turn it onto a plate and chill in the refrigerator. Serve plain or topped with fruit, plain or macerated.

ACKNOWLEDGMENTS

—

This book would not exist without the cooperation of my employers at *The New York Times* and the support of my friends and colleagues there on the food desk, national desk, news desk, culture desk, Sunday magazine, and masthead, past and present. To them and to the Sulzberger family members who own and run the joint, I owe the deepest debt. Thank you.

Thanks are due as well to all the chefs and line cooks, recipe developers, and kitchen wizards I've met and studied during my reporting over the years, and who shared with me their secrets and hacks and advice, in particular John Willoughby, the editor and writer in whose path I have followed since I first walked into a professional kitchen and thought, "There are a lot of stories here."

I owe deep thanks as well to my family and all those who are part of it in spirit and thus in fact: my wife, Tina Fallon, and our children; my mom and brothers; my father, who died before I could finish the work; my stepparents, -brothers, and -sisters; my in-laws and cousins and uncles and aunts; and all those friends in Brooklyn and in Greenport, New York, who have joined me around dinner tables down the years, offering friendship and stories, ideas and debate.

I offer gratitude too to Cynthia Cannell and Andy Ward, who got me started on this project so many years ago, and who have been steadfast in support of it even as I have shifted jobs and blown deadlines, bungling all the way. They made it much better.

Now, here's to Will Conroy, who offered me a room in Arizona to finish the manuscript, along with a friendly ear as I complained about it; to Ally Spier for figuring out how to manage the files; to Maggie Ruggiero for giving me the side-eye on so many recipes and for reminding me always to keep it simple; to the Reverend John Merz, who first got me to cook for strangers; to Poppy Johnson and her staff at the Floyd Memorial Library in Greenport, where most of this book was written; and to the late David Carr, who gave the book its title and slapped the table in glee when he did. I miss him every day.

Without Manny Howard, with whom these dinners started so long ago, I would not be typing now. Without Kim Gougenheim, photo editor at the food desk of the *Times*, I would not have been introduced to the brilliant work of the photographer David Malosh and the food stylist Simon Andrews, whose cooking and images brought this book to life. And here's a final nod to Brendan McCarthy, who made sure to ask about the book's progress only at the moments a striped bass appeared on our skiff's horizon, swimming fat and happy on the surface, a difficult cast away. Thanks so much for that, pal.

INDEX

—

ABOUT THE AUTHOR

SAM SIFTON is the food editor of *The New York Times*,
an "Eat" columnist for *The New York Times Magazine*,
and the founding editor of NYT Cooking, the
newspaper's digital recipe collection and cooking site.
Formerly the chief restaurant critic of the *Times*,
he has also served as editor of the national desk
and the culture desk.

Facebook.com/sam.sifton.58

Twitter: @samsifton

Instagram: @samsifton

This book was set in Fournier, a typeface named for Pierre-Simon Fournier (1712–68), the youngest son of a French printing family. He started out engraving woodblocks and large capitals, then moved on to fonts of type. In 1736 he began his own foundry and made several important contributions in the field of type design; he is said to have cut 147 alphabets of his own creation. Fournier is probably best remembered as the designer of St. Augustine Ordinaire, a face that served as the model for the Monotype Corporation's Fournier, which was released in 1925.